D1555578

THE AESTHETICS OF STRANGENESS

THE AESTHETICS OF STRANGENESS

Eccentricity and Madness in Early Modern Japan

W. PUCK BRECHER

University of Hawai'i Press
Honolulu

© 2013 University of Hawai'i Press
All rights reserved
Printed in the United States of America
18 17 16 15 14 13   6 5 4 3 2 1

Library of Congress Cataloging-in-Publication Data
Brecher, W. Puck
The aesthetics of strangeness : eccentricity and
madness in early modern Japan / W. Puck Brecher.
pages cm
Includes bibliographical references and index.
ISBN 978-0-8248-3666-5 (cloth : alk. paper)
1. Art, Japanese—Edo period, 1600–1868.
2. Eccentrics and eccentricities—Japan.
3. Aesthetics, Japanese—History. I. Title.
N7353.6.E3B74 2013
709.52—dc23
2012048353

University of Hawai'i Press books are printed on
acid-free paper and meet the guidelines for permanence
and durability of the Council on Library Resources.

Designed by Janette Thompson (Jansom)

Printed by Sheridan Books, Inc.

*For Midge Brecher, and
in memory of John Brecher*

CONTENTS

ACKNOWLEDGMENTS

I wish to thank Peter Nosco for his unwavering generosity and guidance over many years. Without his instruction this book would not have been started, and without his encouragement it would not have been completed. In addition, I am grateful for valuable suggestions from David Bialock, Edward Slingerland, Gordon Berger, and Jonathan Reynolds. I am also indebted to Chia-Lan Chang for her assistance with Chinese documents. Kayo Niimi provided me with tremendous logistical and moral support during the process of acquiring image reproduction permissions. My thanks also to Zoe and Rio.

PART I

Contexts of Strangeness

CHAPTER 1

Strange Interpretations

Blessed are the cracked,
for they shall let in the light.
—Groucho Marx

Periodically, circumstances seem to produce, as Nelson Wu describes Ming China, a "perfect breeding ground for eccentrics."[1] At these rare moments strangeness bursts forth to energize and reform mainstream culture. *Kinsei kijinden* (Eccentrics of recent times, 1790), the first biographical compilation of eccentrics (*kijin*) published in Japan, marks just such a moment.[2] But can the literary impact and dazzling commercial success of this work be attributed to certain social or cultural conditions describable as a "perfect breeding ground for eccentrics?" If so, what were the conditions that generated this ethos of eccentricity and what distinguished these *kijin* from the isolated cases of strangeness and genius common to all historical eras? Moreover, how was this strange onslaught tolerated over the course of decades and centuries?

This extraordinary moment in Japan's late eighteenth century has been noted by a multitude of writers. It has been called "the beginnings of decisive change" and "a new age [that was] restless, curious, and receptive."[3] Some go on to posit how this historical moment changed the course of Tokugawa thought: how Dutch studies (*rangaku*) rose to replace China as a repository of knowledge and how Japan rediscovered itself as a repository of spirituality. Others identify it as the first moment in which the Tokugawa government (*bakufu*), recognizing cultural production as a means of controlling public knowledge, successfully utilized historiography, science, and the arts to forge a consolidated national culture.[4] These extraordinary developments in thought, knowledge, and politics were joined by sudden innovative interventions in the cultural field. Late eighteenth-century painting, for example, materialized as "a singular era . . . that witnessed an unprecedented diversity in individual artistic expression. At no time prior . . . did such a remarkable group of artists emerge in Japan."[5]

Historians have called this proliferation of eccentricity a "flourishing," a "new orthodoxy" wherein the term *kijin* became a "fashionable literary catchword" that triggered a "new wave of publishing [*kijinden*]."[6] This explosive convergence of fresh intellectual and cultural energies thus marked a disjuncture in how the nation's most idiosyncratic individuals positioned themselves vis-à-vis state and society. It also forged a conspicuous eccentric presence that was tolerated, even embraced, by the mainstream.[7] Such were the historical conditions—an "era of eccentrics and eccentricities"; a "golden age of Japanese eccentrics"—from which outsiders and oddballs assumed a new position within Tokugawa society.[8]

Aesthetic strangeness during the last century of the Edo period was a society-wide phenomenon buoyed and driven by urbanization, economic growth, intellectual diversity, growing literacy, the expansion of print media, and mounting disillusionment with the Tokugawa state. Though *ki* (extraordinary, marvelous, original, eccentric), the principal signifier of aesthetic eccentricity during this period, was originally expounded as a metaphysical endowment, it was soon swept up in these developments and deployed by biographers and publishers seeking to capitalize on the term's cachet. Eccentric behavior and literary representations of eccentricity thus emerged as parallel phenomena that together would turn strangeness into a cultural sensation.

This study examines aesthetic eccentricity as an emergent feature of identity formation during this new age and traces its trajectory throughout the Edo period (1600–1868). It limits discussion of this timeless phenomenon to a fixed historical era, not to suggest that aesthetic strangeness magically materialized under the Tokugawa or that it was eradicated along with the Tokugawa in 1868, but because broadening its historical scope to include preceding and succeeding events would require introducing new sets of complex historical problems that merit full-length studies in their own right. Rather, the study chooses to focus on a single pivotal era, maintaining that forms of aesthetic strangeness ascendant in the Edo period can be fully addressed within the context of that period alone. Its purpose is to identify certain strains of patterned nonconformity and to discern how they eventually acquired the currency to redefine the cultural landscape. Aesthetic eccentricity refers not only to deviant cultural forms—mainly within the visual arts—but also to subjectivities that privilege individuality, emotion, and intuition over conventional behavior. It tends toward egocentrism and often conveys a subject's desire for detachment from occupational responsibilities, ideological constraints, or commercial pressures.

In Japanese, as in English, the term "eccentricity" is deployed so broadly to signify such sprawling, convoluted phenomena as to present problems of definition and contextualization. It cannot be meaningfully defined in general terms, nor reduced to any representative sample of individuals. What can be evaluated, however, are specific terms (a glossary of which is to follow) used in biographies, diaries, journals, fiction, and other forms of print that signify strange, mad, or idiosyncratic behavior. This lexicon—*ki* in particular—and its changing usage will guide my examination of eccentricity and its reception in early modern Japan. My strategy will be to examine those individuals, both prominent and obscure, from throughout the period who have been most closely associated with these various terms. The greater the sample, the more complex the composite and the sharper the image, and I shall consider as many (several dozen) as is practical.[9] I shall also give considerable space to the intellectual roots of aesthetic eccentricity and to the changing dynamics governing patterns of interaction between individual and society.

Difficulties surrounding historiography and historicization, however, require that the project be further clarified and oriented. The remainder of this chapter will, first, situate our topic within existing English and Japanese scholarship by examining how others have approached eccentricity as a field of study. It then offers a genealogy of the terms commonly used to signify aesthetic eccentricity in the Edo period. This lexicon will frame the study and anchor discussions of the texts and individuals appearing in the chapters that follow. Next, I will introduce some of the historiographical issues that have guided inquiry into aesthetic eccentricity in early modern Japan, including the favored tendency to equate it with later avant-garde movements. The chapter concludes by advancing several counterintuitive arguments that collectively demonstrate how strangeness, particularly during the last century of the Edo period, permeated mainstream ethical values to assume an inviolable position within mainstream culture.

ECCENTRICITY AS A FIELD OF STUDY

Strange behavior and eccentric art in early modern Japan have not stirred much scholarly debate. Studies from the last four decades have come to a nearly consensual view of mad or eccentric artists as, simply, detached and anomalous. Much of this scholarship has been produced by art historians conducting technical analyses of oeuvres and genres, and, while valuable, has not employed any systematic framework for explaining eccentricity historically. Understandably, such work has yielded greater contributions to art history than to our understanding of the individuals in question or to strangeness itself as a sociological phenomenon. The other access point to this field of study is psychology, which frames how we currently tend to apprehend eccentricity generally and artists in particular.

Eccentric individuals do appear to share certain psychological traits that transcend time and place, and modern commentary has viewed these as byproducts of psychological tensions between self and society. It also notes that eccentrics share certain characteristics: they tend to clash with or be excluded from authority and society, causing them to seek independence and expressive freedom; many possess superior intelligence and creativity; they may suffer from physical abnormalities, handicaps, or speech impediments; many are asexual, do not marry or have children, or else have children who commit suicide or exhibit mental problems; and an inordinate number experience trauma or tragedy early in life.[10] Studies also suggest that eccentrics are often thoughtful and disciplined but may not perform well at school, where structure demands conformity. The school environment, it is argued, suffocates idiosyncrasy by denying opportunities for individual experimentation.[11]

Psychological unease is also commonly connected to extraordinary creativity, a notion that has fueled associations between madness and artistic genius. Obsessive-compulsiveness, for example, appears to contribute to creativity by encouraging constant collecting and experimentation. Arnold Ludwig finds that "about one-third of the eminent poets, musical performers, and fiction writers suffered from serious psychological problems as teenagers, a rate that exploded to three-quarters when these people became adults."[12] Clifford Pickover has argued that the unusual creativity of Dostoevsky, Flaubert, van Gogh, and Lewis Carroll, for instance, resulted from altered consciousness due to temporal lobe epilepsy produced by a serotonin imbalance.[13] It is during these seizures, what van Gogh called "the storm within," that individuals generally exhibit heightened clarity, sharpened creativity, greater originality, more expansive thoughts, and are able to work for long periods without a breakdown in concentration.[14] Studies relying on such psychologically based assertions tend to conclude that, while mental disturbance cannot produce important art by itself, in the hands of a talented individual it can lead to creative developments that test the limits of accepted art.

Psychological applications of this sort have contributed to certain mythologies surrounding the mad artist, namely the perception that life and art reflect one another. This notion marks eccentric art as a portal to an eccentric psychology, wedding art to personality. The subsequent romanticization of madness fosters expectations that art (and artists) must of necessity transcend acceptable social boundaries in order to produce anything meaningful. Observers have witnessed this unification of art and psyche in both nineteenth-century Japan and Europe, where artists found a cathartic release of restless energies through aesthetics of unrestrained antirationalism.[15] In both civilizations, the process involved establishing art as a separate realm that enabled engagement with otherwise unacceptable forms of strangeness or, as Habermas put it, as "a sanctuary for the—perhaps merely cerebral— satisfaction of those needs which become quasi illegal in the material life process of bourgeois society."[16]

Among the adoring public, however, the unification of psychology and art has led to the misperception that strange art intimates a strange psychology. The myth of the mad artist required that art and artist alike become anguished, and during the modern era such expectations have helped to buoy periods of bohemianism while simultaneously hastening the destruction of its members.[17] Explaining strangeness through psychology, therefore, has contributed to our knowledge of this subject but also yielded expectations that were in turn imposed upon the individuals in question. It converted eccentricity into a known quantity, neutralizing its strangeness.

One thus finds both benefits and limitations to using psychological inquiry to make sense of historical figures. Many eighteenth- and nineteenth-century Japanese eccentrics indeed had unconventional childhoods, were highly intelligent, and resisted authority. It was also the case that potentialities for individual strangeness were dimmed by the onset of compulsory schooling in the early Meiji period, which sought to "hammer down" protruding nails that upset uniformity. Such findings offer a certain theoretical utility. Yet even with adequate biographical records, psychological inquiry can never yield more than fanciful guesswork about historical figures. It would be easy to imagine that individuals like the *ukiyoe* (pictures of the floating world) artist Katsushika Hokusai (1760–1849), said to have produced thirty to forty thousand pictures, and the poet Ōkuma Kotomichi (1798–1868), who routinely wrote over one hundred *waka* (31-syllable poetry) daily, suffered from some form of obsessive-compulsive disorder. But without trustworthy confessional statements—that is, without psychological data—such analogies lead only to dead ends. Neuropsychologist David Weeks' ambitious ten-year clinical study of historical eccentrics in Europe and the United States, for example, ultimately produced little more than a collection of anecdotes cloaked in guesswork.[18]

These limitations have not deterred some from formulating psychological interpretations of Edo period eccentrics. *A Genealogy of Eccentricity* (*Kisō no keifu,* 1968), art historian Tsuji Nobuo's pioneering work on the topic, makes sporadic use of psychological terminology to suggest that his subjects suffered from psychological abnormalities. The monk Hakuin (1685–1768), Tsuji claims, suffered from neurosis as a teenager; Soga Shōhaku (1730–1781) was brashly obsessive; and Itō Jakuchū (1716–1800) equally so.[19] Interpreting Jakuchū's painting "A Flock of Sparrows by the Dike in Autumn," he sees the single white sparrow amid a flock of darker ones as representing Jakuchū himself, finding here evidence of neurotic tendencies. The fact that Jakuchū never married, had few friends, and lived in self-imposed isolation apparently constituted sufficient evidence for art historian Kanō Hiroyuki to surmise that he was homosexual.[20] Such observations, however, are flimsy and dehistoricize artistic practice. Voluntary isolation, in fact, typified the lifestyles being cultivated by numerous amateur scholars and artists. Obsessiveness like Jakuchū's may indeed manifest a psychological affliction, but it was also an expedient strategy of navigating an otherwise hostile environment. Whether or not it evinced a psychological condition is historically immaterial.

For our purposes, then, eccentricity will be an aesthetic and social phenomenon rather than a scientific one, and our attention will fall on the environmental factors that activate or aggravate it. We will also consider its strange allure. Indeed, for all the political and ideological efforts to eradicate it, nonconformity was continually vindicated by a vague admiration, an intuitive sense among a portion of Tokugawa society that deviance extends and actualizes human potential. This paradoxical admiration of eccentricity, Michel Foucault has argued, lies in our belief that it possesses a truth made inaccessible by our dependence on rationality.[21] Viewed from outside as bestial, it became acceptable only within the more tolerant space of art, wherein it acquired a transcendent truth that attracted consumers. Yanagi Muneyoshi (1889–1961), the central figure behind a revival of folk art (*mingei*) that self-identified as a movement of eccentrics in opposition to modernity, arrived at the same conclusion. "The creative work of a madman does not come from theory," he writes. "Because of this, it appears to contain a truth. It will not do to let the work of the mad be in vain. There are many lessons we can learn from it."[22] The tolerance afforded the eccentric, often at the risk of censure from above, is thus the product of a vague, wistful admiration.

The mystique surrounding strangeness, however, attracts attention that is ultimately thwarted by an intrinsic inaccessibility. As Robert Pirsig has observed, our attempts to study it—madness, for instance—leave us looking only at ourselves: "When you look directly at an insane man, all you see is a reflection of your own knowledge that he's insane, which is not to see him at all. To see him you must see what he saw and when you are trying to see the vision of an insane man, an oblique route is the only way to come at it. Otherwise your own opinions block the way."[23]

Pirsig's observation unveils the fundamental selfishness that has guided how eccentrics are typically viewed. Preconceptions supply the knowledge that observers want or need, reinforcing their understanding of ordinary and extraordinary, centric and eccentric.[24] Inaccessibility, therefore, constitutes our greatest obstacle to theorizing early modern eccentrics (*kijin*), a problem exacerbated by the fact that few of them published treatises or journals confessing private thoughts or deliberating on their own status as outsiders.[25] It was generally those of less talent and vision who produced such documents. Consequently, our knowledge of these individuals comes mainly from observations made by contemporaries or later admirers.

Inaccessibility, however, can be ameliorated by attention to historical context and by plotting eccentrics positionally vis-à-vis more knowable norms. In the Edo period self-discovery and self-invention were carried out through existing social categories (e.g., status, lineage, occupation, and place of residence). *Kijin* and *kyōjin* (mad persons) created and located their own identities beyond these categories, however, and their strategies of doing so afford a valuable vantage point. Positing madness as psychic distance suggests that these individuals occupied distanced spaces of their own invention. Indeed, "the eccentric is, *par excellence,* the inventor," Hess asserts.

"He is the man out of touch . . . sometimes because of his geographical distance from the center of things . . . sometimes because of an interior, psychic distance. . . . His invention is a discovery of self."[26] This assessment, based on physical or psychological detachment, illuminates the problem of eccentricity in the Edo period, when eccentrics were variously condemned, ostracized, celebrated, and venerated according to their perceived distance from the normative. Distance and patterns of self-invention, therefore, will be means of framing how Japanese eccentrics navigated their world.

A GLOSSARY OF STRANGENESS

Melinda Takeuchi is certainly correct when she notes that "within the context of accepted Tokugawa period behavior . . . almost any irregularity was considered a deviation. . . . Only such a rigid age, one suspects, could have produced such a plethora of 'eccentrics.'"[27] And only such a plethora of eccentrics could have elicited such a broad lexicon to represent eccentricity. By 1800, *ki* was the most trendy and provocative such signifier. It was ascribed to a Daoist context, for the original usage of the designation *kijin* is credited to the fourth-century B.C.E. Daoist text *Zhuangzi*. In chapter 6 of that text, Tzukung asks Confucius about the *kijin*: "I venture to ask about the oddball [畸人]." The Master replied: "The oddball may be odd to other men, but he is a pair with heaven. Therefore it is said, 'the villain in heaven is a gentleman among men; the gentleman among men is a villain in heaven.'"[28] Such statements marked *ki* as metaphysically and ethically transcendent, a notion that would become a permanent fixture within East Asian thought. By extension, *kijin* were commonly associated with Zhuangzian values like detachment, playfulness, and useful uselessness (*muyō no yō*).

Zhuangzi's favorite subjects for illustrating this alignment of *kijin* and heaven were the crippled or physically deformed. As deformity disabled one's social utility, for Zhuangzi it enabled one as a sagely eccentric.[29] This association was variously retained during the Edo period. Ueda Akinari's (1734–1809) self-reference as Senshi Kijin (Clipper-hand eccentric) in his preface to *Ugetsu monogatari* (Tales of moonlight and rain, 1776) is accepted as the first native usage of the term *kijin* in early modern Japan.[30] Akinari's childhood bout with smallpox had left him with one atrophied finger on each hand, and the pseudonym Senshi Kijin was a clever double entendre mocking his deformity while bestowing upon himself the loftiness of a Zhuangzian sage.[31]

Ueda's case presented a compelling juxtaposition, for while Zhuangzi had equated deformity with heaven, in Japan deformity had long been viewed as a marker of sin or defilement. The early mythohistories *Kojiki* and *Nihongi* relate how the mythical progenitors Izanami and Izanagi, after circumambulating the land, bore a crippled child and discarded it by setting it adrift in a reed boat.[32] Buddhists explained leprosy, blindness, or disfigurement as karmic retribution for past transgressions, and premodern communities observed this doctrine by banishing the physically handicapped. In the Edo period, commercial culture discovered a way to profit from and "treat" deformity by displaying it as a spectacle.[33] The rationale (or rationalization) held that the sin of disfigurement could be erased and karma ameliorated by having a multitude look upon it. By experiencing the shame of public ridicule the subject could atone for past transgressions.[34] Deformity, then, was a punishment for past sin, and atonement required further punishment. Such were the prevailing attitudes surrounding deformity when the aesthetic of *ki* emerged in the eighteenth century. As *ki* often connoted divinely endowed talent and virtue, however, early modern *kijin* with distinguishing physical attributes were often spared the stigmas imposed on the less fortunate. In fact, the paradox of *ki* as both heavenly and defiled only enhanced the term's power and mystique.

The character 畸 itself, formed by adding the field radical to the more common character 奇 (strange, eccentric, different), acquired certain related associations. The field radical was added from comparisons of *kijin* to leftover scraps of agricultural land too misshapen or unusable to be included within the Confucian well-field system of land apportionment. The character thereby came to signify something left over, neither used nor usable, and later something odd. In reference to humans it also signified the crippled, deformed, or disabled.[35] *Kijin* are thus compared to that which is isolated, nonproductive, and outside the delineations of the social system—a Confucian analogy clearly critical of the eccentric lifestyle as burdensome and socially irresponsible. *Kinsei kijinden* author Ban Kōkei explained that 畸, at that time virtually unused in Japanese texts, should be considered a derivative of the two characters 奇 and 異 (wrong, different), an amalgam signifying something slightly notorious and beyond the safety of the normative.[36] Katharine Burnett's study of the term in the context of Chinese painting confirms that 畸, compared with 奇, carries the more negative subtexts of strangeness.[37]

These two definitions—heavenliness and a more general yet notorious sense of strangeness—were first articulated in Japan by Kōkei's preface to

Kinsei kijinden. Despite his correct recognition of Zhuangzi as both the term's originator and an important archetype of aesthetic reclusion, Kōkei proceeds to bring *ki* closer to his readers' ideological comfort zone by conflating it with the Confucian tenets of striving, self-cultivation, and virtue, an important development to be discussed at length in Chapter 5. Later *kijinden* writers soon dispensed with etymological concerns, however. Annoyed by the exclusivity of Kōkei's designations, the author of *Eccentrics from Tsu* (*Anotsu kijinden,* 1837), Kujaku Rōjin (Old Peacock Man), stated that a *kijin* was simply anyone manifesting unusual qualities.[38] By his time, this simplified, dehistoricized usage of *ki* as an all-purpose marker of strangeness had become part of standard literary practice.

Other *kijinden* authors, aware that many of their entries did not share an affinity for the Daoist aesthetics suggested by the character 畸, opted for the more general character 奇, which also marked unusual or talented individuals. So as not to lose the subtle differences between 畸人 and 奇人, I will use the relevant Chinese character where distinctions are necessary. I will use 畸人 to signify a detached aestheticism and resigned individualism, and 奇人 for individuals exhibiting more general forms of unusual behavior. Admittedly, this is an imperfect solution to the problem given that the two terms are often used interchangeably or randomly. Due to the rarity of the character 畸 in written Japanese, for example, some *kijinden* authors appear to have selected it only to imbue their subjects with a notoriousness or exoticism not carried by the more familiar 奇. One cannot ascertain whether the character 畸 was even recognizable to less learned readers, but there is no doubt that until the late eighteenth century it was both rare and particular to imported Chinese books. The Chinese text *Jiren shipian* (J. *Kijin jippen*), published by the missionary Matteo Ricci in 1608, was a treatise on Roman Catholic ethics rather than eccentricity and as such was subject to the Tokugawa ban on Christian books, but we know that Ogyū Sorai (1666–1728), who had criticized the ban, acquired a copy in 1726. *Zhuangzi* and Chinese commentaries on that text would have been the other obvious sources of exposure to the character 畸.

Contemporary *kijinden* continue to use the term 畸人 ahistorically without acknowledging its Daoist roots, giving it a meaning of 奇人 and 変人 (*henjin*), two terms that contemporary Japanese use together to mean, simply, "weirdo." Some recent *kijinden,* however, have proposed some new and highly reverential designations. In the preface to his *Kinsei shinkijinden* (New eccentrics of recent times, 1977), *kijin* authority Nakano Mitsutoshi states that "the *kijin's* 畸人 defining feature is not resigned withdrawal from the world, but a genuine humanity after his/her external skin has been peeled away."[39] *Kijin,* he continues, are like children sent from Heaven to answer the prayers of the masses. Noted literary critic and *kijinden* author Ishikawa Jun (1899–1987) offers a nearly identical association. For him, *kijin* are those rare souls who—sometimes welcomed, sometimes persecuted—embody resistance from the margins. They answer our prayers, Ishikawa avers, like apostles of the gods who come and go between heaven and earth.[40] The most elaborated definition comes from Koto Yūho, who posits the following six conditions (originally articulated by Jay Robert Nash) as the internationally accepted criteria for eccentricity: (1) though not necessarily respected, *kijin* 奇人 are invariably loved and feared; (2) they must be *kijin* throughout their lives; (3) eccentric behavior must be their everyday behavior; (4) they must be dreamers; (5) their behavior must exert a strong impact on society; and (6) it must also spring naturally from within without striving.[41] To these Koto adds his own stipulations that *kijin* must be unique, noble, and stand as models of righteousness. His final qualification follows Nakano and Ishikawa in invoking the sacrality originally posited by Zhuangzi: *kijin* appear as alienated oddballs but are actually the rare few chosen by heaven.[42]

Ki is the most prominent marker of aesthetic and behavioral deviance and so will be one of this study's central foci. *Kyō* 狂, madness or mental derangement, particularly unrestrained emotion, is a Confucian counterpart to the Daoist discourse on *ki* and thus an important alternate signifier of strangeness.[43] The genealogical position of *kyō* in classical Confucian writings, as well as its distinction from *ki,* will be further introduced in Chapters 2 and 4, and will contextualize our discussion of *Hōsa kyōshaden* (Biographies of Nagoya madmen) in Chapter 5.

In addition to *kijin* and *kyōjin,* we also find the terms *inja* and *itsujin,* usually meaning hermits and recluses but also variously signifying strangeness or deviance. Though theoretically distinct, in practice these disparate terms are often conflated. While *kyō* tends to be reserved for more extreme behavior, for instance, Kōkei's *Kinsei kijinden* does label some of its entries as *kyōjin,* and *Hōsa kyōshaden* does contain references to Zhuangzian *kijin.* By the same token, *Kinsei itsujin gashi* (History of paintings by eccentric persons of recent times, 1824) includes individuals that Kōkei calls *kijin* and others call *kyōjin.* And, in his three-volume exposé of eccentric artists, *Extraordinary Persons* (1999), the most comprehensive treatment of the topic in English, art historian John Rosenfield translates *kijin, itsujin,* and *kiseki* (miraculous) all as "eccentric." It is common, then, to use *kijin* (畸人, 奇人), *itsujin,* and *kyōjin* interchangeably in much the way that the equally generic English term "eccentric" refers to an array of idiosyncratic personae.

Placing eccentrics in cultural context requires close attention to practices of reclusion as well as to literati (*bunjin*) culture, the ethos that most significantly informed aesthetic strangeness during the Edo period. As systemic outsiders, recluses are precursors to *kijin,* and biographies of recluses are forerunners of *kijinden.* In the seventeenth century, some recluses gravitated toward Chinese cultural forms whose gradual popularization fostered a nascent *bunjin* ethos. The implicitly understood genealogical connection between recluses and *bunjin* was then made explicit by *Kinsei kijinden,* which used both terms to codify *ki* and *kijin.*[44] Recluses, *bunjin,* and *kijin* thus share philosophical and experiential ground, and form a chronology of detached aestheticism in the Edo period.[45] While using *kijin* as an umbrella term, Ban Kōkei nonetheless crafts it around a core group of *bunjin.* His preface singles out Ike no Taiga (1723–1776) and Baisaō (1675–1763) as individuals who embody Zhuangzi's original use of the term and whose behaviors exemplify the *kijin* ideal. We must acknowledge the term's dual usage, therefore—as a signifier of general eccentric behavior and as a marker of extraordinary aesthetic and moral accomplishment. Following Kōkei and other *kijinden* writers, our study will focus on the latter usage—that is, of aesthetic eccentricity as an offspring of *bunjin* culture.

In recent years, *bunjin,* long dismissed by Western scholarship, have become subjects of interest. Studies by Anna Beerens, Cheryl Crowley, Patricia Graham, Eiko Ikegami, Lawrence E. Marceau, and Peipei Qiu have done much to improve English scholarship on *bunjin* practice and will be helpful for understanding the cultural milieu in which aesthetic eccentricity flourished. As some have noted, the term *bunjin* itself is ahistorical. Not only is it used rarely in early modern documents, but the individuals in question were more involved in emulating the cultural forms produced by their closest Chinese counterparts (*wenren*) than in intentionally pursuing lives as independent literati. For these reasons, Beerens rejects the term. When *bunjin* composed poetry, painted landscapes, and wrote of themselves as recluses, she argues, they were "play-acting" their own imagined membership within that majestic Chinese world.[46] Conversely, Marceau does not object to the term *bunjin* but rejects its most common English translation, literati, preferring the phrase independent "free" artist.[47]

This study uses the term *bunjin* as the most widely accepted option. It does so, however, while acknowledging its ahistoricity and in recognition that its usage does not signify parity with Chinese *wenren* (all scholar-bureaucrats) but rather refers to individuals who, irrespective of class and occupation, embraced the principles of autonomous aestheticism and amateurism as exemplified by *wenren.* Of particular importance will be contextualizing emergent *kijin* via a prescribed set of attitudes and practices that I shall call a *bunjin* ethos.[48]

The above glossary of terms has served to provide a point of departure for discussing Japan's early modern eccentrics, but we must recognize that the subjects of this study represent an amorphous group that should remain undefined to every possible extent. While progressing from the seventeenth through the nineteenth centuries, we shall find that signifiers lose either their original significance or their relevance. Though I will impose rough definitions on such terms as *kijin* (eccentric) and *kyōjin* (mad person) as a necessity for isolating the central features of aesthetic eccentricity, I do so only to provide the study with a measure of structure and not to impose fixity upon a fluid and variegated phenomenon.

ECCENTRICITY AS A HISTORIOGRAPHICAL PROBLEM

As noted, the year 1790 can serve as a symbolic watershed. It was in this year that chief shogunal regent Matsudaira Sadanobu (1758–1829) promulgated the Prohibition of Heterodox Studies, an administrative gesture reflecting official intolerance for heretical thought, and in which Ban Kōkei published *Kinsei kijinden,* a literary gesture reflecting popular attraction to heretical practice. The coincidental concurrence of these two events, one renouncing deviance and the other celebrating it, responded to ongoing experiments in art and thought. Thereafter, eccentricity would be a social issue affixed to the radar screens of top and bottom alike.

Since then, historians have struggled with how to account for and interpret this influx of early modern oddballs and the biographies written about them. Did eccentric art and behavior amount to nothing more than publicity stunts and commercial gimmicks? On the surface they seemed to serve neither any historically important function nor to exert any enduring impact. And if this was so, what function could be served by muddying history's waters with undue attention on figures like Ishimawari from *Hōsa kyōshaden?*

There was a man who had taken the peculiar nickname Ishimawari. . . .
He liked arithmetic and . . . though he eventually did learn how to use
an abacus, he never understood what it was used for. He was that stupid.
When going out he tried sticking his finger in a knothole in a post at the
front door as he walked by. If his finger didn't slip into the hole on the
first try he would go back inside, come out, and try it again. If it worked
the second time he continued out the gate with a satisfied look and turned
south. His actions were swift and effortless, as if he were riding on the
wind.[49] Before the Wakamiya Gate in Suehirochō there is a particular rock
that he would walk around three times. There is also a stone in front of the
Niōmon gate at Ōsu Kannon Temple that he used to walk around. After
circumambulating these two rocks, he would return home with a joyful
expression. He had no intention of doing anything besides this.[50]

Anomalous oddballs like Ishimawari have been omitted from Edo history, for they appear to have represented nothing more than fallout from late
kinsei's "culture of play" and to contribute little to the historical record.[51]
But this omission exposes a glaring interpretive inconsistency. A corpus
of writing (*kijinden*) from the last century of the Edo period extols these
seemingly useless individuals as moral exemplars. The commercial success
of such publications, moreover, points not only to a perception that these
individuals merited recognition but also to a general warming toward deviance. The ubiquity of this phenomenon calls for reconsideration of how to
explain eccentrics socially and how to position them historically.

The historiographical omission itself is historical. *Kijin* were a national
liability, if not an embarrassment, to the utilitarian interests of Meiji and
Imperial era Japan. Wartime and Cold War historians likewise found them
an irredeemable lot, corroborating the view that, as Arthur Waley put it,
eccentrics constituted "the vagaries of humanity."[52] Artists and writers, it
was assumed, secured their place in history by changing history. Genius or
artistic virtuosity alone could never be "important" without advancing the
cultural field. The field, however, was a centralized institution, the single reference point against which eccentricity's counterpoint could never amount
to more than a flickering annoyance. Marginality by definition precluded
importance. As Paul Moss acknowledges in the case of netsuke carver Ozaki
Kokusai (1835–1894), whose work fostered new aesthetic standards among
netsuke carvers: "The notion of eccentricity in art has long been respected
in Japan but of course, as in the West, the eccentric artist rarely benefits

from this recognition until his new contribution has been established and institutionalized as a new orthodoxy."[53] Deviant art's inherent ephemerality, therefore, eliminated any possibility of its immediate importance to the mainstream.

Indeed, some narratives have ignored its cultural relevance altogether. Koto Yūho, for example, advances the fallacy that traditional Japan did not value individualism and consequentially produced comparatively few *kijin*.[54] For Koto, asserting the *kijin*'s irrelevance yielded a tidier, more easily digestible historical narrative. Others posit *kijin* as failures, verifying this claim by pairing them with Chinese, European, and North American counterparts and then demonstrating their relative passivity and ineffectuality. Tsuji's *Kisō no keifu* was the first to ascertain the essence of Edo period *kijin* by comparing them to European counterparts.[55] Others followed suit. Takahashi Hiromi likened Ike no Taiga to Mozart, for example, and Oda Susumu compared Hiraga Gennai (1728–1779) to Michelangelo and Leonardo da Vinci; but in each case, they contended, strict systemic controls imposed by the *bakufu* suppressed their subjects' true genius.[56] *Kijin*, it is argued, did not incite revolution or overtly overthrow the political, social, or artistic establishments; they neither self-destructed, nor were martyred for their idiosyncrasies; they did not suffer, and in many cases seemed disconcertingly content. They were, in comparison to their counterparts in Europe, less intrepid, less self-sacrificing, and their irreverent shenanigans achieved fewer tangible results. Having failed to meet these modern criteria for success, we are told, Japanese *kijin* generally disappoint. Such are puzzling propositions given the extraordinary success actually enjoyed by many *kijin* during their lifetimes and the decisive impact that aesthetic strangeness would come to exert on Edo culture.[57]

Following scholarship attempting to mine the Edo period for roots of Japanese modernity, from the 1960s a second historiographical movement started interpreting eccentrics as modernizers. Given that reclusive individuals tended to be strong-willed and introspective, it is understandable that historians would see in them many of the qualities attached to modern subjectivity: that is, rationality, self-empowerment, existential crisis, or individuation. Edo period *kijin* indeed exemplified such traits, seemingly manifesting the self-consciousness and autonomy that Maruyama Masao has attributed to modern subjectivity.[58] Seeking for evidence of self-invention was thus common historiographical practice in 1968 when Tsuji introduced the term *kisō* (eccentricity) to the study of early modern Japanese aesthetics. Building on work by ethnologists and folklorists like Yanagita Kunio (1875–1962) and Yanagi Sōetsu (1889–1961), Tsuji reversed the view of *kijin* as failures, instead positing some as individualists and "discoverers" of Japanese art.[59] He excavated, for example, a cohort of "eccentric painters"—Itō Jakuchū, Soga Shōhaku, and Nagasawa Rosetsu in particular—as well as previously uncategorizable "individualist" artists like Ike no Taiga. Despite his troubling devotion to an essentialistic Japanism (*nihonjinron*), Tsuji nonetheless redeemed the aesthetic and cultural value of strangeness by equating it with modernization.

Ascribing a modern consciousness to historical individuals, however, is anachronistic and historically unhelpful. Commentary surrounding the *bunjin* and Rinpa revivalist Sakai Hōitsu (1761–1828) exemplifies some of the misrepresentations produced by such historiography. Hōitsu was the second son to the daimyo of the Harima domain, near Kobe, but was born and educated at the family compound in Edo. At thirty-five he withdrew from official life to enter the Nishi Honganji monastery, accepting a consolation salary of one thousand *koku* and fifty attendants. Two weeks later, now sufficiently severed from official responsibilities, he left the monastery for a life of leisure and aesthetic pursuits. Hōitsu's irreverence toward the elite arts practiced by his own social class, his (alleged) rejection of wealth and status, and his preference for plebian artistic circles were consistent with the bohemianism popular among literati of his age. Nonetheless, it is for such apparently strange preferences that Hōitsu is anthologized as a *kijin* in *Zoku zoku meijin kijin* (Even more prominent eccentrics, 1920) and other *kijinden*.[60] Modern historians focus on what they interpret to be Hōitsu's "modern" psychology: his unsettled mind, his rejection of feudal institutions, his life of play and separation, and his artistic originality. They conclude that he exhibited, as did many of the free-spirited literati of his time, evidence of a modern consciousness.[61]

Yet we cannot simply conclude, as historian Haga Tōru has, that Hōitsu was an enlightened individual who wished to dispense with the elitism of hereditary status and the backwardness of feudalism. Both his art and his lifestyle indicate that at times he was quite comfortable taking advantage of the material comforts afforded by his birthright. Moreover, Haga's view that Hōitsu's rejection of his elite status marks him as a recluse and social dropout overlooks the fact that he continued to lead a life of leisure consistent with that status. While Haga does present an interesting case for him as a modern figure, Hōitsu was best known as a revivalist of Rinpa School aesthetics and as disinclined to produce art and poetry that meaningfully departed from those traditions. Given the nature of his chosen lifestyle and pastimes, one can just as easily view Hōitsu as a conservative and a traditionalist.

More recently, scholarship reducing cultural phenomena to political means and ends has determined that *kijin* represent dissent. Such interpretations have no difficulty distilling political messages from deviance by simply reading it as veiled protest, or, as Patricia Graham describes the *kijin* Baisaō's behavior, as carrying "strong antiestablishment sociopolitical implications."[62] Deviant individuals, these studies argue, constitute further evidence of how the restrictive nature of the Tokugawa status system and the ideological nature of state power wrought a restless desire for freer expression. John Rosenfield, for example, maintains that the *kijin* phenomenon was a response to the conformity being forged by state control, an instinctive reaction that was in any case far less successful than comparable movements in the West.[63] Eccentricity was but a cathartic venting. This view complements rather than replaces the perception of eccentrics as modernizers. In fact, scholarship attaching deviance to politics continues to see "mad" poetry, painting, or behavior in early modern Japan as outpourings of an enlightened cohort whose attitudes most closely approximated the "modern" ideals of self-discovery and self-determination.[64] Such discussions are vested in the importance of their subjects and quickly turn laudatory, thereby continuing the hagiographic tone of the *kijinden* themselves. Paradoxically, therefore, *kijin* have received both criticism as failures and uncritical acclaim as the outstanding figures of their day.

Notions of eccentricity as political dissent have, for some, justified applying the term "avant-garde" to a broad swath of Edo period intellectuals and artists. While most Western scholarship has disallowed the term in reference to analogous pre–twentieth-century cultural movements, Japanese scholarship has not hesitated to apply it to earlier genres. In reference to Edo period eccentric artists, Tsuji writes that "the most avant-garde forms of modern expression—comics, posters, murals, etc., are strangely consistent with the obscure artworks of the eccentrics' school."[65] Tsuji's pioneering *Kisō no keifu,* in fact, was originally serialized in *Bijutsu techo* with the subtitle *Edo no abagyarudo* (Edo's avant-garde). Intellectual historian Kurozumi Makoto describes early seventeenth-century Confucians as "a rootless cultural avant-garde that society had thrown up."[66] The 2003 exhibition "Ukiyo-e Avant-garde" also deployed the term to refer to the playful, unconventional subject matter favored by certain *ukiyoe* artists.[67] Koji Kawamoto explains this usage by proposing "an avant-garde with no modernist strings attached or . . . a view of the avant-garde conforming to a minimal definition."[68] Kawamoto's open interpretation of the term allows him to reassess Matsuo Bashō's poetics, and *haikai* (17-syllable poetry) generally. *Haikai's* semantic indeterminacy (its favorability to multiple possible interpretations), its intention to open new aesthetic ground, and its active engagement with the past, he argues, imbue it with distinctively avant-garde qualities. "If we understand 'avant-garde' to refer to any group of writers or artists unorthodox or untraditional in their approach," Kawamoto continues, "we are able to see how the term applies throughout the history of the haiku, the most popular poetic form in Japan for the past four centuries."[69]

Kawamoto's is a courageous position. The various plebian genres of oppositional literature that emerged as derivatives of higher literary forms in the Edo period—*haikai* from *ushin renga; kyōka* from *waka,* and *kyōbun* from classical *kanbun* and *wabun*—indeed aggregated through countercultural energies that would seem analogous to the more counterhegemonic avant-garde movements of the twentieth century. Yet such movements, what might be more aptly styled Edo's proto-avant-garde, go only halfway. The forms of amateur, independent art and literature produced by *kijin* created autonomous spaces within the cultural field whence a critique of that field (the institution of mainstream art) became possible. In this narrow sense they were countercultural. But the great majority of such art did not self-position with politically destabilizing intentions. Rather, it sought political disengagement and so was fundamentally distinct from the more revolutionary, counterhegemonic avant-garde energies that deployed art as a means of reorganizing twentieth-century society.[70] As Tsuji avers, aesthetic eccentricity in early modern Japan emerged from a genealogy fueled by conventional values and buoyed by mainstream tastes.[71] It was, as Haruo Shirane writes of *haikai,* "not the creation of an oppositional culture that attempted . . . to invert the social and literary hierarchy, but rather a commoner culture that existed largely within and sometimes became indistinguishable from the cultural orthodoxy."[72] Paradoxically, then, we find that most eccentric art positioned itself to orbit existing conventions rather than as a medium of political opposition.

If early modern Japan's growing fascination with eccentricity was indeed fueled by conventional tastes and connected to an existing cultural orthodoxy, it cannot be viewed as a marginal, anomalous, or failed experiment.

Rather, it indicates evidence of an emergent paradigm that valued strangeness for its own sake. This study seeks to demystify this phenomenon by illuminating the conditions and tensions under which certain rubrics of strangeness—*ki* and *kyō* particularly—were appropriated as aesthetic and behavioral criteria. In doing so it revises histories that variously attach eccentricity exclusively to freedom, failure, or protest.

The chapters that follow propose that Edo society progressively developed an attraction to and tolerance for strangeness, and that by the early eighteenth century a confluence of intellectual, aesthetic, and social energies created conditions that enabled it as a sustainable cultural force. This subcultural movement, as such movements do, acquired a currency that eventually undermined its authenticity. Becoming a legitimate participant in this movement required that one master a set of compelling foreign aesthetic tropes and conventions. In most cases, applying these to expressions of individual freedom was secondary. In other words, it variously involved capturing an alternate orthodoxy rather than developing a protestant heterodoxy.

For many, China was the logical doorway to this movement. It is true that China boasts a long, rich textual discourse on *ki* and *kyō*, produced official dynastic histories that included sections on recluses (C. *yinyi;* J. *in'itsu*), and generated a large body of manuals, treatises, and essays that extolled aesthetic strangeness. Such was not the case in the early Tokugawa Japan, however, whose engagement with such concepts was comparatively passive. Few Japanese recluses and eccentric artists endeavored to develop and document their teachings as transmissible schools of thought. Until Kōkei's *Kinsei kijinden* found a way to domesticate eccentricity by incorporating it with discourses on native ethics, therefore, the only established theoretical frameworks for defining aesthetic strangeness were Chinese. It is this process of domestication that attracts our attention.

As we examine the numerous eccentrics who lived during the three centuries in question, it would be simple enough to fill these pages with biographical accounts of strange antics and extraordinary exploits. Doing so, however, would yield only another *kijinden*. It is equally tempting to leave the discourse on eccentric artists within the field of art history, which currently claims the most developed scholarship on these individuals, and to analyze them through artistic style.[73] This book, however, does not purport to position itself either as biography or art criticism, its purpose being an interdisciplinary reconsideration of how aesthetic eccentricity emerged, evolved as a social identity, and exerted lasting impacts on Edo society.

The study will organize Tokugawa period eccentric artists into generations, as Japanese and Western scholars have for amateur independent artists
(*bunjin*).[74] Doing so not only classifies these individuals chronologically, it
enables us to identify traits particular to respective generations and thereby
establish a provisional trajectory of cultural tastes and practices. It was *bunjin*
who most vigorously explored difference and strangeness, and so it follows
that the generational model applied to them bears utility for eccentric artists
as well. The generational model focuses history's diffusion by introducing
a chronological and contextual logic; it enables comparisons between the
collective attitudes of contemporaries with those of their successors; and it
makes possible considerations of causation without which our study could
not move beyond mere discourse. In using this generational organization, I
preserve the general time frame used to periodize each generation of *bunjin*.
The pioneers of the initial movement (late seventeenth to mid-eighteenth
century) were undeniably the mentors of the second generation (mid- to
late eighteenth century), the cluster of extraordinarily talented individuals
through whom aesthetic strangeness acquired mass public appeal. The third
generation, active during the early and mid-nineteenth century, occupies the
period of commercialization and politicization and is usually judged to possess less artistic merit than its predecessors. Of particular interest, then, will
be theorizing the experiential divide between earlier and later generations.

It should be evident by now that this book will focus less on personality—
on random, individualized quirkiness and idiosyncratic character traits—
and more on the process through which an aesthetics of eccentricity became
codified and recognizable within networks and across generations. While
personality cannot be removed from our discussion, neither can it be meaningfully scrutinized as an access point to our topic. I will require a more
systematic, historical approach. The study begins, in Chapter 2, by contextualizing types of strangeness during the early Edo period and examining how secular, emotional forms of deviance informed a nascent *bunjin*
ethos in the seventeenth century. Although aesthetics like madness (*kyō*)
and uselessness (*muyō*) had already become literary and artistic conventions,
they initially confronted a measure of social intolerance in Edo society.
Chapter 3 examines how a small cohort of early *bunjin* and *nanga* (*bunjinga*) painters first engaged with *ki* as an aesthetic in the early eighteenth
century. Their immediate successors, including important prototypical
kijin like Ike no Taiga and Soga Shōhaku, epitomized what later *kijin* and

kijinden writers would herald as the golden age of *ki*. Aesthetic eccentricity is further contextualized in Chapter 4 through a discussion of intellectual eccentricity, a parallel phenomenon that crystallized in the eighteenth century. Confucianism, usually overlooked as a philosophical justification for deviance, is discussed within the context of *kyō*. The role of eccentricity within Daoism, Wang Yangming (Yōmeigaku), and Nativism (Kokugaku) is also examined, along with a selection of individuals who used those creeds to advance intellectual justifications for strangeness. Chapter 5 introduces and compares three of the earliest biographical compilations of eccentrics: *Hōsa kyōshaden* (Biographies of Nagoya madmen, 1778); *Ochiguri monogatari* (Fallen chestnuts tales, 1780s); and *Kinsei kijinden* (Eccentrics of recent times, 1790). It examines how these publications, *Kinsei kijinden* most prominently, adapted eccentricity to contemporary conditions by conflating Daoist with Confucian ethics and ultimately (and ironically) establishing eccentrics as archetypes of moral virtue. The third generation, the topic of Chapters 6 and 7, battled conflicting receptions of strangeness in the early and mid-nineteenth century. Here I theorize aesthetic change during this period and note how treatise (*garon*) writing, commercialization, and politicization transformed eccentric practice. My findings lead us to conclude that aesthetic strangeness was neither a marginal nor a failed phenomenon, but rather an emergent paradigm that guided Edo culture. I shall begin by examining the complex array of contexts within which strangeness crystallized in the seventeenth century.

CHAPTER 2

Contexts of Strangeness in Seventeenth-Century Japan

Tokugawa Ieyasu and his immediate successors were taking no chances. Having witnessed Oda Nobunaga and Toyotomi Hideyoshi's attempt to unite the country with only temporary success, Ieyasu undertook national unification with an understandable measure of paranoia. Ensuring the longevity of Tokugawa supremacy, he realized, would require bringing aspects of his subjects' daily lives—the arts included—under political control.

Attempts at consolidation of power during the Momoyama years (1573–1600) had left the arts with considerable autonomy. Fueled in part by active cultural exchange with continental Asia and Europe, painting, lacquerware, ceramics, textiles, prints, and publishing all thrived. As people discovered new possibilities for self-expression, new forms of culture germinated and individuals expanded their spheres of participation. For the Tokugawa, this "renaissance," or culture, of social surplus and diversification necessitated a reappropriation of control. By likening themselves to ancient Chinese models of virtuous rule, Ieyasu and his successors recouped the arts as tools of political legitimation. Artists' guilds (*za*) were dissolved and replaced by independent masters and apprentices whose aesthetic vision was comparatively less innovative and more proprietary. Kyoto's lacquerware industry, for example, whose innovations and commercial success owed much to the patronage of Hideyoshi, dwindled and moved to Edo after the regime change.[1] The professional Kanō School painters also followed the Tokugawa to Edo, while the courtly Tosa School was temporarily deposed and forced to adopt a more military aesthetic.

Such assertions of control over culture allowed early Tokugawa shoguns to secure the politicization of art by depoliticizing the arbiters of art.
Such was the price of peace; but strangeness remained as a backdoor for
those unwilling to submit to such initiatives. This chapter will examine how
strangeness was received in the early Edo period and how three key tropes
of eccentric behavior—reclusion (*insei; inton*), madness (*kyō*), and uselessness (*muyō*)—were successfully inserted into this culture of intolerance and
came to infiltrate the arts. Doing so will require visiting, and then revisiting,
aspects of thought and culture from Ming and Qing period China. It also
will invite discussion of how a *bunjin* ethos crystallized in Japan and how
this phenomenon informed an emergent aesthetics of eccentricity.

STRANGENESS IN THE SEVENTEENTH CENTURY:
A PRELIMINARY TYPOLOGY

The Tokugawa shoguns aligned their statecraft with a Neo-Confucian logic
that prioritized longevity and fixity. Longevity would be assured by assigning
subjects with fixed responsibilities and obligations as determined by constel-
lations of familial and occupational relationships. Service to the collective
constituted an ethical mandate, a norm by which eccentricity would be
defined. By underscoring public benefit, this systemic model eliminated all
ambiguity surrounding forms of antisocial nonconformity, which hereafter
would be equated with moral corruption. The *bakufu* targeted street toughs
(*kabukimono*), for example, which it defined as people of low status who
wore clothes with velvet collars, grew long beards, sported upswept or ostentatious hairdos, and carried oversized swords. Such individuals were townsmen and masterless samurai (*rōnin*) emulating the swaggering postures and
arrogant behavior being displayed on stage by kabuki actors. Viewing them
as instigators of moral degeneracy, in 1652 the *bakufu* announced that in
Edo it would arrest all *kabukimono* on sight.[2] Eccentricity would need to be,
if not useful, at least sociopolitically benign.

Indeed, the longevity of the Neo-Confucian discourse itself in East Asia
is evidence of a doctrinal hostility toward antisocial forms of strangeness.
Neo-Confucian thinkers as diverse as *Vegetable Roots Discourse* (*Caigentan*)
author Hong Zicheng (fl. 1572–1620) and Meiji social critic Yagi Sōsaburō
(1866–1942) shared the Tokugawa's suspicion of nonconformity. "Secret
schemes, strange habits, eccentric conduct, and peculiar accomplishments—
all these are wombs of calamity in the course of human affairs," Hong

asserts. "It is just ordinary virtue and conduct that give rise to harmony."[3] Deliberating on the matter of social value in his 1912 essay "Ijin to kijin no betsu" (The distinction between heroes and eccentrics), Yagi notes that many eccentrics exist only for the amusement of others and so must not be considered authentic. They reject common sense, are overcome by selfish abandon, and demonstrate no regard for public benefit. "Put bluntly," he concludes, "they are unhealthy (*byōteki*)."[4] Heroes (*ijin*), in contrast, adhere to the commonsensical values of common people but accomplish far more.

Social value does not disqualify the strange as a barometer of virtue, however, for strangeness assumes a broad array of forms. What of the myriad eccentrics whose existence claimed neither public benefit nor social injury? Consider how a harmless oddball like Striped Kanjūrō (Fig. 2.1) would be publicly received in the seventeenth century:

> A man named Sakuragi Kanjūrō lived by Muromachi-dōri at Sanjō in Kyoto during the Genroku period [1688–1704]. He was an appraiser of antiques and scrolls who liked rare and strange items—especially striped items. From his clothes to his sash to his fan, wallet, and sandals, he wore nothing that was not striped. For breakfast and dinner he cut strips of long items like *daikon* or burdock and arranged them in stripes on his bowl or tray. His house also contained a number of unusual features. Using various types of imported wood, he integrated a striped pattern into the lattice around the front of the second floor. In front he erected a Sakai lattice, alternating vertical boards with blue shells in an arabesque pattern, and overhead he decorated the rafters under the eaves with stripes of thin lengths of purple bamboo. There was also a pond in the courtyard filled with goldfish, and from it to the second floor of the living room extended a stairway whose handrail was decorated with imported onion-capped pillars. In addition, the entire courtyard, from the north side to the wall, was painted in stripes. For these reasons everyone called him Striped Kanjūrō.[5]

Yagi's view dismisses as irrelevant individuals like Striped Kanjūrō, whose obsessive-compulsive antics would have offered onlookers comic relief but little social value per se. And while Kanjūrō's unexplained behavioral strangeness was a curiosity that held minimal social utility, it was appreciated for its own sake in much the way it would be today. Even when public benefit and other ideological criteria are removed, benign strangeness has always been greeted with a mixture of amusement, amazement, admiration, and trepidation. The fact that Kanjūrō's story survived the centuries, resurrected first by Yajima Gogaku in *Hyakka kikōden* (A miscellany of eccentricities, 1835) and then by Yagi himself, indicates that strangeness for its own sake holds lasting interest and is neither invisible nor socially irrelevant.

In addition to the sort of generic behavioral idiosyncrasies represented by Striped Kanjūrō, the cultural field in early Edo accommodated a breadth and diversity of observable strangeness: derangement resulting from spirit possession or excessive emotion, outsider status, physical distinctiveness, religious detachment, and aesthetic reclusion. Signs of derangement were potentially explained, first, by animal or spirit possession (*monotsuki*), of which the inhabiting entity (*mono*) might or might not be identified.[6]

FIGURE 2.1   Residence of Striped Kanjūrō. Yajima Gogaku, *Hyakka kikōden*. Digital Library from the Meiji Era, National Diet Library, Japan.

Alternatively, derangement (*monogurui*), to be revisited later, was attributed to excessive stress or grief. Such cases of emotional displacement might render one socially dysfunctional or, as explained in the opening words of Yoshida Kenkō's (ca. 1283–1352) *Tsurezuregusa*, produce merely "a strange sense of disturbance" (*ayashū koso monoguruoshikere*).

Foreigners and outsiders possessed a related, if less dramatic, sense of strangeness. China was one such source, for its mysteries were not easily imagined or known. Accordingly, certain tales of the strange (*kaidan*) invoked China, and products like Chinese medicines and saké were attributed with magical qualities. Appeal for supernatural strangeness grew through the seventeenth century through the publication of several *kaidan,* including *Kaidan zensho* (Complete works of strange tales, ca. 1627) by the important Confucian ideologue Hayashi Razan (1583–1657). It was believed that gatherings convened at midnight to tell one hundred of these tales (*hyaku-monogatari kaidankai*) would elicit a close encounter with the supernatural, and such events enjoyed growing popularity from the mid-1600s.[7]

Strangers need not be foreigners or supernatural entities, however. In his study of outsiders and folk religion in the Tokugawa period, Yoshida Teigo has noted that in rural communities, newcomers, as well as itinerant merchants and peddlers traveling between villages, generated suspicion and were variously feared, chastised, or worshipped. Often viewed as magico-religious adepts (*gyōja*) able to inflict spirit possession on others, they were commonly blamed or credited for a range of unexplainable phenomena, for causing madness in some and bestowing good fortune on others, for example. To assuage such fears, some villages required newcomers to erase their outsider status by fabricating kinship relations with existing village households.[8]

Although itinerant ascetics (*hijiri*) were also feared for their reputation of attacking and stealing from travelers, their strangeness was tempered by assumptions of religious potency. The Jōdō-shin monk Enkū (1632–1695), anthologized in *Kinsei kijinden,* provides an apt example (Fig. 2.2). Enkū practiced a personalized version of Buddhist worship similar to mountain asceticism (*shugendō*), and from his early thirties spent his years traveling through the country's wildest, most severe locations, including several extended trips to Ezo (Hokkaido and portions of northern Honshū). Traveling with nothing but his carving hatchet and chisels, he left behind thousands of statues and carvings of Buddhist and Shinto deities.[9] He also transcribed thousands of scrolls' worth of Buddhist sutras.[10] Distinctive among normally solemn Buddhist artworks, these wild yet affectionate talismans and idols ranged from elaborate pillars to abstract, minimalistic carvings.[11] Using the wood's original shape to produce elongated or distorted features and leaving many of his works in stages of incompletion, Enkū intentionally experimented with artistic strangeness.[12]

Mountain ascetic (*shugenja*) training included learning magic incantations and healing spells, as well as engaging in rigorous austerities. The mystery surrounding Enkū as a *shugenja* engendered belief in his protective powers, and communities erected his statues to ward off misfortune. *Kinsei kijinden* author Ban Kōkei showcases Enkū's religious potency and strangeness with anecdotal evidence of his ability to foretell the arrival of people and events. Upon visiting Lake Ōnyu (present-day Takayama in Gifu prefecture),

FIGURE 2.2   Enkū. Ban Kōkei and Mikuma Katen, *Kinsei kijinden.* International Research Center for Japanese Studies Library.

whose waters were protected by a guardian deity believed to attack lone travelers, Kōkei relates, Enkū warned locals that the lake had an ominous aura and that a disaster would soon befall them. When they implored him for help, he quickly carved one thousand Buddhist images, which he then cast into the lake, placating the deity and protecting the locals from mishap.[13] Enkū's status as a stranger in such accounts lends credence to his ability to discern portents and his power to harmonize the human and supernatural realms. His legend concludes with an account of his death from *nyūjō*, a process of self-mummification through the gradual elimination of various foods until the body becomes a desiccated, indestructible husk. *Nyūjō*, it was believed, enabled both transcendence as a Buddha and the preservation of one's carnal body until Shakamuni returned to the earth to grant salvation.[14]

Physical abnormalities, handicaps, or deformities constitute a third variety of strangeness. Traditionally, deformity was explained as a physical manifestation of defilement inflicted upon the individual as karmic retribution for past transgressions. This physical evidence of an immoral constitution justified the banishment or relegation of offending individuals to liminal outlying spaces. Yet exclusion for physical difference again carried the presumption of magico-religious abilities that empowered these individuals in divination, exorcism, and the placation of spirits. Blind lute-playing priests (*biwahōshi*) are an easy and well-known example. A number of the eccentrics anthologized in Edo period *kijinden* reiterate correlations between physical distinctiveness and mystical abilities. Seemingly extending Zhuangzi's assertion about the use of the useless, several subjects in *Hōsa kyōshaden* (Biographies of Nagoya madmen, 1778), for example, derive their "mad" identities from physical abnormalities: Hechikan is "a crooked fellow"; Nobō is a grotesquely deformed monk; Shinrokubō is crippled; and other characters are blind, shockingly unkempt, or simply strange-looking.[15] Having deformed fingers on both hands allowed Ueda Akinari to use the term *kijin* in self-reference. Ebisu, the god of commerce whose name comes from the cognate term for outsider or foreigner, was worshipped as a deformed stranger who had crossed the sea bearing good fortune. Occasionally he is represented as "one-eyed, deaf, hunchbacked, or left-handed," Yoshida finds, and in some regions is believed to be hermaphroditic.[16] Such traits are allusions to his status as stranger and invoke him as an intermediary between the mundane and the mystical.

Strangeness deriving from detachment, whether religious reclusion practiced by "mad" monks (*kyōsō*) or secular aesthetic reclusion sought by amateur literati, constitutes a final type of eccentricity. The preponderance of monks who earned fame by connecting strangeness to religiosity during the preceding centuries left deep marks on perceptions of detachment during the Edo period. As illustrated repeatedly in Kamo no Chōmei's (1155–1216) *Hosshinshū* (Collection of religious awakenings, ca. 1214), the uncompromising piety of certain wild, antisocial, antiauthoritarian monks earned them credence as otherworldly strangers. But their preference for wandering in mountains and forests where *kami* commingled with the defiled and the banished was also evidence of madness.[17] In the poetic tradition, mountains had long been synonymous with religious reclusion, and entering such wild spaces connected one with the wildness of those who resided there. Close associations between reclusion, madness, and religious transcendence are most famously exemplified by the earlier monk Zōga Shōnin (917–1003), who used unruliness and outrage as means of rejecting monastic practice. Zōga seemed to take pleasure in shocking people. His outlandish antics—his rejection of an imperial summons, allusions to his generous sexual endowment, and self-professed madness, however, were interpreted as expedient devices (*hōben*) that allowed him to overcome mundane encumbrances and attain karmic merit.[18]

The logistical difficulties of reclusion had, to an extent, been reconciled in the fourteenth century by Yoshida Kenkō. For most people, Kenkō realized, endeavoring to shed personal attachments merely induced a physical and mental inertia that numbed the very mindfulness and devotion demanded by the Buddhist Way. Kenkō, who sought reclusion on Mount Hiei in 1319 but soon returned to the city, arrived at an interpretation of world rejection that utilized everyday practices as expedient means of spirituality. When one directs one's focus upon arts or crafts in ways that allow self and art to become undifferentiated, he concluded, such practices could acquire the same spiritual functions and benefits as Buddhist austerities.[19] Kenkō's view of complete detachment as an unrealistic and unnatural contrivance thus inspired his eventual adoption of a secular reclusion that presaged practices of aesthetic reclusion common during the seventeenth century.

Chōmei and Kenkō modeled themselves after important archetypes from China, of course, where strangeness had long been embedded in cultural practice. Since at least the Wei-Jin era (220–465), reclusion and "cultivated eccentricity" had flourished as established tropes among iconic figures famed for their unkempt appearances, sexual freedom, and indulgence in drinking, music, nature appreciation, and the scholarly arts. Indeed, aesthetic reclusion was a concept ambiguous enough to support a variety of odd behaviors.[20]

ECCENTRICITY AND CONVENTION: THE CHINESE MODEL

Early Edo life thus inherited various forms of religious, behavioral, and aesthetic strangeness. Many of these would be further elaborated in the coming years, but always with due recognition of their standing as cultural traditions. Whether generic behavioral eccentricity, derangement, outsider status, physical distinctiveness, religious detachment, or aesthetic reclusion (disassociation from officialdom), strangeness was sustainable only as a convention and only if perceived as socially benign. Our ability to identify types of strange practices that were sustained throughout the medieval and early modern eras suggests that these were learned and transmitted topoi. The need to make strangeness recognizable and identifiable obliged those who aspired to distance themselves from mainstream life to replace old identity markers with new ones. Changing one's identity thereby ensued through prescribed procedures.

Once again, Chinese models proved indispensable. Political turbulence surrounding the Qing takeover in 1644 created a social volatility conducive to the formation and tolerance of eccentricity, particularly among former Ming scholar bureaucrats. Intellectuals and Ming officials trained in Confucian ethics found the proposition of employment under their new rulers morally and emotionally intolerable. For many, the only viable solution lay in self-imposed exile. Some committed suicide to avoid servitude under the Qing. Others lived their remaining years in guilt for not having done so, while others withdrew from public life and became monks. Self-reinvention of this nature was contingent upon renunciation of the position held previously, including the clothing, names, and other markers used while holding that position.[21] As these former bureaucrats donned the robes and yellow caps of Daoist priests they gave themselves new names reflective of their new status as recluses. Not to do so, Wu notes, would have been ethically improper given that establishing a new identity was a social act requiring new social observances.[22] Only through the somewhat formal protocol of accepting new duties and responsibilities would one become reenabled as a social being.

Secular reclusion was itself a learned convention that in practice was fraught with contradiction. First, while isolation and communion with nature were themes that perpetually informed the arts, artistic practice itself—in particular painting and poetry composition—was generally enjoyed within a group context. Second, although reclusion denoted aesthetic authenticity, it also tended to magnify one's celebrity. Eminent *bunjin* Kinryū Keiyū's (1712–1782) lament that unwanted visits from admirers constantly disturbed his retirement would have been a common complaint.[23]

Nonetheless, detachment did afford opportunities for cultural innovations, including those that would prove most inspirational to Edo period eccentrics. Dong Qichang's (1555–1636) group of Southern School artists, for instance, recovered impressionism and originality by breaking from the stolid traditionalism of professional (Northern School) painting. Its experimentation with abstraction, distortion, and the spiritual integration of subject and object ultimately revitalized painting and calligraphy by combining classical aesthetics with individual creativity. Indeed, the central principle of the Six Laws of Painting, introduced earlier by Xie He (early sixth c.), was capturing the "spirit consonance" (*ki* 気) of the object.[24] As had long been the case with poetry and calligraphy, literati painting did not endeavor to reproduce objects in realistic detail. To do so would be to exhibit dull-witted ignorance, or, as statesman and painter Su Shi (1037–1101) put it: "To judge a painting by its verisimilitude shows the mental level of a child."[25] Literati painting must express one's subjectivity while also recognizing and capturing the object's inner nature.[26] Su maintained that even objects without constant form—clouds, ripples, bamboo—possessed a constant inner nature, and the skillful, attentive artist should paint so as not to corrupt either constant form or inner nature. The following analogy drawn by Su was to become fundamental to later *wenren* painting theory: "Nowadays the artists construct bamboo, joint by joint and leaf by leaf. Where is the bamboo? Therefore in painting bamboos, one must have bamboo formed in one's breast; at the time of painting, one concentrates and sees what one wants to paint. Immediately one follows the idea . . . like a hawk swooping down on a rabbit. With a moment's hesitation it would be lost."[27] Artistic excellence, therefore, was judged by the ability to connect spiritually with an object and then to capture it spontaneously. This not only provided the core literati arts—painting, poetry, and calligraphy—with thematic and technical inspiration, it obliged artists to look more closely at their local scenery and to internalize nature's contours and movements.

Dong's Southern School used this principle of internalization to produce fantasy, grotesquery, and distortion in order to recast the world as something unfamiliar and unsettling but also as a place where the impossible became possible. It was the otherworldly, uncanny qualities of this art that earned it its reputation for strangeness.[28] As eccentric scholar-artists also experimented with dry-brush techniques, the uncanny acquired an aesthetic of intentional deformity and ugliness. Pale, dim, desiccated landscapes were fitting to those who constructed their new identities around the enlightened cripples and outcasts modeled in *Zhuangzi*. Dong's group subsequently became synonymous with amateur literati painting (C. *wenrenhua; J. bunjinga,* or *nanga*), the genre that would provide philosophical and technical validation for aesthetic strangeness in early modern Japan.

While these subversive aesthetic forms marked a qualified revival of the unorthodox in China, literati functioned without incurring undue condemnation and thus came to represent an orthodoxy in their own right. "Eccentric artists were usually left alone," Wu notes, "roaming the community drunk, living inexplicably between tears and laughter."[29] By the late seventeenth century, the original impetus for protestant, eccentric painting thus faded under its own popularity. Preserving freshness was a purely artistic problem for so-called eccentric artists like Dao Qi (1641–1717), for example, and not necessarily connected to a genuinely strange interior. Dao's perceived idiosyncrasies were not contingent upon cultivating a specific public image but upon exceeding his contemporaries in artistic originality.[30] The view of *wenren* artists as amateurs who rejected any notion of mixing art and commerce, moreover, had now all but faded. The Eight Eccentrics of Yanzhou (Yanzhou baguai), who sat atop their field as the foremost painters of the eighteenth century, reversed the sanctity of amateurism by attaching their purported eccentricity to self-promotion.[31] Zheng Xie (1693–1765), for instance, advertised by posting his prices, but cautioned: "If you present cold, hard cash, then my heart swells with joy and everything I write or paint is excellent. . . . Honied talk of old friendships and past companions is only the autumn wind blowing past my ear."[32] James Cahill wonders if popularity caused a self-consciousness among these painters that elicited forms of artificial posturing. The fact that eccentric masters took pupils, making strangeness transmissible, is certainly a paradoxical development unless we acknowledge eccentricity as a convention in its own right.

Growing receptivity of aesthetic strangeness presented writers with similar opportunities to challenge the boundaries of literary heterodoxy. Like Dao Qi, the novelist Pu Songling (1640–1715) sensed a constant need to shift the contours of strangeness to preserve the freshness of his writing.[33]

"When the strange becomes ossified," writes Judith Zeitlin of Pu's *Liaozhai zhiyi* (Liaozhai's records of the strange), "it is in imminent danger of disappearing altogether. . . . By the late Ming and early Qing . . . accounts of the strange inevitably began to lose their sense of novelty and to seem stereotyped both in their thematic range and literary expression."[34] Pu's estrangement from the strange, in other words, sought to overcome processes of conventionalization that were commodifying strangeness as a literary trope.

Cao Xueqin's (1715–1763) towering work *Hong lou meng* (The Story of the Stone) deploys intentional detachment as just this sort of trope. Widely considered China's greatest novel, and well known in Japan, the work portrays an array of aristocratic characters who find reprieve from the tedium of their routines in reclusive, antisocial behavior. Playing with aesthetic detachment as a convention learned through their studies of the classics, they delight in constructing and inhabiting gardens and utopian realms detached from the nuisances of mundane affairs. Adamantina (Miao Yu), for example, is a lay Buddhist nun living alone in a family temple. She is talented, knows the classics by heart, and is a proud, strange, and contrary person. Cao's use of counterpoint between worldly and otherworldly is illustrative in his description of Adamantina, here delivered by Xiu-yan:

> Her favourite prose-writer is Zhuangzi, so sometimes she calls herself "The Outsider" (畸人), after Zhuangzi's "outsider . . . wandering beyond the realm." The way to please her is to refer to yourself modestly as someone still trapped in the toils of the wicked world while she is floating freely somewhere above them. If she'd called herself "The Outsider" in this note she's sent you, the right response would have been to call yourself "The Worldling" in your reply. As she's called herself "The Dweller Beyond the Threshold," you should refer to yourself in answering as "The Dweller Behind the Threshold," to indicate that you have understood the reference.[35]

Adamantina represents herself as a Zhuangzian eccentric and believes herself to be faithfully following the reclusive identity so valued by early modern Chinese and Japanese *kijin*. Her purposive striving, however, is inconsistent with the playful effortlessness of this calling, and her open disdain for mundane affairs prevents her, despite Xiu-yan's assurances, from "floating freely" above them. Nonetheless, Adamantina's references to Zhuangzi are universally recognized, establishing her eccentric veneer as a literary trope that need not manifest genuine strangeness.

Having lost its protestant bite, detached strangeness became attractive to an array of social classes. Even Emperor Qianlong (r. 1735–1796) was pleased to represent himself publicly through paintings that exhibited his spontaneity, individualism, and contempt for convention. One such image dresses him in Daoist garb with one hand on a deer, the mount of the Daoist master, and the other holding *lingzhi* mushrooms signifying immortality and magic powers. It posits him, not merely as a Daoist immortal, but as a messianic figure empowered with an otherworldly mystique that selflessly remains earthbound as a guardian of the people. Tolerance, Qianlong's example reveals, operates in both directions. Eccentricity is not only a strategy of coping with intolerance but also a strategy of tolerance adopted by the especially powerful.

EMOTION (*QING*) AND STRANGENESS IN MING CHINA

By now it is clear that developments within China's cultural field nourished the roots of aesthetic eccentricity in seventeenth-century Japan. Discussion of Japan's outsiders and oddballs likewise requires extensive reference to Ming and Qing period thought. For our purposes, the most compelling intellectual development was the thought of Wang Yangming (1472–1529), which justified the sorts of cultural strangeness already discussed by lending moral legitimacy to individual emotion. Drawing heavily from Mencius, Wang maintained that sagehood dwelt not in dogma but within the individual, a proposition that made moral self-cultivation both a private affair and a social obligation. He also asserted that standards of goodness, while universal, were ultimately apprehended individually, meaning that personal convictions in no way conflicted with universal moral knowledge.[36] The premise that the moral potential of innate knowledge was to be actualized through action, even seemingly immoral action, was a mandate to follow instinctive predispositions like *qing* (J. *jō*). *Qing* was not a chaotic explosion of primal, unregulated emotion, but an ardent, universal sympathy informed by human relationships. It enabled one's moral and intellectual capacity for virtue.[37] By positing emotion as a supreme moral force, Wang reformulated Confucian ethics to tolerate difference.

Wang's theories, which will be discussed further in Chapter 4, were taken in liberal directions, most notably by the radical Taizhou or Realization School. By advancing the individual as the root of all moral knowledge, this populist, grassroots contingent promoted individualism and extreme forms of rationalism among people of all classes.[38] Though a large number of its leaders had earned the highest civil service degree, thereby giving the group a measure of immunity from official sanction, its popularity emerged mainly through the efforts of commoner proselytizers. Li Zhi (1527–1602), remembered as one of China's preeminent heretics, was the Taizhou's stand-out figure. A foremost iconoclast of his day, his celebration of human passions exemplifies late Ming individualism. In *Zhuangzi jie* (Interpretations of the *Zhuangzi*) he highlights that text's alignment of *kijin* and Heaven. Li was no detached Daoist eccentric, however. He was an activist whose belief in the inherent divinity of individual knowledge and action tolerated no pretensions. Notorious for his outspoken contempt for corrupt officials and specious Confucian scholars, he was particularly critical of certain reclusive contemporaries ("mountain-men") who feigned aestheticism as false evidence of moral superiority. He writes:

> Those who consider themselves sages today are no different from the mountain-men—it is all a matter of luck. If it is a man's luck that he can compose poetry he calls himself a "mountain-man"; if it is not and he cannot compose poetry and become a mountain-man, he calls himself a sage. . . . They turn around and reverse themselves in order to deceive the world and secure their own gain. They call themselves "mountain-men" but their hearts are those of merchants. Their lips are full of the Way and virtue, but their ambition is to become "thieves of virtue."[39]

Li's venomous attacks were tolerated to a point, but further antics led to his eventual undoing. A mob, incited by one of his essays, burned his house; his books were censored, seized, and also burned. In 1601 he was finally thrown in prison, where he committed suicide the following year.

Li Zhi recognized that the value of individual endowments is endorsed by all major East Asian creeds: Mencius famously articulates the individual's inherent goodness; Zhu Xi Confucianism notes the indistinguishability of original nature (*honzen no sei*) from principle (*ri*); and Wang Yangming prioritizes the centrality of intuition (*ryōchi*). All intone agreement concerning the individual's innate potential for moral virtue. Likewise, Mahayana Buddhism teaches "original enlightenment" (*hongaku*) as a universal endowment consistent with the dharma, while Zen explains Buddha nature in nearly identical terms. Such parallels constitute important philosophical agreement concerning the individual's intrinsic moral potentialities.[40]

Li sought to activate these consensual ideas through unchecked, instinctive action. *Qing* informs art, he argued, and art emanates from individual emotion. "There is no impurity in the passions," Li continued, echoing Nâgârjuna's assertion that human passions are consistent with Buddha nature. "Neither wine, women, wealth, nor disposition place any obstacle to following the Bodhisattva path."[41] Disdainful of stolid conformity in art and literature, he lauded the creativity and "emotional genuineness" of folk and vernacular cultural forms.[42]

Feng Menglong (1574–1646), whose acquaintances called him the *kijin* or *kyōshi* (madman) living near the Tiger Hills market, is a second important archetype of aesthetic eccentricity. Feng was one of few publicly self-declared *kijin*, taking the studio name Hainai Jishi (Eccentric within the Four Seas) while also referring to himself as "the *kijin* of Eastern Wu."[43] Such a person, he explained, is one who follows an unorthodox Way and who delights in unusual thoughts and behaviors.[44] For Feng, the term *kijin* connoted a strong attraction to *qing* as a criterion for aesthetic and moral cultivation. Not only was *qing* the most genuine of human dispositions, Feng felt that it was also the trait most effectively converted into action. Its spontaneity, moreover, aligned it most naturally with the inherent goodness of human nature.[45] Feng explains the *kijin*'s natural affinity for *qing* in *Qingshi* (Anatomy of love), which identifies four types of people differentiated by the nature of their souls as reflected in dreams: "A superior person has no dreams," he begins, "because he has freed himself from his emotions [*qing*] and his soul is therefore calm. A most stupid person also has no dreams; this is so because his emotions are dull and his soul is withered. An ordinary person, however, has many dreams, because his emotions are mixed and confused and his soul, therefore, is unsettled.

Finally, an unusual person [畸人] has extraordinary dreams; this is so because his emotions are concentrated and his soul, therefore, is pure."[46] Here Feng proposes that both emotions and soul are integrated components of subjectivity. The superior person's soul finds calm through freedom from emotion; the *kijin*'s soul is purified by intense emotion. Feng's subsequent passage clarifies this apparent inconsistency: "Those who excel at painting can put souls into their paintings; and those who excel at magic can use it to command souls. In this vast universe, really, what has not been accomplished by the soul?"[47] For Feng, then, the soul is an emotional outlet. While the superior person finds calm, it is likely that this precludes superior literary or artistic expression. Likewise, while the *kijin* is aesthetically enabled by concentrated emotion, this is a constitution that precludes any possibility for internal stillness.

Wang Yangming, Li Zhi, and Feng Menglong each endeavored to erect *qing* against the rational utilitarianism advanced by Zhu Xi Confucianism. *Qing*'s justification of subjective feelings also opened up possibilities for introspection and experimentation in poetry, painting, and literature, creating a more receptive environment for the unconventional.

Meanwhile, the transmission of this "cult of *qing*" to late seventeenth-century Japan was helping proto-literati assert individualism and strangeness as philosophically viable.[48] The relationship between the Confucian Way and human emotion would become an ongoing discourse in Japan that ultimately framed how eccentricity would be conceptualized. Confucians recognized the Way as formulated to align with people's emotional dispositions and to nurture those emotions for the benefit of society at large. They saw no value in gratuitous emotionalism independent of a civic context. Revisionist interpretations of Confucian texts by Ancient Learning (Kogaku) scholars Itō Jinsai (1627–1705) and Ogyū Sorai (1666–1728) broke from the staunch rationalism of Zhu Xi-ism by positing the ethical validity of human emotion. For Jinsai, emotional responses, whether to daily events or to the experience of reading poetry, had both cathartic and morally beneficial effects. Sorai, who gained notoriety for historicizing ancient Confucian texts by explaining them as merely responses to specific historical problems, agreed that human passions were a valuable resource for moral good. "The Way of the ancient kings was established through human emotion," he wrote, and Japanese could internalize the moral benefits of emotion by reading ancient Chinese texts and engaging with the language contained therein.[49] Sorai went on to affirm emotion as an undeniable component of human nature, a proposition that both freed it from the political and moral rationalism of Zhu Xi-ism and ratified it as a valuable part of human experience.

Sorai's ideas proved infectious to many schools of eighteenth-century thought, National Learning (Kokugaku) in particular. Echoing Sorai, leading National Learning thinkers Kamo no Mabuchi (1697–1769) and Mootori Norinaga (1730–1801) found apolitical value in poetry's capacity to express the emotional contents of the human heart. They also found that cases of emotional release expressed in literature had, since ancient times, helped people understand one another better.[50] Such propositions directed the ensuing National Learning movement toward recovering a native ancient Way (*kodō*) characterized by unadulterated human feelings.[51]

The benefits that Ancient Learning and National Learning thinkers found in intuition and emotional intensity were easily extended to a spectrum of eccentric behaviors. *Kijin* and *kyōjin,* whether admired or reviled, have been provocative largely for their emotional intensity and unpredicatiblity, a sentiment articulated later by Miyazaki Tōten (1870–1922) in *Kyōjindan* (Discussions of the mad, 1902).[52] Miyazaki invokes Edo period *kijinden* by equating *kyōjin* with enlightened beings whose moral rectitude is ill suited to the corruption of contemporary society. The mad, he begins, are distinctive for "their extraordinary intellect, emotion, and volition."[53] This view of *kyōjin* as struggling with passions and ambitions distinguishes them from—and elevates them above—the unfeeling, unthinking, complacent masses. Miyazaki elaborates:

> They wish to . . . arrive at the natural world of the self, stamp out self-consciousness, sweep aside the turmoil of worldly desires, and embrace the beautiful flower of raw emotion. They are people who revel in sentiments emanating from the natural self. Thus, when they feel grief they cry, when they feel joy they laugh, and when they feel success they are fulfilled. Whether crying, laughing or fulfilled, never is there an impetus to reflect on these feelings, and without an impetus for thoughtfulness evil passions never arise. For them the present is a dream, and dream and reality are one. This is their state, their reality, and they don't care how they appear to others. They want nothing to do with words and deeds; they merely follow their feelings without hesitation or fear of what others will say.[54]

For Miyazaki, then, *kyōjin* are active, talented, and emotional, though unable to regulate these impulses. Regulation, after all, reduces one to mediocrity, and so while *kyōjin* may fail in their ambitions, they at least remain true to their instincts. Centuries after Wang Yangming articulated the moral value of individual emotion and action, sentiments like Miyazaki's speak to its continuing importance within Japanese thought.[55]

JAPAN'S EMERGENT *BUNJIN* ETHOS

During the Muromachi period, recluses bore sufficient cultural prestige to serve as authorities of Chinese taste for the Ashikaga shoguns and as hired hosts for parties, linked verse (*renga*) gatherings, and tea competitions.[56] Signifying not merely detachment from officialdom but strangeness itself, aesthetic reclusion remained the primary manifestation of eccentricity in the seventeenth century, and throughout the centuries that followed, recluses were commonly represented as eccentric. The first biographical collections of eccentrics, in fact, were biographies of recluses—for example, Gensei's (1623–1668) *Fusō in'itsuden* (Biographies of Japanese recluses, 1664) and Hayashi Dokkōsai's (1625–1661) *Honchō tonshi* (Histories of Japanese recluses, 1664). *Kinsei kijinden,* along with the numerous *kijinden* that followed, continued to invoke and glorify Japan's prominent recluses.[57] Meiji and Taisho documents like Hosokawa Junjirō's *In'itsu zenden* (Complete accounts of reclusion, 1878) and Motoyama Tekishū's *Meijin kijin* (Notables and eccentrics, 1926) perpetuated this practice of representing prototypical *kijin* like Matsuo Bashō and Ike no Taiga as recluses.[58] Detached aestheticism would thus remain a core feature of early modern Japan's developing ethos of eccentricity.

From its outset, the Edo era's inhospitable political and cultural climate necessitated reclusion. Indeed, its first important recluses were educated political refugees, aristocrats, and warriors who had been disenfranchised following the consolidation of power under the Tokugawa shogunate. Withdrawal would be their means of neutralizing themselves as political liabilities. Patterning their retreat after the secular withdrawal of Chinese cultural icons like the Four Greybeards of Mount Shang (C. *Shangshan sihao;* J. *Shōzan shikō*), the Seven Sages of the Bamboo Grove (C. *Julin qixian;* J. *Chikurin shichiken*), Tao Qian (365–427), and native forebears like Yoshida Kenkō, these individuals became the progenitors of Japanese *bunjin.*

The *bakufu's* overtures toward custodianship of the arts also caused some of the country's most accomplished aesthetes to leave official service. Tea culture offers an apt example. Tea reached its zenith in the early seventeenth century, largely through the influence of the Rikyū's Seven Worthies (*Rikyū shichitetsu*)—seven daimyo, most of them Christian, who emulated the tea style of the preeminent Sen no Rikyū (1502–1591). The *shichitetsu's* affiliation with the controversial Rikyū, as well as with Christianity, posed a potential threat to Tokugawa legitimacy, however. In 1613, a 1587 prohibition against Christian activities was reissued, and the following year several Christian daimyo, including the tea master Takayama Ukon (1552–1615), were expelled from Japan.[59] The collective threat posed by the *shichitetsu* extended beyond their religion and former ties to the Toyotomi, for their combined wealth—3.88 million *koku*—approached the Tokugawa family's 4.1 million *koku.*[60] In 1615, Ieyasu forced the celebrated warrior and tea master Furuta Oribe (1544–1615), to commit ritual suicide (*seppuku*) for his suspected involvement in Toyotomi Hideyori's insurgency earlier that year. First a warrior under Nobunaga and then a general to whom Hideyoshi had awarded the domain of Yamashiro (35,000 *koku*), Oribe was also a disciple of Rikyū and considered one of Kyoto's leading tea masters. Though later summoned to teach tea ceremony to the second Tokugawa shogun, Hidetada (1579–1632), his lingering loyalties to the Toyotomi were apparently revealed during Hideyori's campaign. The Christian expulsion and Oribe's death thus ended tea's cultural independence from politics.

They also sent a clear message to others with similarly ambiguous affiliations. The year of Oribe's death, Ieyasu granted to the eclectic artist Hon'ami Kōetsu (1558–1637), also Hideyoshi's former retainer, a piece of land on the outskirts of Kyoto where, he said, Kōetsu might better devote himself to artistic pursuits. Kōetsu, who had befriended and studied with Oribe and who had just declined a job offer from Ieyasu, understood this land grant as an unstated demand to remove himself from Kyoto's political center.[61] Sen no Rikyū's grandson Sen no Sōtan (1578–1658) was also careful to distance himself from political circles and influential families, opting to live quietly in Kyoto as a reclusive tea master.[62] Responding to the same confluence of political events, Tosa School painter and *ukiyoe* pioneer Iwasa Matabei (1578–1650) withdrew from Kyoto to Echizen in 1617 in order to situate himself on safer ground among Tokugawa allies. Shōkadō Shōjō (1584–1639), a priest, tea master, painter, and calligrapher who would share with Kōetsu claim as one of the Three Great Calligraphers of Kan'ei (1624–1644) (*Kan'ei no sanpitsu*) had acted as an intermediary between the *bakufu* and the court, but later retreated to a small hut outside of Kyoto.[63] Within the new political climate, clearly, conspicuous participation within the higher echelons of cultural practice was an unwise presumption. The result was a diverse group of nouveaux literati desiring to break from established professional or official schools to pursue independent modes of artistic expression.

The transmission of cultural knowledge and artifacts from China also served as a formative catalyst for Japan's nascent *bunjin* ethos. While identifying themselves as Sinophiles, many contemporary *bunjin* acquired knowledge of the *wenren* arts from antiquated or unreliable models. Access to Chinese literati painting was particularly problematic. This deficiency would be addressed, however imperfectly, by two sources: Ōbaku Zen temples and imported painting manuals. Ōbaku, a sect of Rinzai, arrived in

Japan through Ingen Ryūki (C. Yinyuan, 1592–1673), who immigrated to Nagasaki in 1654. Ingen traveled to Edo to meet the shogun Tokugawa Ietsuna (1641–1680), who permitted him to construct Manpukuji temple in Uji, south of Kyoto. Established in 1663, Manpukuji became the headquarters of Ōbaku Zen in Japan, and outreach by its resident Chinese monks provided interested locals with access to forms of Chinese literati culture, including infused green tea (*sencha*). *Sencha,* which Patricia Graham calls "the central component of an eccentric and Sinophile lifestyle," served as a cultural conduit by which Chinese tastes entered and circulated among Japanese literati. Its introduction corresponded to a time when Sinophiles were seeking a fresh alternative to the tea ceremony (*chanoyu*), which had become increasingly popular among wealthy patrons who placed exaggerated importance on collecting and displaying expensive utensils. *Sencha* rejected *chanoyu*'s ritualistic pretensions by resurrecting interest in the elegance of drinking and appreciating the flavor of tea.[64]

Ōbaku temples were also a crucial point of access to Chinese paintings and manuals. The most ubiquitous and influential Chinese painting manual was *The Eight Kinds of Painting Manual* (C: *Bazhong huapu,* 1621), translated into Japanese in 1672 as *Hasshu gafu*. Also of interest to Japanese literati was *The Mustard Seed Garden Manual* (C. *Jieziyuan huazhuan,* 1679), translated as *Kaishien gaden* in 1748, though the Chinese original likely reached Japan during the Genroku period.[65] While contact with these sources unquestionably ignited a fascination with aesthetic strangeness, art historians disagree about the extent to which first- and second-generation Japanese literati artists emulated Chinese models. Patricia Graham and Joan Stanley-Baker come down on opposite sides of this question. Graham posits that the cultural forms transmitted by painting manuals and Ōbaku monks were, in general, uncritically embraced by adoring Japanese *bunjin,* while Stanley-Baker asserts that Chinese culture was adopted selectively and experienced a gradual process of domestication. Japanese painters, she notes, were aware that manuals were distorted during the process of reprinting and so resisted uncritical emulation. For this reason, the primary influence of these manuals was topical and thematic rather than technical.[66]

An additional factor contributing to the emergence of a *bunjin* ethos in the seventeenth century was a surplus of educated would-be bureaucrats who either voluntarily rejected placement in official service or, due to limited available positions, were denied posts. For individuals opting to retire from service, aesthetic reclusion offered both freedom and cultural prestige.

Already financially secure, Kinoshita Chōshōshi (1569–1649) and Ishikawa Jōzan (1583–1672) retreated to semireclusive lives in hermitages on the outskirts of Kyoto, where they immersed themselves in poetry and painting. Chōshōshi was Ieyasu's in-law but also Toyotomi Hideyoshi's nephew. When the Tokugawa engaged a coalition of Toyotomi loyalists at the Battle of Sekigahara (1600), conflicting loyalties compelled Chōshōshi to abandon his military duties, for which he was stripped of his fief. He retreated happily to a quiet life, which he describes fondly in *Sanka no ki* (An account of my hut in the mountains), amassing a gigantic private library of Chinese and Japanese books and cultivating friendships with such important contemporaries as Neo-Confucian scholar Fujiwara Seika (1561–1619) and tea master Kobori Enshū (1579–1647). Jōzan sought for his own retirement a similar balance between isolation and social engagement, for after taking residence in a hut on the eastern edge of Kyoto he remained active within a circle of local literati. Emulating Chinese recluses, he became an early proponent of *sencha* and would later be credited as a core progenitor of *bunjin* culture.

Reclusion earned both Chōshōshi and Jōzan reputations as eccentrics, and they would serve as bookends in Ban Kōkei's *Zoku-kinsei kijinden* (1798).[67] But their sociocultural position was not uncontested. As proto-*bunjin* who predated the development of an established *bunjin* ethos, from a Neo-Confucian perspective they showcased the aforementioned problem of social legitimacy. Their social irrelevance—the use of their uselessness—had yet to be widely appreciated for its own sake. Confucian ideologues held that art must bear practical, utilitarian functions. Its grandeur was achieved only if it existed in some useful capacity for public and political good. The strange Chinese aesthetics being advanced by *bunjin,* they maintained, contained no such utility.[68] While this position echoed the Neo-Confucian perspective on difference embraced by government officials and professional artists, it was not uncontested. In opposition to this view, Ogyū Sorai legitimized the concept of art for art's sake by proposing that the value of literature and poetry lay in their merit as recreation. Not until the eighteenth century, after Sorai had distanced Confucian morality from the arts, was commercially supported "amateurism" made possible as a career choice of sorts.[69] For many, this laid to rest the problem of social utility faced by Chōshōshi and Jōzan and enabled further artistic interventions toward establishing the *bunjin* ethos as a prominent cultural force.

It was within the context of this discourse that the aesthetics of detachment and autonomy infiltrated early modern Japan. The influx of political refugees seeking asylum after the Tokugawas' assumption of power; the establishment of Chinese Ōbaku Zen temples in Kyoto, Nagasaki, and Gifu; and the increasing demand for foreign prints and painting manuals that packaged originality and heterodoxy as high art all helped to introduce the unconventional and original as viable aesthetic criteria.

KYŌ AND *MUYŌ* AS AESTHETICS OF ECCENTRICITY

If aesthetic reclusion framed seventeenth-century Japan's preferred form of eccentric practice, the terms *kyō* (along with its variants *kuruu* and *kyōki*) and *muyō* topped the lexicon that signified eccentricity. *Kyō* was a general term indicating a state of emotional abandon.[70] In Confucian classics like the *Book of Songs* and *The Analects* it referred to suffering from the passions of romantic love, usually by young, unmarried men.[71] *The Analects* 17:8, for instance, uses the term in reference to certain young disciples exhibiting a deficiency of emotional control. "Love of courage without love of learning," it warned, "degenerates into mere recklessness [*kyō*]."[72] But it made no difference whether this recklessness was genuine or contrived. As from the Confucian perspective one is defined by one's social utility, even disingenuous recklessness or feigned madness (*yōkyō*) were indistinguishable from true lunacy. "Even one who runs through the streets imitating a madman (*kyōjin*) is in fact a madman," Yoshida Kenkō writes in *Tsurezuregusa,* for such behavior defied constructive social involvement.[73]

In contrast to the standard Confucian view of *kyō* as an unregulated and therefore potentially disruptive state, Japanese folk traditions variously embraced *kyō*'s potential to induce a state of transcendental ecstasy. The term appears in reference to the emotional derangement experienced in thaumaturgy and shamanism, liminal states of consciousness, as well as the sorts of performative religious rituals that formed the basis of *dengaku* and *sarugaku,* carnivalesque theatrical forms that presaged Nō. As noted above, associations between madness and the supernatural also extended to descriptions of spirit possession by a ghostly or demonic entity.[74] From the fourteenth and fifteenth centuries, emotional abandon or supernatural possession were depicted in Nō through the prominent theme of derangement (*monogurui*). The madness depicted in this genre of plays was generally triggered by an intense sense of loss, either of a husband as in the play *Kinuta* (The fulling block), a child as in *Sumidagawa* (Sumida River), or of one's youth as in *Sotoba Komachi* (Komachi on the Stupa). In such cases, the rapture of *kyō* allowed the mind to break free from conventional thought, aligning it with or rendering it receptive to Buddhist truths. Buddhism's backhanded appreciation for derangement thus validated *kyō* as a device able to ameliorate life's uncertainties and expedite enlightenment.

Whereas derangement and spirit possession posited madness as an altered state of consciousness, Zhu Xi Confucianism advanced a metaphysical explanation. The term *kichigai* (lunacy), for instance, gained credence from the fifteenth century through a metaphysics that recognized an interplay between *ri* (C. *li,* Principle) and *ki* (C. *qi,* material force) within the individual. Distorted or incorrect *ki* (*kichigai*), it explained, was a psychoemotional disturbance that differentiated the individual from others. As *ki* was a universally shared endowment, *kichigai* disrupted the self's connection with that universality, alienating the self from human society and undermining social relations.[75] This explanation enabled perceptions of strange individuals through a lens of natural, innate endowments and provided a framework to reconsider the particularities of individual character. And although *kyō,* like the term *monogurui,* often referred to antisocial, illegal, or immoral behavior, this metaphysical explanation enabled its eventual association with natural endowments such as extraordinary ability, intelligence, creativity, and Buddhistic piety. Interpreting strangeness as a natural gift would prove critical to its popular reception later in the Edo period.[76]

Zhu Xi's metaphysics also enabled Wang Yangming to take an activistic interpretation of *kyō* as a metaphysical endowment, finding within *kyō* utility for embracing rather than extinguishing individual will. For Wang, *kyō* was the free expression of intuitive knowledge, the human heart's natural state. This implicit validation of a more emotionally liberated and independent self gained popular support with Wang's more liberal proponents and helped establish *kyō* as an intellectually viable aesthetic criterion.[77] The liberal adventurousness informing Wang's thought thus legitimized a generation of literati disposed to challenging standing aesthetic conventions. As Wang's thought infiltrated the cultural field, *kyō* subsequently emerged as a standard feature of Ming art and literature.[78]

Neo-Confucian metaphysics not only provided qualified intellectual validation to *kyō* but also lent moral authority to eccentric practices like deliberate uselessness (*muyō*). Social disengagement and carefree wandering (*shōyōyū*)—particularly scandalous propositions for Confucian societies advocating individual responsibility—had long since been elucidated in *Zhuangzi.* Section 4 of that text, "In the World of Men," extols the utility of uselessness through a series of misfits whose deformities both entitled them to special treatment and released them from social responsibilities. "It is this unusableness," the text asserts, "that the Holy Man makes use of!"[79] Zhuangzi concludes his discussion of uselessness by rewriting *The Analects* 18:5, wherein Jieyu, the madman of Chu, warns of the state's imminent political decline. In Zhuangzi's reinterpretation, Jieyu reverses Confucius' position by noting the benefits of the useless and the misfortunes of utility, learning, and virtue. His lament that "Nobody knows the use of the useless," thus carried "useful" antisocial subtexts for seventeenth-century Japanese whose own utility had been eroded under the Tokugawa order.[80]

Zhuangzi had been known in Japan since the Nara era, but was not a favored textual resource until the early Edo period when Danrin and Teimon *haikai* poets were drawn to it as a font of cultural validation and comic irony.[81] As Peipei Qiu has demonstrated, *Zhuangzi* provided a source of intertextuality to progenitors of *haikai,* who then proceeded to create a culture of uselessness around their art. Danrin School founder Nishiyama Sōin (1605–1682), who surrendered his samurai status to assume the identity of a *muyōsha,* represents himself as such in *Shakkyō hyakuin* (One hundred Buddhist verses, 1674):

> A useless monk on a pilgrimage to the western provinces, I know the use of uselessness and the pleasures of pleasurelessness. Without purpose or discriminations, I know only the virtue of good health. Cared for by villagers and spring blossoms, and teased by the autumn foliage, I pass the years wandering wherever my heart and feet may lead me. As for the idle hours of my journey, I fritter them away composing *haikai*. . . . Above all, the way of *haikai* is to put emptiness first and substance last.[82]

Here, Sōin's practical embodiment of uselessness and emptiness are extended as aesthetic values and poetic ideals. Not only must verse emanate from deprived, empty circumstances, it must be positioned outside the utility of status and wealth. Rendered socially irrelevant, both poet and verse attain the desired condition of *muyō.*

Sōin's acquaintance Matsuo Bashō (1644–1694) proceeded to develop and popularize an aesthetics of eccentricity around uselessness. By invoking, for example, the Zen monk Sōgi (1421–1502), a wandering poet known mainly for his *renga,* Bashō connects himself to *haikai*'s earlier lineages of *muyō, shōyōyū,* and poetic madness.[83] He did this primarily by openly emulating Daoist works and incorporating into his verses principles gleaned from the *Laozi* and the *Zhuangzi*. Paraphrasing Zhuangzi, he notes the uselessness of the *bashō* tree from which he took his sobriquet, thereby hinting at his own irrelevance. Subsequent references to his personal eccentricity in verse and in prose, as here in *Genjūan no ki* (On the unreal dwelling, 1690), reinforce the point: "I have not led a clerical life, nor have I served in normal pursuits. Ever since I was very young I have been fond of my eccentric ways, and once I had come to make them the source of a livelihood, temporarily I thought, I discovered myself bound for life to the one line of my art, incapable and talentless as I am."[84] In such statements Bashō explicitly aligns himself with Chinese and Japanese icons like Zhang Hengqu (1020–1077), Huaisu (725–785), Kamo no Chōmei, Yoshida Kenkō, and Zen master Ikkyū Sōjun (1394–1481), all of whom united eccentricity and aestheticism through carefree detachment. Including himself among a vaunted cohort known for putting Zen and Daoist principles into practice imbued his *haikai* with greater philosophical depth.[85]

Kyō, whose usage had now expanded to include both humor and technical deviation, was also a favored poetic trait among *haikai* poets. Those exhibiting an ostensibly mad devotion to that calling were variously referred to as "mad recluses" (*kyōinja*) or "masters of crazy verse" (*kyōka no saishi*), but only Bashō, styling himself both a *muyōsha,* "a hermit and socially useless soul who had forgotten the world," and a *kyōsha,* made *kyō* a fundamental part of his poetics.[86] In the linked verse collection *Fuyu no hi* (Winter days, 1684), he writes:

> My bamboo hat had worn out in the rains of the long journey, and my paper jacket had become crumpled in the storms. A poor man utterly destitute, even I felt pity for myself. Suddenly I remembered that a gifted man of eccentric poetry had visited this province in the past, and I uttered:
>> With a crazy verse
>> and the wintry winds—I must look
>> much like Chikusai.[87]

Bashō's self-comparison to Chikusai, a fictional character from Tomiyama Dōya's (1585–1634) *Chikusai monogatari* (Tale of Chikusai) with a crazed love of *kyōka,* implies his own devotion to *haikai* as a comparable form of madness.[88] By emulating the reclusive, eccentric lifestyles of noted archetypes, Bashō both weds *haikai* to tropes of madness and uselessness, and raises it to a technically and aesthetically superior form unsullied by commercial motives. Prior to this, *kyō* had consisted of comic aberration, vulgarity, or wildness that used existing literary genres—comic *tanka* (*kyōka*), comic prose (*kyōbun*), and comic drama (*kyōgen*)—to deliver humor. "In order to transform *haikai* into poetry of profound meaning," Peipei Qiu asserts, "Bashō and his followers reinvented the *kyō* of *haikai* by creating the personae of unworldly recluse and carefree wanderer."[89]

Bashō felt that eccentricity was a quality to which poets should intentionally aspire, and that even strong verses could be improved by adding elements of strangeness. The aesthetic qualities of *fūryū* (windblown elegance), *fūkyō* (windblown eccentricity), and *kyōken* (eccentric and nonconforming) constitute the core of Bashō's poetics.[90] *Fūryū*, Qiu notes, advocates poetic sensibilities that place emphasis on strangeness—or more precisely, on "transcending the 'worldly' by being eccentric and unconventional."[91] Shōmon (Bashō School) disciple Mukai Kyorai's (1651–1704) notes reveal how Bashō taught his students to deliberately and actively pursue *fūryū* and *kyō* as poetic standards.[92] Once he had grasped *fūryū*, Kyorai reports, his poetry progressed quickly. Close disciples Hattori Ransetsu (1654–1707) and Naito Jōsō (1662–1704) also earned reputations as eccentrics by relinquishing their samurai status and following the master's self-described uselessness. Ransetsu would later be labeled a *muyōsha* in *Haika kijindan* (Accounts of eccentric haikai poets, 1816), and Jōsō would be anthologized as a *kijin* in *Kinsei kijinden*. Bashō was so successful in his efforts to promote an aesthetics of eccentricity that by the 1680s it was becoming an established criterion for aesthetic achievement generally. Within the restlessness of the Genroku period the will for uninhibited play was pervasive, writes Takahashi: "*kyō* was a declaration of detachment from the world order, a space in which the mind was free to play uninhibited."[93]

Eccentricity did not enjoy unqualified tolerance, however. As suggested, it required observance of certain boundaries, and Bashō earned kudos by revising those boundaries within the purview of amateurism. While the celebrity and commercial success of contemporaries like Ihara Saikaku (1642–1693, about whom more later) proved intermittent, Bashō became a permanent icon of early modern Japanese literature by choosing to move his art toward artistic purity, which he viewed as antithetical and aesthetically incompatible with commerce. Originally, *haikai* practice required a physical gathering (*za*) of poets to create linked verses, and on such occasions a master might award points to students for meritorious compositions.

During Bashō's day, however, many poets found it preferable to send their verses to professional graders (*tenja*) via courier and thereby receive points without the inconvenience of attending the *za*. An influx of commercial activity, movement, and road building allowed this practice of "distance learning," called *tentori* (point-procuring) *haikai,* to flourish both as a diversion and a pedagogical tool. By enabling remote poets to win acclaim and receive prizes, it encouraged competition among students.[94] But it also led to the erosion of the poetry circles and recast *haikai* training as an industry wherein masters competed with one another for recognition. Bashō rejected this sort of activity. By shielding *haikai* practice from commercialism and advancing the poetic merits of strangeness, his Shōmon School emerged as a vanguard of Edo period *haikai.*

The mixed reception of Ihara Saikaku's life and work is an instructive counterpoint. Early in his career Saikaku adhered to the Danrin School of *haikai,* considered scandalous for its independence, wittiness, and disregard for traditional poetics. By 1673, Saikaku had earned the epithet Oranda Saikaku for his unusual, eccentric verses. (Terms associated with Westerners—*Oranda, bateren* [Jesuit missionary], *kōmō* [redheaded]— were deployed as pejorative signifiers of strangeness.) Though occasionally unpopular, his bizarre feats of literary prowess—as in 1684 when he composed 23,500 haikai in twenty-four hours—helped establish him as a prose writer. His works sold well among townspeople, but intellectual circles did not look favorably upon his populist bent. Intellectuals condemned his literary eccentricity for two reasons: his flagrantly smutty subject matter violated existing literary standards of moral decency, and his brazen self-promotion suggested the mentality of a scribbler more than a man of letters.[95]

Saikaku and Bashō thus occupied opposite ends of the continuum between heteronomous (market-driven) and autonomous art. Both men cultivated identities of strangeness, but Bashō's legacy carried two innovations that were to prove critical for subsequent generations. First, his lifestyle and teachings refined *haikai* poetics through an aesthetics of eccentricity (detachment, *kyō,* and *muyō*) that in China had long enjoyed considerable prestige. Second, he situated himself within the cultural field as a champion of aesthetic purity by vigorously resisting the artificialities of commercialism. For these reasons Bashō merits inclusion among the most influential eccentrics of the Edo period.

While the early Tokugawa *bakufu* did regulate many aspects of daily life, it did not unilaterally suppress nonconformity. It paid comparatively less attention to benign forms of strangeness, including unusual artistic tastes. But this did not free eccentric artists from suspicion altogether, for talent alone was insufficient to win public or commercial recognition. The Chinese literati painter Chen Yuanyun (1587–1671), who migrated to Japan in 1638, was unable to earn a living as a painter because his work was too strange to attract buyers and students. Reduced to working as a potter and kung-fu teacher, he ultimately gave up painting, aware, perhaps, that the Japanese were as yet unprepared to appreciate the Chinese literati style.[96] Stanley-Baker affirms that newer devices, styles, and techniques were initially "too unfamiliar, too abstract" for Japanese painters to accept.[97] Only later, as Chinese literati aesthetics grew more accessible, she argues, did Japanese begin a selective process of assimilation. When the painter Yi Fujiu (1698–after 1747) arrived in Japan a century after Chen, his art was embraced by local literati despite being similar in style and in no way superior to Chen's.

A culture of suspicion fomenting within both the official and the public realms thus compelled Edo's early outsiders to reinvent themselves in ways that allayed potential hostility. It necessitated that strangeness be passive and, for some, tempered by withdrawal. While retreat was often politically motivated, it represented a benign dissent that bore little political threat. Following their retirement, certainly, Chōshōshi and Jōzan incited no meaningfully subversive sentiment, and the *bakufu* harbored no suspicions against them. As Kendall Brown notes, aesthetic reclusion actually served to preserve the Tokugawa order by removing discontents from a social context and rendering them politically irrelevant.[98] By assuaging suspicion, irrelevance also afforded them an important degree of artistic freedom.

In addition to wandering and nature appreciation, *muyō* could be displayed by dissipation or alcohol consumption. Alcohol was originally associated with festivals and rites related to ancestor worship, and though drinking developed into a form of secular recreation during the Edo period, it was normally enjoyed as a communal activity.[99] Indeed, solitary public drinking was a mildly scandalous expression of nonconformity that could complement one's standing as an eccentric. The retired screen maker Hyōta (d. 1712), for example, was well known for his tendency to roam the Kyoto countryside gazing upon the changing brilliance of the seasons.[100] His reputation as a wino, however, cast him as a genuine oddball. As related in Kōkei's *Kinsei kijinden* (Fig. 2.3), Hyōta, bent over on his staff with saké gourd tied to his waist, was variously sighted traipsing about, singing in the rain, sketching, sipping wine under the blossoms, or scrutinizing passersby through his spectacles. At the time, Kōkei relates, his incessant drinking and wandering qualified him as Kyoto's most prominent *kijin*.[101] Kōkei's entry closes with a *kyōka,* presumed to be Hyōta's, about the pleasures of drinking alone. The same verse accompanies Hyōta's entry in *Kijin hyakunin isshu* (One hundred verses from one hundred eccentrics, 1852). Kanazawa Tokō's *Okinagusa* (An old man's jottings, 1772, 1788) also portrays Hyōta as a wandering wino, though more of a public embarrassment than an icon. Before closing with a different alcohol-related verse, it relates that his gravestone "is in the shape of a wine bottle, and the roof is a wine chalice."[102] In each of these texts Hyōta's practice of solitary drinking accentuates his

FIGURE 2.3 Hyōta. Ban Kōkei and Mikuma Katen
Kinsei kijinden. International Research Center for Japanese
Studies Library.

notoriety, and his submission to the natural course of things invokes the sort of *muyō* lifestyle popularized by Chinese recluses.[103]

By the end of the 1600s, an aesthetics of eccentricity had emerged as a subcultural byproduct of political control and societal stringency. As urbanization, economic prosperity, and cultural liberalism were generating an explosion of popular cultural forms, each running headlong in its own direction under its own economic power, a nascent *bunjin* ethos struggled to preserve amateurism and artistic purity. Detached, aesthetically minded individuals like Jōzan, Bashō, and Hyōta negotiated a culture of intolerance by turning to *fūryū, kyō,* and *muyō* as tried-and-true aesthetic principles. In this sense, aesthetic eccentricity was a consciously adopted taste, a set of conventions that established strangeness as a recognized style. This convergence of developments helped permanently to anchor individuality, originality, and emotion as aesthetic ideals within Edo culture. The proliferation of eccentricity observable during the late 1700s, clearly, was merely the interim phase of a movement already well under way a century earlier.

PART II

Discourses on Difference in the Eighteenth Century

CHAPTER 3

Strange Tastes

Cultural Eccentricity and Its Vanguard

*Strangeness, eccentricity, foolishness, and
madness are the keywords for explaining
eighteenth-century Kyoto's art world.*

—Kanō Hiroyuku

Post-Genroku Japan witnessed growing cultural independence, and had the aforementioned Chen Yuanyun lived several generations later one suspects his work would have encountered a warmer reception. This softening climate also nurtured broader interest in *bunjin* culture: a packaged nonconformity informed by Chinese tastes, amateurism, and detached playfulness. Such were the conditions catalyzing successive developments in art, philosophy, and print that collectively buoyed aesthetic strangeness throughout the second half of the Tokugawa period.

This chapter identifies an escalating attraction to strangeness that fundamentally differed from the isolated cases of aesthetic reclusion evident in the seventeenth century. It examines how the cultural field moved toward tolerance and inclusivity that afforded certain talented individuals considerable latitude to establish eccentricity as a legitimate moral force. Not all succeeded in such efforts, and we begin by demonstrating how certain members of Bashō's Shōmon School failed to inherit and sustain the master's aesthetics of strangeness. Discussion then turns to a sampling of *bunjin,* including some of early modern Japan's most celebrated individualists, who brought energy and prestige to this growing culture of eccentricity. We consider how the first two generations of eccentric artists (flourishing in the mid- and late eighteenth century) positioned themselves as a cultural vanguard that challenged the rigidity and conformity characteristic of Tokugawa life. The two chapters that follow contextualize these findings. Chapter 4 examines how concurrent scholarship reinterpreted Confucian knowledge through a host of heterodoxies that supported qualified nonconformity. Chapter 5 then explores how these developments were perceived and popularized through biography.

MASTER DEPRAVITY: A SHŌMON SHOWOFF

Individual idiosyncrasies cannot be transmitted to even the most devoted disciple. For this reason obsessive-compulsive behavior like Striped Kanjūrō's, extraordinary devotion like Enkū's, or uncommon aesthetic sensitivity like Bashō's are isolated cases of strangeness that, however inspirational, must inevitably lose potency in the process of transmission. Bashō's followers offer an apt example. The Shōmon "school" was a nationwide collective of admirers and self-designated followers who may or may not have interacted with the master. That these enthusiasts were united more by their reverence for Bashō than by adherence to his philosophical or poetic teachings made this collective more of a cult than a school per se. The overly cerebral and esoteric nature of Bashō's mentorship, moreover, had cultivated a purposefulness among his pupils. As a result, even the most capable of Bashō's disciples were unable to demonstrate adequately either the poetic sensitivity or the spontaneous "windblown eccentricity" (fūkyō) that the master had exhibited. Because many concentrated more on compiling and transmitting his teachings than on actualizing them, the school's vitality suffered. Bashō anticipated this deficiency himself. As often noted, a poem composed weeks before his death laments that his disciples had not acquired the skill to carry on his aesthetic vision:

kono michi ya	none is traveling
yuku hito nashi ni	here along this way but I,
aki no kure	this autumn evening[1]

While retaining the master's devotion to *haikai* and penchant for wandering, his heirs variously interpreted *fūkyō* and *fūryū* (windblown elegance), his signature aesthetics of eccentricity, as austerity, playfulness, or hedonism. Some earned celebrity and later became immortalized in *Kinsei kijinden* (*KKD*), but they did so by converting Bashō's aesthetic strangeness into behavioral strangeness or self-indulgence. *KKD* claims, for example, that the disciple Hirose Izen (d. 1711) wandered directionless throughout the provinces leading a lifestyle that indeed manifested a visage of *fūkyō*.[2] He rejected wealth, status, family, and possessions, preferring the simple, unencumbered life of a beggar. Motoyama relates that his ragged clothing, torn hat, and glazed eyes made him a frightful sight and incited heckling from children: "Beggar monk, beggar monk! Madman, madman!" His alleged reply was: "Beggar? Madman? How funny! I'm neither of those; I'm a long-nosed mountain goblin (*tengu*)! Ha ha ha . . . Praise Amida."[3] Izen was especially known for what he called his Bashō-esque prayer (*Fūra nenbutsu*), refrains cobbled together from Bashō's poems. *KKD* gives the following example:

mazu tanomu mazu tanomu shii	For now, for now, I will turn to the
no ki mo ari natsu kodachi	large oak tree—a grove in summer
oto ya arare no hinokigasa	How harsh it sounds! [The hail] on
	my travelling hat
namu amida namu amida.[4]	Praise Amida, praise Amida

This verse combines the *nenbutsu,* a Pure Land Buddhist prayer to Amida, with two of Bashō's *haikai,* and although it carries a certain logic—both the large oak and the traveling hat provide shelter from the elements, the same protection asked of Amida—it was heretical to standard *nenbutsu* recitation.[5] It similarly sullied the integrity of Bashō's originals. As a poet, then, Izen departed radically from the studied subtlety characterizing the poetic principles—that is, lightness (*karumi*) or objective loneliness (*sabi*)—advanced by Bashō. As a public personality, his reckless demeanor transposed Bashō's aesthetics of eccentricity from art to behavior, perhaps diverting attention from his insecurities over inadequate poetic prowess.

Although Izen openly revered Bashō and emulated his lifestyle, it was his distinctive character rather than poetic skill that secures him a place among memorable Shōmon poets. The same pattern applies to Shōmon eccentrics like Teramachi Hyakuan (1695–1781), a *bakufu* official who devoted his retirement to restoring the school's credibility. Hyakuan (one hundred hermitages—so named for his desire to move one hundred times before dying) was a self-indulgent youth. Spending much of his time in Edo's pleasure quarters, he earned a reputation around the city as both a playboy and a poet. Until his marriage at age thirty-three, Hyakuan continued what he describes in *Gō no aki* (Autumn hair, 1735) as an astonishingly irresponsible lifestyle—carousing through the nights and napping through the days. Hyakuan's associates also document his unpredictability and "scandalous behavior" (*hōitsu muzan naru furumai*). *Tsuno moji* (Horn letters, 1739) notes that at a public Setsubun festival, during which one purifies and invites good luck into an establishment by throwing beans, Hyakuan filled his square box with coins instead of beans and proceeded to fling them about.[6] While this seems far from "scandalous," Hyakuan's inclusion in *Zoku haika kijindan* (More accounts of eccentric *haikai* poets, 1833) and *Kijin hyakunin isshu* (One hundred verses from one hundred eccentrics, 1852) bespeaks his reputation as an oddball.

Later in life Hyakuan was demoted for coveting his *renga* teacher's position, and at age sixty-one he withdrew to concentrate on *haikai* and *waka*. In his theoretical treatises on *haikai*, Hyakuan voices reverence for Bashō while ridiculing contemporary Shōmon practitioners.[7] Decrying the vulgar quality of contemporary *haikai*, his texts proclaim a desire to eradicate the ineffectual poetic practices of recent years and reestablish the "correct" way.[8] Neither these laments nor his own poetry proved widely inspirational, however, and he is memorialized in works like Katsushika Hokusai's *Kijin hyakunin isshu* (Fig. 3.1) more for his singular personality than his literary talents.

During the first half of the eighteenth century the Shōmon School lacked the charismatic leadership to reestablish its credibility. It even became the target of satire. Satirical, yellow-covered comic book (*kibyōshi*) originator Koikawa Harumachi's (1744–1789) parodic work *Kachō kakurenbō* (Hide and seek among flowers and birds, 1776), for example, focuses on the Shōmon poet Yamazaki Hokka (1700–1746), popularly called Jidaraku sensei (Master Depravity).[9] By any measure Hokka was an eccentric fellow. Born in Edo, from age twenty-two he worked as a retainer for five different samurai families. Hokka was temperamentally ill suited for official service, however, and, claiming poor health, retired at age thirty-eight to become a physician and *haikai* master. In 1739, the year after his retirement, Hokka famously staged his own funeral. According to prominent *bunjin* Ōta Nanpo (1749–1823), his coffin was carried through the streets to Yōfuku-ji Temple in the Edo suburb of Yanaka. Then, following the priest's prayers and just prior to the cremation, Hokka jumped out of his coffin. His friends broke out food and drink, and all "enjoyed themselves singing and dancing, to the astonishment of everyone."[10] The gravestone erected at this mock funeral remains Hokka's only observed tomb, and we know of his actual death in 1746 only from records at Hongō Sannenji temple in Ochanomizu.[11]

Hokka's poetics were heavily influenced by Kagami Shikō (1665–1731), one of the *Shōmon no jittetsu*—Bashō's "ten great disciples." And, not only did he emulate the master by retracing parts of the journey chronicled in Bashō's famous *Oku no hosomichi* (Narrow road to the interior, 1789), but he presented himself as Bashō's successor, giving his diary *Chō no asobi* (Frolic of the butterfly, 1746) the subtitle *Zoku-oku no hosomichi* (Sequel to Narrow road to the interior). But clearly Hokka could not match Bashō as a model of elegance, and this allowed Harumachi's *Kachō kakurenbō* to satirize him as a paragon of selfishness. The work opens by positing Hokka (Jidaraku sensei) as a formidable talent. As a child he chides his teachers and betters his elders at swordsmanship; as an adult he outwits a group of bandits and cavorts with Edo's most imminent poets and kabuki actors. But he is also a degenerate showoff whose disreputable comportment humorously conflicts with his alleged celebrity.

FIGURE 3.1   Teramachi Hyakuan. Katsushika Hokusai, *Kijin hyakunin isshu*. Tokyo Gakugei University Library.

Once he became a *haikai* poet, people came to recognize his name and face wherever he went. It was his habit to doze past noon, rousing himself only when his attendants brought in saké and fish. Those around him subsequently dubbed him Master Depravity. . . . He was a completely selfish master, but loaded with money.[12]

In each of the illustrations, Jidaraku sensei is identified by the character for "self" (自: *ji; mizukara*) displayed prominently on his robe like a crest (Fig. 3.2). This is both the first character in Jidaraku and visual affirmation of the egotism elaborated in the text. By literally wearing his selfishness on his sleeve, he offers a visible marker of eccentricity that celebrates personal interest over all else. For all his devotion to Bashō—or pride in his affiliation with the Shōmon School—he converts *fūryū* into a foolishness constructed from the acclaim he receives as a public spectacle.

Master Depravity grew his beard long and scented his clothing with incense, and this fragrance followed him as he wandered through various provinces practicing austerities. He was just like the Chinese scholars Cheng Hao and Guan Yu.[13] Penetrating the provinces to the north (*michinoku*), he once pushed as far as Matsushima. As for his appearance, he bound his hair up in a ball on his head, grew his beard long, and carried tooth dye to blacken his teeth.[14]

Ōta Nanpo calls Hokka a fake madman (*yōkyō*), implying that his objectives were directed outward for the amusement of others. Hokka's mock funeral, certainly, was contrived and carried out for this purpose. Hokka also gave himself and his dwellings perversely humorous names intended to invite comment. His house (*ken*) was called Furyōken (a homonym for Evil Dwelling), his hermitage (*an*) was Mushian (homonym for Thoughtless Hut and Bug-infested Hut), his meditation room (*sai*) was Sharakusai (a homonym for Impudent Room), and his Buddhist name (*bō*) was Kakurenbō (Hide-and-Seek). Like names, appearance is also fundamental to crafting a public identity, and Hokka's scented clothing, long beard, hairstyle, and dyed teeth all underscored his strangeness. And, in case any observer had missed these bizarre manifestations, Hokka admitted to his madness in his collection of essays *Fūzoku bunshū* (A miscellany of manners, 1744): "Some people ask me why my usual manner of speaking and acting is different from that of others. Others tell me that I am mad. To them I reply: 'Yes, I truly *am* mad.' Then, when they who called me mad agree with me on that point, I grab a pillow and take a nap."[15]

In addition to recounting extraordinary episodes from Hokka's life, *Kachō kakurenbō* connects him with a cavalcade of Shōmon royalty who also become targets of Harumachi's mockery. Takarai Kikaku (1661–1707) and Hattori Ransetu (1654–1707), two of Bashō's "ten great disciples," appear in the text, Kikaku cavorting in the Yoshiwara and Yanagibashi pleasure quarters together with Hokka. Ichikawa Danjūrō (1660–1704), the celebrated kabuki actor, is similarly depicted. Collectively they form a laughable trio of boors who revel in base pleasures, perhaps to compensate for their lack of poetic talent. Jidaraku also crosses paths with kabuki actors Nakamura Denkurō (1662–1713) and Nakamura Shichizaburō (1668?–1725), as well as two famous female *haikai* masters Shūshiki (d. 1725) and Shiba Sonome (1664–1726).[16]

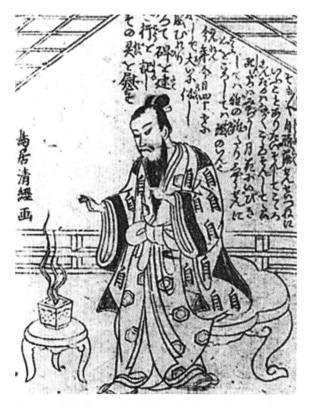

FIGURE 3.2   Yamazaki Hokka. Koikawa Harumachi,
Kachō kakurenbō. Dai-Tōkyū Memorial Library.

Being continually surrounded by Edo's cultural elite makes Hokka an elite himself, but his interactions with these individuals always occur within the context of decadent behavior. And while the text includes a number of *haikai,* all but one are composed by his drinking companions. Hokka's own poetic voice is nearly unheard, adding an additional layer of parody. In the end, his eccentricity (selfishness) becomes a source of both mirth and revulsion: "This man of elegance always enjoyed eating fish and fowl, and he knew the taste of saké better than Li Bai (701–762) and Tao Qian (365–427). With no shortage of pleasures during each of the four seasons, he seemed destined to enjoy longevity. How regrettable, then, that he suddenly caught a slight cold and passed away."[17]

Master Depravity is surely a unique individual, but he is not the eccentric that Striped Kanjūrō was. Though claiming inheritance from Bashō, a self-seeker, his own quest culminates in self-indulgence. His treatment in *Kachō kakurenbō,* therefore, clarifies the Shōmon School's ambivalent status in the eighteenth century prior to its revival under Yosa Buson (1716–1783). While the school provided an affiliation that valued the behavioral deviance of individuals like Izen, Hyakuan, and Hokka, it was not a principal source of aesthetic eccentricity during the eighteenth century. We find, rather, that sustained, transmissible patterns of strangeness were concurrently being discerned through closer inspection of Chinese tastes.

Now, I shall examine how these patterns informed strangeness in two related ways: through the "taste" of *ki* connected to imported Chinese aesthetics like *fūryū* and *fūkyō,* and as a means of self-discovery and self-expression. Sinophilia and subjectivity, then, will be the two rubrics through which I shall interpret aesthetic eccentricity. While *bunjin* like Gion Nankai (1677–1751), Yanagisawa Kien (1704–1758), Baisaō (1675–1763), and Ike no Taiga (1723–1776) accessed strangeness through the former, the individualistic Rinzai monk Hakuin (1685–1768) and the mountain ascetic (*yamabushi*) Yokoi Kinkoku (1761–1832) engaged with strange art for more cathartic reasons. Itō Jakuchū (1716–1800), Soga Shōhaku (1730–1781), and Nagasawa Rosetsu (1754–1799), falling between these two categories, tempered their affection for Chinese aesthetics with devotion to painting as a means of self-preservation.[18] Adhering to these two rubrics, I shall discuss these nine individuals as either "eccentric *bunjin*" (Sinophilia) or "individualists" (subjectivity). As all nine are artists loosely construed as *bunjin,* and all nine demonstrate unusual strength of character, these categories are not to be understood as mutually exclusive. Nor do they suggest that members of the respective groupings are philosophically aligned. Rather, this division will assist us in discerning two separate features of eighteenth-century eccentric art.

ECCENTRIC *BUNJIN:* NANKAI, KIEN, BAISAŌ, AND TAIGA

Nakata Yūjirō locates Japan's initial stage of literati painting (*nanga*) treatise writing between the Genroku and Kyōho eras (1688–1736), a period that corresponds to an innovative cohort that is considered the first generation of *bunjin.*[19] Not only did these early treatises (*garon*) tend to echo and affirm Chinese writings about art, they represented greater engagement with Chinese texts generally.[20] Tokugawa Yoshimune (r. 1716–1745), the fifth shogun, had catalyzed the prestige of continental sources by establishing an institute for the study of Chinese texts (1716) and lifting the ban on foreign books (1720) imposed ninety years earlier. The philosophical validation of art for art's sake advanced by Ancient Learning thinkers like Itō Jinsai and Ogyū Sorai, moreover, had contributed to a more hospitable environment for Chinese materials, enabling commercially supported "amateurism" as a career choice of sorts for post-Genroku aesthetes.[21]

Chinese tastes were absorbed through a selective process, however. Joan Stanley-Baker has shown that newer devices, styles, and techniques depicted in the paintings and manuals being supplied through Ōbaku centers were "too unfamiliar, too abstract" for early *bunjin* painters to accept.[22] Not only did they seem emotionally deficient, they clashed with native visual and poetic tastes. It is no wonder that as a young man even the celebrated Ike no Taiga had trouble selling fans decorated with his "strange" Chinese pictures.

Strangeness, however, was an intended effect, and *bunjin* fostered it on two levels: in artistic style, and in daily practice. Artistically, eighteenth-century Japanese *nanga* painters embraced the "free expression, spontaneous and inspired, abbreviated, wash oriented, and nonlinear" qualities characteristic of so-called *ippin* (C. *i-p'in;* untrammeled) painting from the Song and Yuen eras (960–1468).[23] Taiga's pupil Kuwayama Gyokushū (1746–1799) summarized admiration for this *ippin* aesthetic in *Kaiji higen* (Modest chats on painting, 1799): "The sublime category *ippin* is classified above the three classes of Divine, Marvelous, and Competent. What is meant by this *ippin* is a category free of the ordinary rules of painting and imbued with clarity, wonder, mystery, and marvel."[24] Though a heterodox aesthetic, *ippin* was nonetheless considered the culmination of artistic accomplishment for encapsulating the extraordinary. In other words, it advanced a carefully crafted eccentricity.

Bunjin also sought eccentricity by placing themselves in escapist, utopian circumstances. For urban samurai officials, however, adopting such lifestyles posed a theoretical contradiction: it conflicted with their obligations to live in a city, serve a lord, and receive monetary compensation. Fortunately, early Chinese scholar-bureaucrats in similar positions had long since provided discursive justifications for administrative spaces as idealized aesthetic spaces. Reclusion at court and in urban areas was couched as "great reclusion" (*taiin*), suggesting officialdom as a form of utopian detachment in itself.[25] Japanese *bunjin* like the poet Hattori Nankaku (1683–1759) did not hesitate to deploy similar assertions. A retainer of the Kōfu daimyoYanagisawa Yoshiyasu (1658–1714), Nankaku was an inveterate urbanite, but from his residence in Edo he adopted the guise of a transient, nature-loving recluse. Late in life he wrote *Biinben* (On sleeping and hiding), in which he admits to his dependence on the comforts of city living and his abhorrence of the menacing mountains and forests. To be released from society's burdens and annoyances, he maintains, does not require self-exile to the hardships of the wilderness. One is able to do this while sleeping. Reclusion, he continues, entails cultivating a sleeplike state that transports one from a condition of encumbrance to one of freedom.[26] Nankaku considered himself a useless person (*muyōsha*), and indeed the unfettered passivity extolled in his defense of sleep invokes Zhuangzi's own defense of uselessness.[27]

Ōta Nanpo, the *bakufu* official who had maligned Yamazaki Hokka, arrived at a similar conclusion. In *Neboke sensei bunshū* (Master Sleepyhead's miscellaneous writings, 1767), Nanpo puzzles over whether he is real, a dream, or an illusion. Clearly inspired by Zhuangzi as well, Nanpo posits dreaming as a pivotal point between his real and illusory selves.[28] Having discovered the utility of multiple selves, Nanpo is able to reconcile official obligations with cultural pursuits by placing himself between dream and reality as a "recluse in government" (*riin*). This internalization of *bunjin* aesthetics was an important development, for by rendering aestheticism a state of mind it enabled individuals from all social classes to participate as custodians of culture. By simply constructing a literary alter ego, officials and townsmen alike were able to pose as mountain hermits and write about their loneliness, friendships with warblers, conversations with chirping crickets, or longing for winter's first snow.

It was this detached state of mind, moreover, that most vigorously explored difference and strangeness. Our representative sample of first- and second-generation eccentric *bunjin*—Gion Nankai, Yanagisawa Kien, Baisaō, and Ike no Taiga, exemplify this psychic detachment. Anthologized in *Kinsei kijinden* and subsequent publications as among Japan's most celebrated oddballs, collectively they represent the vanguard of eighteenth-century subcultural art. All lived unassuming or reclusive lives; many found inspiration in Ōbaku Zen thought and aesthetics; and all attracted disciples while remaining uncorrupted by the allure of celebrity and wealth. Finally, all positioned themselves outside the mainstream of their respective callings while opening artistic and philosophical spaces that embraced human emotion.

Gion Nankai (1677–1751) and Yanagisawa Kien (1704–1758) were among those who converted Chinese literati painting into *nanga,* an emergent pictorial form that would develop and transmit aesthetic eccentricity to Tokugawa society. Born in Edo to a samurai from Kii, Nankai lived in Edo until 1697, when he was dispatched to his domain. Several years later he was exiled and imprisoned for misconduct unbecoming his rank, most likely for his recurrent escapades in the pleasure quarters. This oddly severe punishment could only have been elicited by habitual and unrepentant transgressions on Nankai's part. He was not exonerated until 1710, when he returned to serve Kii as a Confucian scholar. At age thirty-eight he was appointed head of the domain's official school. His lessons departed from traditional Neo-Confucian dogma, however, instead advocating individual self-expression through poetry and painting. He was instrumental in popularizing the Ming and Qing painting styles detailed in the *Hasshu gafu* and *Kaishien gaden* manuals, and in turn influenced important second-generation artists like Taiga and Buson.

In *Shōun sango* (1726), Nankai also issued one of the Edo period's most explicit statements regarding the aesthetics of eccentricity:

> We should call people's attraction to the strange (*ki*) a kind of "illness." The strange stands in opposition to correctness (*sei*) and is what turns the ordinary into its opposite. From the beginning, the Way of the Sages lay in revering correctness and defending normalcy. . . . Having said as much, wherein lays the taste (*omomuki*) of putting correctness and normalcy into practice? On the contrary, it is only because of the strange that taste exists. People have an attraction for what possesses taste but have no interest in that which lacks it. Those unconventional people living beyond the bounds of common sense appreciate taste all the more, while philistines know nothing of it. Furthermore, while the latter busy themselves chasing fame and fortune they learn nothing of the elegant delights of the strange.

So while there is no question that people's attraction to the strange is a kind of "illness," it is also true that where there is no strangeness neither is there anything to taste.[29]

While influential, this was not a revolutionary sentiment. It echoed the eccentric aesthetics of *fūryū, fūkyō,* and *kyōken* advanced by Bashō; it also invoked various existing strains of antirationalism within the arts that sought to stave off formulism by elevating the strange over the familiar.[30] The importance of Nankai's statement validating strangeness lay in its encapsulation of the existing *bunjin* ideal. Its juxtaposition of opposites as a means of scrutinizing existing aesthetic values excavated Bashō's "awaken to the high and return to the low" (*kōgo kizoku*) while also invoking the inversion of correctness characteristic of contemporary satirical literature. Strangeness coexisted with the normative, and its effectiveness as satire derived from exposing the normative as artificial and "tasteless."[31] Nankai's praise of *ki* was thus emblematic of an expanding desire to recover strangeness for the purpose of returning freshness to cultural practice.

Nankai's statement requires some qualification, however. Seventeenth-century aesthetes like Ishikawa Jōzan and Matsuo Bashō adopted the Chinese notion of *fūryū* as a tried-and-true artistic standard. Yet this was an uncritical adoption, and in this sense a vanity—a way of becoming more sophisticated by becoming more Chinese. For Nankai as well, the taste (*omomuki*) of strangeness was a consciously adopted taste, a matter of style. This meant that strangeness was an established and codified end in itself that was independent of uniqueness or originality. In fact, as we saw in Teramachi Hyakuan's writings on the proper way of Shōmon poetry, artistic technique continued to be couched in terms of correct and incorrect. Aesthetic eccentricity, then, was concerned with affirming or revising an existing Way, about grasping and capturing a correct (*sei*) strangeness. What remained was for *ki* to be taken into unknown, more personal, territory.

Yanagisawa Kien, a poet-painter and student of both Ogyū Sorai and Nankai, attempted to do so. At the age of twelve or thirteen, Kien examined the merit of the irrational in an essay analyzing Zhuangzi's story *Bisei no shin* (Weisheng's faith), the tale of a young man who, having promised to meet a woman at low tide under a bridge, continues waiting in vain long after the appointed hour. The tide rises and Bisei drowns, clutching faith to his own end. Kien proposed that, though Bisei was undoubtedly guilty of foolishness, it is only such foolishness—in this case inflicted by love—that genuinely investigates life's true feelings. Following Bashō and Nankai, young Kien's defense of unconventional wisdom demonstrates belief in the need to shed conventional common sense to access a greater, more spiritually fulfilling truth.[32]

Kien's prioritization of private feelings, the stranger the better, put him at odds with his social position. His father was a chief adviser to the daimyo of Kōriyama, and Kien took on administrative duties there from age twenty, receiving an exorbitant salary of 2,500 *koku*. This elite status was an obstacle to the sort of bohemian, independent lifestyle that Kien craved. Well-educated and adept at numerous arts, he was drawn to cultural activities and pleasure seeking. His ironically titled *Hitorine* (Sleeping alone, 1725), most notably, advocated immersion in the sensual delights of the pleasure quarters. Comportment of this sort was particularly scandalous for one of his pedigree and elicited a strong reaction from his parents, who disinherited him for recurrent instances of "unrefined conduct."[33] Though his birthright and stipend were returned several years later, Kien remained impetuous and unpredictable. Small wonder, then, to find in Kien's *Unpyō zasshi* (a collection of essays published posthumously by Kimura Kenkadō in 1796) an entry extolling the ten virtues of drinking: "Saké corrects etiquette, dismisses troubles, dispels worry, shakes off depression, revives spirits, prevents illness, neutralizes poisons, fosters intimacy, solidifies relations, and extends felicitations."[34] *Kinsei kijinden* describes him as one who pleased everyone by constantly doing the unexpected. Continuing, it relates that he was so famous for his generosity and fondness for companionship that beggars and pilgrims, including one man chased off his own land for gambling, flocked to his door seeking food and shelter, some of whom stayed on for years. His kindness, it claims, eventually drove him to ruin, an unlikely assertion given Kien's affluence.[35]

KKD opts to divert its readers with a series of anecdotes depicting Kien as an epicurean and polymath with tastes for music, gambling, and women. Its illustration (Fig. 3.3), more appropriately, showcases his appetite for recreation and his wide circle of associates. Too broadly educated to tolerate the relative vulgarity exhibited by Japanese professional schools, he directed his energies toward emulating Chinese painting manuals. He studied under the Chinese Ōbaku monk Eppō Dōshō (1655–1734), the abbot of Manpukuji, as well as with the Chinese painter Ying Yuanzhang (J. Ei Genshō; Yoshida Shūsetsu) in Nagasaki. Though he never became an important painter himself, Kien was extraordinarily successful as a popularizer of Chinese Southern School painting.

Nankai and Kien were influential as highly conspicuous delinquents who found ways to actualize a measure of freedom and then inject it into *bunjin* practice. While occupying prominent public posts, they created spaces outside officialdom for self-indulgent aesthetic activities, demonstrating that self, even strange selves, can coexist with bureaucratic obligations. It was Kō Yūgai (1675–1763) and second-generation *bunjin* Ike no Taiga, however, who became Kyoto's most important arbiters of Chinese taste. Ban Kōkei invoked both Yūgai, known as Baisaō (Old Tea Seller), and Taiga in his preface to *KKD*, immortalizing them as the two exemplary *kijin* of the eighteenth century. (Their respective entries in *KKD* will be discussed in Chapter 5.) Baisaō was an Ōbaku monk from Hizen who served at several temples, including Manpukuji, where he studied under the Chinese painter Duzhan (1628–1706). A man of learning and piety, at age sixty he

FIGURE 3.3   Yanagisawa Kien. Ban Kōkei and Mikuma Katen, *Kinsei kijinden.* International Research Center for Japanese Studies Library.

voluntarily left the security of the temple to proselytize his way of *sencha* on the streets of Kyoto. His tea stand was recognizable for its banner reading *seifū,* short for *seifūryū* (pure elegance), and for a bamboo container to collect whatever payment patrons wished to donate.[36]

For the uninitiated, *sencha*'s simplicity and affordability facilitated exposure to Chinese literati culture, making Baisaō a pivotal figure in this capacity. Takahashi suggests that he and his affiliates were more responsible than any other for injecting an appreciation for freedom into cultural practices and activities around the city.[37] For *bunjin* and others accustomed to practicing the arts inside the comfort of studios and salons, Baisaō's honorable poverty (*seihin*) positioned him as an archetype of *furyū.* He attracted a wide following, including the important *nanga* painter Sakaki Hyakusen (1698–1753) and noted eccentrics Taiga and Itō Jakuchū, who collectively produced a small body of literary and pictorial tributes to him. In his preface to *Baisaō gego* (Verses of Baisaō, 1763), the *bunjin* Kinryū Keiyū writes of Baisaō: "He has white hair and a beard, and is a bright-faced person of extremely calm temperament. The clothes on his body are modest and disheveled. From his tendency to drink too much saké, at one glance, you can discern his character."[38] Baisaō described himself more humbly: as "just a wanderer who laughs at himself and makes the whole world his home."[39] Many sent him their poems for appraisal, believing, as his friend Daiten Kenjō (1719–1801) put it, that he possessed an ancient and therefore unmatched level of poetic sensibility.[40] More than any other individual in mid-eighteenth-century Kyoto, Baisaō showed the *bunjin* ethos to be a lived rather than an academic calling.

Baisaō's friend Taiga was a true heir and custodian of this ethos. Though most celebrated as a painter, he was also an accomplished calligrapher; a *kanshi, waka,* and *haikai* poet; a lutist and an herbalist.[41] He cultivated friendships with Hakuin, Kien, Nankai, Shōhaku, and other important representatives of Kyoto's *bunjin* circles. Taiga created lasting impressions upon people throughout his life. Born to a farmer who had moved to Kyoto and found work in the silver mint, he was pronounced an "infant genius" at age six, and by fourteen his name had reached the ears of prominent Confucian intellectuals. Stories of Taiga's strange behavior accompanied his reputation as an artist.[42] Sources relate that he abstained from alcohol, which may have been a curiosity in itself. He showed an oddly strict observance of certain social customs and utter disregard for others. Though generally reclusive, by all accounts he had a well-mannered, sociable nature and enjoyed guests.

He mounted a sign over his gate that read "Please come in. All passersby welcome."[43] Yet he also nursed a fierce dislike for the wealthy. When expecting a prosperous visitor, Melinda Takeuchi relates, he would place his urinal bucket at the front gate. Contempt for wealth affected his own finances, for he occasionally failed to collect money owed him, failed to charge for some of his works, and often donated whatever money he did acquire. Both Kōkei and painter Tanomura Chikuden (1777–1835) relate that he was unkempt and easily mistaken for a beggar, and yet was always exceedingly polite to people, to some annoyingly so. They also relate that his impetuousness caused annoyance, for he was prone to sudden urges to wander the countryside, disappearing while in the middle of jobs and not returning for hours or days. His wife Tokuyama Gyokuran's (1727–1789) eccentricity matched his own. Like Taiga, Gyokuran became an accomplished painter under the tutelage of Kien and Nankai, was strongly independent, and was disinterested in money. Before marrying she aspired to become a Chinese-style painter, a remarkable ambition considering Japan's convention of viewing Chinese studies as an exclusively male realm of endeavor. She also kept her surname after marriage and, by some accounts, maintained a separate residence. Disinclined toward norms of respectability, she smoked and did not shave her eyebrows, wear makeup or fine clothes, or keep a clean house.[44] Ueda Akinari, not one to miss an opportunity for ridicule, notes that their home was so disheveled that he was unable to sit down in it.[45]

For these reasons Taiga is often called the Edo period's archetypal *kijin*. But he is also cited as the most important *nanga* painter of his day and invoked by later artists as personifying the pinnacle of *bunjin* accomplishment. Taiga studied Chinese manuals and painting collections and occasionally experimented with Chinese brushwork and other techniques. Ultimately, though, his technique developed in ways that integrated these with native aesthetics. Clearly disinterested in copying Chinese methods, Taiga's style and brushwork exhibit distinctly Japanese "wet, expressive, moist, and fluid" qualities reminiscent of Rinpa style painting.[46] In his treatise *Kaiji Higen* (Talks on rustic painting, 1799), eminent *nanga* theorist Kuwayama Gyokushū (1746–1799) avers that Nankai and Kien were the first artists to introduce *nanga* to Japan but it was Taiga who attained its ultimate potential. Taiga, he felt, was the singular artist of his generation, whose painting attained the level of *ippin* while also capturing the substance of Japanese art. Those who considered Taiga's art to be peculiar, he added, failed to understand the essence of literati painting.[47]

From the time he was brought to Manpukuji at age seven to demonstrate his calligraphy, Taiga's was an unfathomable genius. Nankai describes witnessing a demonstration of his finger painting: "The minute I saw him I knew he was not [an artist] of the common [order]. When I watched him do finger painting I was doubly astonished. [In such paintings] he does not use the brush but dips his fingertips into ink and dribbles [across the paper] this way and that, following his inspiration. . . . Such indeed is the accomplishment of an age."[48] Nankai's estimation of Taiga's painting recalls his own mandate for strangeness as an artistic criterion. For the young Taiga, Takeuchi suggests, this meeting with the iconic Nankai likely "reinforced his penchant for eccentricity" and encouraged him to further develop this wondrous technique of finger painting, which he probably learned from Kien.[49]

Subsequently, Taiga's innovations were to set new standards for literati painting. His topographical scenes were so distinct from other landscapes that they necessitated a new descriptor: *shinkeizu* (true-view picture), which transcended conventional landscape art by infusing the work with a realism "filtered through [the] individual character and experiences of the artist."[50] Such innovations confirmed his mysterious talent, evoking such reactions as this one by Kien: "There is an adage: 'poverty of talent is not to be regretted, but over-abundance is to be feared.' Only since meeting you have I come to believe this proverb."[51]

Enduring esteem for Taiga as an artist was inseparable from his status as an eccentric. As already noted, the term *kijin* 畸人 was absent in print culture before Ueda Akinari's *Ugetsu monogatari* in 1776, the year of Taiga's death. Though numerous accounts testify to his eccentricity, Melinda Takeuchi's exhaustive research on Taiga finds only two references to him as a *kijin* 奇人 by his contemporaries: one in Taiga's epitaph by the Abbot Daiten and the other by Yosa Buson in a letter to Ashida Kafu telling of Taiga's death.[52] Taiga's strangeness, therefore, was not wrapped in any preexisting discourse represented by the *ki* aesthetic. Nor was it a gratuitous or irresponsible strangeness. Rather, he was responsible for personifying aesthetic eccentricity, doing for *ki* what Bashō had done for *fūryū*.

Fourteen years after his death, *Kinsei kijinden* would showcase Taiga to establish the *kijin* as a discursive identity. Thereafter, his name would be featured in numerous *kijinden* and painting treatises. He and Gyokuran (also mentioned in *KKD*) are anthologized as follows in *Zoku-haika kijin-dan* (More accounts of eccentric *haikai* poets, 1833): "They were poor and unabashedly wore each others' clothes, though Gyokuran also used to play the zither (*koto*) in the nude. They both were carefree, open-hearted, and famous for being so."[53] Of Taiga, Tanomura Chikuden wrote in *Sanchūjin jōzetsu* (A mountain dweller's chatter, 1813): "Master Taiga Ike's calligraphy and painting are both very good, but people did not acknowledge him during his lifetime. After his death, his fame rose and everyone knew about him; he is now praised as first rate. . . . He had a pure and unconventional heart and was untroubled by [petty] things."[54] The preceding citations are representative for integrating Taiga's high moral character, artistic talent, and untrammeledness. One is not mentioned without the other, supporting Chikuden's great-grandson Tansmura Shōchiku's statement that "A man of high quality will produce painting of high quality."[55] *Ki* is not mere wildness; it weds moral character, eccentric behavior, and artistic genius.

Yosa Buson's example further illustrates nuances of the *ki* aesthetic as conceptualized at this time, clarifying Taiga's status as a *kijin*. Those who speak of a zenith in the *bunjin* movement invoke Taiga and Buson as the two who most successfully exemplify that ethos during the eighteenth century. Though highly regarded as a *nanga* painter—during the last several decades of his life the *Heian jinbutsushi* (Record of Heian notables) consistently ranked him among the top five painters in Kyoto—Buson longed to be recognized for his *haikai*. He led the typically rootless life of a *haikai* poet, traveling throughout Japan, studying with other masters, and experimenting with poetic styles. Some may have viewed him and Taiga similarly, and judging by Buson's own accounts both his art and his behavior may have appeared strange. In *Momosumomo* (Peaches and plums, 1780), for example, he recalls being challenged by one who did not recognize the elegance of his poetry. He was told: "'The kind of eccentric thing you're doing deviates from the basic essence [of *haikai*]. Why don't you abandon this and give into human feeling?' I listened to these words, and coming to a realization, I finally went to the northeast and spent some time traveling around."[56] But despite his prominence and obvious talent, the comparatively few references to him as an eccentric indicate that his contemporaries likely viewed him as less of one. Kōkei, for instance, selected *bunjin* of lesser talent for his *kijinden* but passed over Buson.

Both Nakabayashi Chikutō (1776–1853) and Tanomura Chikuden also compared Buson unfavorably to Taiga.[57] Okada Chōken does praise Buson in *Kinsei itsujin gashi* (History of paintings by eccentric persons of recent times, 1824), saying that his pictures demonstrate *kyō*, but others detect a striving in Buson that is antithetical to the self-absorbed indifference and effortlessness for which Taiga is so acclaimed. Indeed, Buson, as Cheryl Crowley has shown, demonstrated an obsessive preoccupation with his reputation and artistic legacy as a *haikai* poet. A leader of the Bashō revival, he was caught between the perceived need to remain current and his desire to recover the high level of refinement exhibited by Bashō.[58] Instead of steadfastly pursuing a detached aestheticism, he occupied himself with such projects as copying and illustrating the *Oku no hosomichi* and erecting a hall—the Bashō-an—for poetry gatherings in Kyoto. Insecurity over his public image and a desire to be compared favorably to Bashō thus beset Buson with doubts that precluded him from reaching a "depth of character and attainment of transcendence," as the priest Rikunyo (1734–1801) described Taiga.[59] Poet and literary critic Miki Rofū (1889–1964) explained it as follows: "Buson had the temperament of an artist. For this reason, his work captures the exterior radiance, the shading, the fragrance that rises from the shadows of the trees. . . . Yet this capturing, this redistribution, are properties of the surface and are in fact not properties of the self. In this, Buson is perceptual, but does not open his perceptual eye."[60] Of interest here is Rofū's position that Buson's "temperament of an artist" is responsible for perceptual practices that blind his view of himself. Taiga, rather, exhibits a subjectivity detached from technique. This detachment imbues both the artist and the artwork with an untrammeledness that informs his identity as an eccentric.

THE INDIVIDUALISTS: HAKUIN, THE THREE ECCENTRICS, AND KINKOKU

The individualistic but conflicted monk Hakuin (1685–1768) is credited with revitalizing the declining sect of Rinzai Zen. Hakuin's piety and willfulness, certainly, were inspirational, but his charismatic strangeness also helped to restore the sect's vitality. Throughout his life, Hakuin struggled to overcome his preoccupation with self. Determined to conquer self-consciousness once and for all, *Kinsei kijinden* relates, he resolved to abstain from food and sleep for one month. His innards burned while his extremities turned ice cold; he grew weak, hallucinated, perspired, and wept unceasingly, but in the end failed to overcome his uncertainties.[61]

Of particular interest are Hakuin's autobiographical essays, rare in the Edo period, reflecting on parts of his life and some of his paintings. It is within these pages that we find rare glimpses of the emotional origins of the man's strangeness. *Itsumadegusa* (Ivy on the wall, 1765), written in seven-character Chinese verse resembling *kyōshi* (mad verse), is extraordinary for the private, confessional nature of its content. Claims that as a boy Hakuin suffered from neurosis undoubtedly derive from accounts in this text, which relate his tormented obsession with hell.[62] Upon first learning of the eight Buddhist hells, he relates: "my whole body shook with mortal terror. When I went to bed that night, even in the security of my mother's bosom my mind was in a terrible turmoil. I lay awake sobbing miserably all night, my eyes choked with tears."[63] It was an obsession that would torment him throughout his life. Even after becoming a monk, he confessed to being "at the end of [his] rope," ashamed of his fear and emotional instability.[64]

The work itself is deeply self-conscious and indicates that Hakuin has constructed his own self-image around a succession of deeply emotional events, including his tearful elation at reaching enlightenment. It presents his life as a spiritual journey undertaken and completed through psychological struggle. Though intended as a guide to proper Zen practice, it is also a confession of personal failures and achievements. It depicts a Zen master who, in obvious contradiction to Zen teachings, has pushed through the doctrine of No-Self (*muga*) and come out the other side, where he is reunited with Self. One who is weak and fearful will, in the pursuit of No-Self, deny one's emotions and submit to serendipitous external events. "This habitual fool and dullard . . . experiences nothing," Hakuin writes. He, on the other hand, had fully attained this state and then gone on to capture the true No-Self. To do so, he continues, one "must necessarily let go of one's hold on the steep precipice and then, after dying, come to life again. Only then will one directly experience the True and Real Self."[65] Hakuin's subversion of mainstay Buddhist doctrine (No-Self) recovers and honors subjectivity. Though a profane proposition for both Buddhist and Neo-Confucian ethics, recovering selfhood resonated with the psychological struggles of human experience, and for this Hakuin is heralded as the preeminent Rinzai monk of the Tokugawa period.

A nonartist (unaffiliated with any school or stylistic lineage), Hakuin also used art as a tool to transmit religious devotion. Though his temple in Kyoto, Myōshinji, had a close relationship with Manpukuji, and he was likely influenced by the portraiture of the Ōbaku Chinese painter Duzhan, Baisaō's teacher, Hakuin created superb paintings by discarding rules and techniques and simply painting as he wished. His prioritization of personality over technique not only subverted orthodox Buddhist art, it aligned religious practice with personal taste. Bold but playful, austere but affectionate, it created a personalized aestheticism that embraced simplicity and passion.

As Bashō, Nankai, Kien, and Taiga all demonstrate, emotional expressiveness was quickly gaining support among literati and Confucian scholars. Hakuin's art, however, is emblematic of an opening within religious practice to the spiritual benefits of subjective expression. Notably, he produced several self-portraits that suggest struggles with personal demons and a view of himself as resurrected from hell.[66] His portrayals of Bodhidharma appear grizzled, bitter, and half-defeated, as if they too had been resurrected; and his depiction of Daitō Kokushi (1282–1337), leader of the Rinzai sect, as a worn-down, crazed beggar intimates the misery society inflicts upon the individual (Fig. 3.4).[67]

FIGURE 3.4   Hakuin, *Daitō Kokushi*. Eisei Bunko Museum.

It is unusual for a nonartist to release interiority through art, asserts Yajima, but equally extraordinary is Hakuin's profound effect on even the greatest of *bunjin* painters.[68] Soga Shōhaku's *Four Sages of Mount Shang,* for instance, was influenced by Hakuin, as were many of Nagasawa Rosetsu's works. With Taiga and Itō Jakuchū, this exceptionally talented cohort has been grouped, for convenience rather than for stylistic commonalities, under the heading of "the eccentrics" or "the individualists." Though their body of work defies definition, collectively they represent eccentricity in early modern Japanese painting the way Kōkei's *Kinsei kijinden* represents eccentricity in Japanese literature. To this extent, Hakuin can be credited with helping to infuse painting with a passionate subjectivity.

As an outstanding personality, Soga Shōhaku (1730–1781) is a reflection of his extraordinary painting, and a discussion of his eccentricity is best begun there. Critics spare few superlatives on Shōhaku. J. Hillier calls his work "as remarkable as any in the history of oriental art. . . . Shōhaku is possibly the most outrageous of all in his flouting of accepted conventions in ink-painting, and vents the extremist expression of revolutionary willfulness."[69] He worked with intense passion, favoring strong, dark, wild lines over refined brushwork. But wildness was not wielded as a substitute for talent. Some of his paintings appear to have been created by dipping straw into ink and smearing it over the paper; but Shōhaku also demonstrated a remarkable precision and technical virtuosity.[70] He painted beauty with a madness that overturned academic compositions and attacked prevailing aesthetic conventions such as *iki* (chic) and *karumi* (light and ever-changing). This crystallized as a dark, degenerate yet reverential style. His painting *Bijin* (Beauty, 1765), for instance, depicts a barefoot, ragged woman with a crazed grimace clutching a tattered letter, a representation that redefines the conventional allure of female beauty as mania or tragedy. Also noteworthy are his works that convert conventional Chinese settings into terrifying landscapes and Daoist sages into monsters.[71] His *Tekkai-zu* (Portrait of Li Tieguai, ca. 1770) is typical in its depiction of this Daoist immortal, identifiable by his iron crutch, as a frayed, comically disreputable character whose chaotic features reflect the turbulence of his surroundings (Fig. 3.5). Known as an irascible, eccentric healer, here Tekkai exhales a cloud of vapor containing a miniature, disembodied, and therefore transcendent incarnation of himself.

Relatively little is known of Shōhaku's life, and many have filled the gaps with stories of antics that would contextualize his paintings. Allegedly

Figure 3.5 Soga Shōhaku, *Tekkai-zu*. Photograph © 2012 Museum of Fine Arts, Boston.

he was often seen loitering around temples like a beggar, ragged and starving, asking for food or saké in exchange for pictures; riding in palanquins backwards while playing a samisen; painting with rags or straw; and amazing onlookers by getting drunk and then producing large works with a torrent of frenzied energy.[72] In all likelihood, some of these stories are apocryphal, devised later to explain his paintings' strangeness.[73] It is true that Shōhaku gravitated toward a bohemian lifestyle for much of his professional career, traveling and selling or exchanging paintings for daily necessities. But, Tsuji writes, his was an off-kilter (*yokozama*) existence that constantly startled people. He was regularly mistaken for a vagrant, exhibited bad temper, shouted at passersby, and abused alcohol. Tsuji surmises that his hair and clothing probably fit the image of the man that people envisioned when they saw his work, and for such reasons he was regarded as a madman.[74]

The two questions of interest to us are how—or whether—to interpret the man from his art and how he was received artistically and socially. Contemporary scholarship on Shōhaku is divided over the first question—whether his brashness was the result of "demonic passions spilling forth from within" or an intentional ploy to attract attention.[75] Tsuji asserts that Shōhaku transferred his own emotional instability into his paintings, which developed in a "mad" way out of tune with the art of his times but nonetheless attracted public fascination.[76] Certainly his methods of operating within society were more erratic than any other individual we shall consider here, and the extent to which this quality was deliberate will never be clear. Even if his wildness was a deliberate and feigned strategy of garnering attention, Tsuji continues, his construction of parody through the demonic, ugly, and grotesque was empowering to him in ways that would have been possible only through a genuine madness.[77]

Satō Yasuhiro believes that Shōhaku knowingly cultivated an identity of craziness in emulation of certain known Chinese *kijin* and *kyōjin,* and that his public behavior was intentionally antisocial.[78] Indeed, Shōhaku's remark that the eminent painter Maruyama Ōkyo's works were mere picture copies (*ezu*), and that anyone desiring a true painting should come to him instead, shows him making little effort to position himself strategically within the field.[79] This indictment of the day's most celebrated artist (Ōkyo was ranked first in the 1775 *Heian jinbutsushi* while Shōhaku was ranked fifteenth) was tantamount to intentional infamy. Furthermore, it demonstrates a willingness to incite controversy and invite scorn from literati circles.

Money Hickman takes the position that Shōhaku was less creative and eccentric than he is usually depicted as being. Shōhaku, he argues, was orthodox, serious, and not inspired solely by strangeness.[80] It is likely that his style was acquired over a lifetime of influences. A sense of personal tragedy may have followed the experiences of losing his parents and a brother early in life, and then a young son in 1777. The prominence of Daoist immortals in his paintings leaves no doubt that his antisocial, bizarre behavior was at least partially modeled after Daoist exemplars. He is also thought to have befriended and learned of aesthetic madness from Wang Yangming advocate Akutagawa Tankyū (1710–1785).[81] Shōhaku's painting style, finally, was certainly influenced by the wandering painter Takada Keiho (1674–1755), whose own idiosyncrasies earned him an entry in *Zoku-kinsei kijinden.*

Shōhaku would never have achieved artistic notoriety without making certain concessions to standing artistic practice, and in some important ways he was careful to operate within conventional boundaries. He did maintain relationships with certain peers. He cultivated a friendship with Taiga and a rivalry with Ōkyo, and seems to have been well known to a number of others within that circle. He also recognized the necessity of associating himself with an artistic lineage. Born to a merchant family in Kyoto, he did not receive the privilege of studying at the foremost studios, which, in any case, would have quashed his artistic independence. Nonetheless, he adopted the name Soga, probably out of admiration for the strange, defiant painter Soga Jasoku (d. 1483), who relinquished his samurai status to become a Zen monk under the eminent iconoclast Ikkyū Sōjun (1394–1481). This affiliation allowed Shōhaku to claim descent from samurai stock and become a successor to a recognized painting "school," without which he would have been unrecognized and thus unable to operate as an artist.[82]

The uniqueness of Shōhaku's personality could only have grown from the anxiety of existence itself, for it is not enough merely to mention the monstrous figures that dominate his paintings. Other artists also wielded an aesthetic of monstrosity, but they exhibit an emotional harmony that Shōhaku does not. If he is to be labeled a painter of monsters, he must be distinguished from others by this lack of inner peace. From the normative perspective, those who paint the monstrous can be said to be monsters themselves; but Shōhaku's indifference to convention was actually a purging of his sensitivities to which the world was so abrasive. Nonconformity in his case was a result of extraordinary sensitivity.[83] If anecdotes about him are true—that he used to call from inside that he wasn't home when guests knocked at his gate, or that once invited for a meal he became so engrossed in conversation that he talked late into the night and forgot to eat—then they indeed indicate a disregard for decorum that would have been considered eccentric.[84] They suggest a highly focused, possibly obsessive personality that turned to disdainful brashness when he was interrupted by demands for social niceties.

Answers to the second question, that concerning Shōhaku's reception by the public, are as surprising as the man himself. Consensus holds that Shōhaku enjoyed popularity during his own lifetime. His strange and startling demons, his vulgarity and coarseness, were backed by strong public support, according to Tsuji.[85] Satō concurs that Shōhaku was well known and favorably viewed in his day, and finds no evidence of him being socially ostracized for his art. He had a circle of *bunjin* admirers, and his paintings were widely copied and in demand around the Kansai area.[86] In 1775, when he was forty-six, his name was listed alongside other contemporary celebrities in *Heian jinbutsushi*. It thus appears that, although his erratic behavior was scandalous and earned him a reputation for madness, his strange art also brought him a measure of critical acclaim.[87] In this respect, Shōhaku illustrates more clearly than any other late eighteenth-century figure that eccentrics were generally respected as social agents and cultural producers. Even antisocial behavior could find a habitable space within Tokugawa society if it was accompanied by extraordinary talent.

After his death, Shōhaku came to be treated more critically, in part because he had never become a formal disciple of an established painter. Despite his appearance in *Heian jinbutsushi,* for example, he is not included in Kōkei's *Kinsei kijinden*. His notoriety and talent as an artist and eccentric would seem more than sufficient to qualify him for inclusion. The fact that he was not suggests that Kōkei judged him to be an irredeemable persona lacking the requisite moral virtue. Shōhaku fit neither the model of the Daoist *kijin* nor that of the virtuous Confucian; he occupied an irrecoverable position outside these categories. He is depicted as a *kyōjin*—scornfully in this case—in Okada Chōken's *Kinsei itsujin gashi* (History of paintings by eccentric persons of recent times, 1824), and in *Gajō yōryaku* (Concise annals of painting, 1831) Shirai Kayo relates that Shōhaku's "figures are unearthly in appearance and because of this strange, bizarre quality he became a school unto himself."[88] While acknowledging the extraordinary power of Shōhaku's art, the prominent *bunjin* Nakabayashi Chikutō (1776–1853) wrote that Shōhaku's art was vulgar and that he was "a man full of talent who treaded a road of evil."[89] Finally, Maruyama Ōkyo's apprentice Shibata Gitō (1780–1819) assessed Shōhaku as a "hallmark of difference" in the world, certainly a derogatory comment given Ōkyo's palpable dislike of Shōhaku.[90]

Shōhaku's contemporary Itō Jakuchū was equally detached but more prudent about his public image. Significantly, Jakuchū was one of the only eccentrics of his own or later generations to actually refer to himself as a *kijin*. He writes: "As for painting these days, there are many who paint but few who look at things closely. They endeavor to create sellable works through technique alone, but none are able to surpass the limitations of technique. That's what is strange (畸) about me."[91] These were not words of grandeur, though they do reveal a self-aggrandizing recognition of artistic talent. More likely, they were an apologetic attempt to explain his chosen lifestyle and peculiar painting style. As Satō surmises, it may well have been that Jakuchū was troubled about being labeled an outsider but deployed the term *ki* as a resigned affirmation of such.[92]

The son of a Kyoto grocer, Jakuchū initially took over the family business but at age thirty-six shaved his head and became a lay monk. His obsession was painting, which he learned by imitating Chinese artworks. A friendship with the Zen priest Daiten (1720–1802) and close associations with several Ōbaku monks allowed him access to collections of imported paintings at various temples; he also maintained a close friendship with Baisaō, through whom we imagine he developed an appreciation for the simple, pious aesthetic life. Despite these associations Jakuchū remained unmarried and lived in quiet, reclusive, penurious circumstances that occasionally forced him to trade his paintings for food.[93]

Also despite these associations, Jakuchū, like Hakuin and Shōhaku, developed an exotic style. His eccentricity derived not from open contempt for artistic convention, however, but from an ability to transcend those standards through technical precision and obsessive detail. Daily, Jakuchū spent hours observing and sketching chickens, fish, birds, or plants and earned fame for his ability to capture the lifelike essence of those subjects with unparalleled accuracy.[94] His precision was such that the exact time of year a work was produced is discernable from the detail with which he depicted his plants and animals. Botanists have also discerned the gender of certain flora in his paintings. This close attention to detail suggests a compulsive perfectionism that we do not see in any of his contemporaries. By wielding his mastery of technique through the whims of his own personality he was able to produce realism that was unprecedented in either Chinese or Japanese art.

One cannot claim that Jakuchū's obsessions were manifestations of mental illness, as some do. He was no agoraphobe, for he actively marketed his paintings. Elizabeth Lillehoj asserts that he even oversaw his own painting studio, though little is known of this.[95] It is nonetheless clear that both his painting style and his solitary lifestyle were tactics aimed at securing a level of psychological comfort within what Jakuchū himself feared would otherwise have been an uncomfortable existence.[96] He has been viewed as an eccentric for the same reasons that Jakuchū styled himself as a *kijin:* perfectionism (his infatuated pursuit of realism), individualism (privileging personal aesthetics over normative ones), and the talent to actualize these without extensive training.

If Jakuchū's was an eccentricity of quietude and Shōhaku's was one of struggle, then Nagasawa Rosetsu's was an eccentricity of expulsion, Suzuki Susumu suggests.[97] Rosetsu studied under Maruyama Ōkyo, but a "penchant for heavy drinking and brawling" made him a poor fit for disciplined life within a prestigious atelier.[98] His impatience with the master's criticisms, in particular, strained their relationship. Allegedly, Rosetsu once brought one of Ōkyo's own drawings to him for critique and revealed his ruse only after the master had thoroughly condemned it.[99] Though Rosetsu was expelled from the studio, he wasted little time making a name for himself. Nearby he established his own atelier and before long was receiving commissions from high-ranking officials, including one at the Imperial Summer Palace in Kyoto. His virtuosity earned him mention in the 1782 edition of *Heian jinbutsushi.* He died at age forty-five, by some accounts poisoned by jealous competitors.

Rosetsu's range of styles defies classification, making his oeuvre a violation of artistic orthodoxy. This indefinability rendered his body of work decipherable only through comparisons to a spectrum of traditions, including Sesshū's (1420–1506) "splashed-ink" technique; the spontaneous but understated *satori*-like immediacy of Zen painting; the playfulness of untrammeled early Chinese Daoists; and the various styles used by Chinese eccentric painters of later centuries.[100] An emotional extremism underlies Rosetsu's undefinability, but is tempered by a talent for portraying surprising motifs with warmth and humor. Often his strange expressionism is realized through an irreverent playfulness, as in his portrayal of the monks Kanzan and Jittoku (Fig. 3.6) as slovenly, vagabond-like figures, or through juxtapositions or inversions of categories, as in his portrait of a miniature boy flautist perched on the back of the immense ox.[101] In *Mount Fuji* (Fig. 3.7), the mountain is tucked into the bottom lefthand corner overhung by an imposing plum tree rendered by a thick diagonal slash across the paper. The mountain's symbolic importance, which by artistic convention required that it be centered and prominent, is subverted by the size, power, and central position of the plum.[102] But whereas convention provides guidance for the average, for the extraordinary it stirs impatience. Shōhaku, Jakuchū, and Rosetsu—all social outsiders—mounted separate challenges to artistic convention. That they were lauded rather than ostracized for doing so is further evidence of extraordinary public tolerance for defiant art at this time.

Yokoi Kinkoku (1761–1832), our final archetype of strange individualism, was a monk turned mountain ascetic (*yamabushi*) turned painter who was reputed to possess mystical powers and a formidable intelligence. Though not a true literatus, he has been evaluated by art historians through comparisons to contemporary *bunjin* painters.[103] To some he is "baffling," and for others he is "one of the most eccentric and fascinating personalities in the history of Japanese art."[104] Fujimori Seikichi views him as a self-obsessed individual whose willfulness overcame external obstacles and internal deficiencies. If his eventful life was, in Fujimori's words, "a performance of personality," it was more a comedy than a tragedy judging by the light-hearted style of Kinkoku's autobiographical *Kinkoku shōnin gyōjōki* (Annals of the eminent priest Kinkoku) and *Kinkoku shōnin goichidaiki* (Record of the life of the eminent priest Kinkoku, 1809).[105] These works were part of the performance, as Kinkoku took pleasure in using them to expound on

FIGURE 3.6 Nagasawa Rosetsu, *Kanzan and Jittoku*. Kōzanji Temple, Wakayama.

FIGURE 3.7   Nagasawa Rosetsu, *Mount Fuji.* Mana
Maeda Design Association.

his eccentricity. In the former, Kinkoku confesses to being born a "terribly strange" (*kikimyōmyō*) son, and, as he relates it, the strangeness of his early childhood set the tone for the rest of his life:

> Though my mother did not neglect her devotion to the Three Treasures [the Buddha, the Dharma, and the monastic order] . . . I was nonetheless born in her eighth month of pregnancy.[106] At just that moment a strange cloud carrying a terribly noxious odor fell over the birthing chamber. Someone had farted. . . . Then, when I was two years old my mother secretly dropped me down the latrine, after which everyone called me Kusomatsu-dono (Master Crappy). Clearly my strange karmic connection to foul odors was apparent from the beginning.[107]

Confessional "performances" of this sort earned him a celebrity that contributed to his reputation as an eccentric. His self-promotional skills allowed him to cultivate a distinctive aestheticism that straddled the spiritual and the secular.

Although Kinkoku spent most of his professional life in the Nagoya area, he was born in Shiga, where he entered a Pure Land Buddhist monastery at age nine. His nature was too restless and capricious for monastic life, however. Variously attracted to and repulsed by the priesthood, he sought spiritualism in other creeds, probably to satisfy an introspective rather than an intellectual curiosity. Though appointed chief priest at Gokurakuji at the age of twenty-one, he was drawn to the asceticism and less doctrinaire practices of *shugendō*. Contrary to monastic Buddhism, this sect advocated activistic forms of religious practice and training in magico-religious powers, both of which suited his restless temperament.[108]

The defining moment in his life as a spiritual and public figure occurred in 1804 when he was offered the coveted position of axe-bearer on a particularly prestigious *shugendō* pilgrimage. Led by an Imperial prince, the two-month expedition traveled to the sacred peaks of Ōmine, Katsuragi, and Kumano to perform esoteric rituals. For his service, Kinkoku received a ceremonial purple robe and the prestigious title Hōin Daisendatsu (Great Leader of the Seal of the Law). Thereafter he identified himself as a mountain ascetic and earned money by selling paintings and hiring himself out as a guide for officials and pilgrims. He also began signing his paintings *Taihō shūjin* (Master of the Great Treasure) and with other self-aggrandizing pseudonyms. The sudden notoriety received for his service as axe-bearer increased the demand for his paintings, which may have been believed to possess some of the mystical powers Kinkoku himself had acquired at the sacred sites he had visited.[109]

As with Shōhaku, whose paintings appear to have received more attention from local literati circles than elsewhere, Kinkoku's popularity in the Nagoya area was probably not reciprocated in Kyoto, where he was likely dismissed as a *yamabushi* bumpkin.[110] Though a self-taught painter and an undistinguished poet, he took pains to maintain friendly relations with accomplished literati in Nagoya and elsewhere. His painting was a haphazard mixture of many styles he had come across, and he resisted overtly copying from Chinese or other models. He was thus able to escape the conventionalism that plagued his contemporaries who, he felt, were unable to recapture the originality of earlier masters. In fact, Kinkoku had little knowledge of past masters and no use for genre art. He waved off art critics, allegedly snapping that they were welcome to evaluate his work after his death.[111] His paintings are strong, rustic, fragmented, and closely resemble Rosetsu's in their obsessive energy. In comparison, he says, Kinkoku made no attempt to suppress his derangement (*monogurui*). "There is fierce emotion lurking beneath," Furukawa notes. "Kinkoku's strength is his vehement madness."[112]

While painting was a source of income for Kinkoku, it was also a medium of self-reflection. In addition to his autobiographical *Ichidaiki,* he produced at least two self-portraits and numerous poems ruminating, curiously, on his estrangement from the world he sought to transcend. Some landscapes bear inscriptions revealing, instead of nature imagery as would be customary, the cogitations of an unsettled mind. His isolation and self-absorption are evident, for example, in a verse that Patricia Fister interprets as an outcry of isolation.

> *kangetsu ya*   cold moon–
> *atari he kumo mo*   even clouds
> *yosetsukezu*   are kept at a distance[113]

As a *yamabushi,* isolation was the very aesthetic he sought, but self-obsession variously denied him its spiritual benefits. The following poem is a remarkably straightforward confession of this emotional state:

> I was born without intelligence or virtue,
> Among Confucians, Buddhists, and Taoists I have no friends.
> With my three-foot sword I cut away the rights and wrongs,
> Embracing all misfortunes and accepting people's animosity.[114]

Here, Kinkoku claims to be philosophically alienated from mainstream thought, enabling him to "cut away" the artificial restrictions it imposed. If this estrangement, as he claims, attracted contempt, it may have both caused him anguish and steeled his determination to persevere.

In some respects Kinkoku's restless discomfort is characteristic of other eccentrics; his brashness mirrors Taiga and Shōhaku, and his impatience with institutionalized religious practice evokes Baisaō and Hakuin. Kinkoku was enigmatic, however, for he coveted status and social recognition in ways that would have defiled the aesthetic sensibilities of other clerics. Bashō's open disdain for the commercialization of art even while relying on it as a source of revenue had been an unchallenged pillar of reclusive aestheticism throughout the eighteenth century. Kinkoku, however, was shamelessly self-promoting. To advance his own fame, he asked a friend to circulate a statement listing his accomplishments and asking for alms in exchange for paintings. "When people present small donations of money or goods," he wrote, "I give them landscape or figure paintings as desired. All contain power. . . . [Through them] dangers will be chased far away and the sounds of happiness will rebound."[115]

Kinkoku's claims to possessing mystical power echoed what his contemporaries wrote of him. The noted literatus Nakajima Sōin (d. 1856) knew Kinkoku and was greatly impressed by his journeys to sacred sites. He exalted him as a Daoist immortal who used art as a medium for disseminating his power:

Holy mountains and sacred peaks—he must have already visited them all.
It is not strange that smoke and mist arise from his colorful brush

And yet I think that at his waist was a heavy axe—
Splitting open mountain cliffs, he frightened away dragons.[116]

Although Kinkoku admired and cultivated associations within *bunjin* circles, he was an outsider there as well. One imagines that his ties to local literati were secured through his eccentric image, that his painting and poetry attracted more curiosity than admiration.

It is clear that Kinkoku utilized his reputation as a mystic for personal benefit. He not only assumed those mystical powers ascribed to *yamabushi* and peddled his art by imbuing it with magical blessings, he also coveted the attention and recognition afforded by this publicity. And though some may have accused him of feigning eccentricity for attention and financial gain, it would be improper to conclude that Kinkoku's was a disingenuous aestheticism. Emotional conflict between his social detachment and his desire for recognition suggests frustration arising from a failure to receive the respect he felt his intelligence and talents deserved. The magico-religious empowerment he derived through his practice of *shugendō* may have mediated this conflict by providing him with both spiritual distance and public prestige, but his restlessness would be a lifelong affliction.

CELEBRATING SELVES AND MAKING SPACES

Kinkoku's self-obsession may have been distinctive in his day but is consistent with the eccentric lives introduced in this chapter. As will be discussed later, greater portions of Edo society were arriving at greater appreciations of self and individual peculiarities. In contrast to pre-Genroku, pre-Sorai years, when the cultural field was guided by a more stringent moralism that drove outsiders like Ishikawa Jōzan into "stylish reclusion," after the Kyōhō era (1716–1736) a new *bunjin* consciousness afforded greater engagement with the diverse emotions of human experience. With this newfound autonomy, cultural practice moved toward constructing independent aesthetic realms for individual pleasure. Such spaces enjoyed relative independence from social structures like status and occupation. "Off-duty" spaces such as calligraphy and painting gatherings (*shogakai*), tea gatherings, and *haikai* salons thus allowed men and women of diverse status and occupational groups to study and interact with relative freedom.[117]

Although a clear numerical minority, female *haikai* poets, for instance, were comparatively less restricted within *haikai* schools and networks than they were in mainstream society.[118] The most accomplished would be heralded as *kijin*, not only for their talent as poets but for devoting themselves to poetry rather than succumbing to the conventional role of good wives and wise mothers (*ryōsai kenbo*). Indeed, many are anthologized in Takeuchi Gengen'ichi's (1742–1804) *Haika kijindan* (Accounts of eccentric *haikai* poets, 1816).[119] Most were nuns, widows, or single women, which facilitated mobility and study with *haikai* masters. Some—for example, Shiba Sonome (1664–1726) and Taniguchi Denjo (d. 1779)—worked as *haikai* graders (*tenja*); others, like Chiyo-ni (1703?–1775), published poetry anthologies. Many others traveled widely, some—for instance, Arii Shokyū (1714–1781) and Togami Kikusha (1753–1826)—retracing Bashō's journeys and producing travelogues modeled after his *Oku no hosomichi*.[120]

The comparatively free and egalitarian forms of participation occurring within aesthetic spaces were directed toward two general objectives: exploring personal feelings and acquiring cultural refinement (*ga*). The two bore no sense of conflict, for *ga* was a mutable and easily coopted aesthetic. Indeed, it was through *ga* that the experiential passions of human life informed the aesthetics of strangeness. The seeming incompatibility between emotions and refinement was easily explained away with nondualistic logic asserting the inseparability of *ga* and *zoku* (vulgarity). Bashō had united them in his endeavor to raise *zoku* to the level of *ga* via his mandate to "awaken to the high and return to the low" (*kōgo kizoku*). Ogyū Sorai endorsed a similar view; and Gion Nankai had proclaimed that human feelings were best conveyed with *ga* words, the words of past masters.[121] Nankai had also designated *ki* as a requisite for successful art. As noted, Kuwayama Gyokushū in turn asserted that the deviant aesthetic *ippin* (untrammeledness) was "the sublime category . . . [of] wonder, mystery, and marvel."[122] Ōta Nanpo then eradicated any lingering doubts by declaring simply that "When a *ga* person engages with *zoku* it becomes *ga*."[123] Each of these statements reiterated and extended what had long been intuitive to many eccentric artists: that *ga* and the alleged vulgarity of human passions were interdependent and, ideally, indistinguishable.

The spirit of strangeness deriving from individual passions and particularities, moreover, was consciously sustained, bequeathed either from parent to child or from master to pupil. In such cases, eccentricity became the property of an esoteric tradition that perpetuated a sort of guild of the strange. Nearly all eccentric artists studied with masters, receiving and transmitting their artistic techniques. The painters Soga Chokuan (fl. ca. 1596–1610) and his son Nichokuan (fl. ca. 1625–1660), for example, both known for their rebelliousness and violent imagery, were independent progenitors of the Echizen Soga School, also known for eccentric art. In their case, eccentricity was an aesthetic tradition transmitted generationally to which Shōhaku later claimed entitlement; likewise the Three Women of Gion. Gyokuran, Taiga's wife, was an accomplished *nanga* painter but also the third generation of women to run the famous Matsuya teahouse in Kyoto's Gion entertainment district. She, her mother Yuri (1694–1764), and grandmother Kaji (late seventeeth–early eighteenth c.) all succeeded in earning reputations as talented poets. Kaji and Yuri, known for their *waka*, never married, and all three remained singularly devoted to their teahouse and art. That Gyokuran opted to be buried not with the husband with whom she had lived happily for several decades but at the gravesite of her natal family is indicative of this independent spirit.[124]

The formation of aesthetic spaces, greater focus on particularities emanating from within, and proprietary transmissions of eccentricity all helped sustain a valuation of strangeness for the remainder of the Edo period. Sustainability was aided by tendencies among *kijin* to convert the potential dangers of deviance to benign ends. From the Meiji ideologue Ernest Fenollosa (1853–1908), who viewed *nanga* as a "heresy," to writers as recent as art historian Patricia Graham, who see Baisaō and his followers as advancing a "political agenda," idiosyncratic art and strange behavior have consistently been assumed to connote open political dissent.[125] However, one finds no evidence that the artists discussed here either espoused overt political interests or were considered notorious for their unusual ways. We know of the generally warm reception enjoyed by Taiga and Jakuchū in their communities. The unruly Shōhaku was guardedly well received in his day, as was the flamboyant Kinkoku. Though eccentricity implies marginalization, therefore, in many cases disenfranchisement appears to have been an assumption of later writers and one perpetuated by historiographical bias. The low incidence of censure or indictment among *kijin* indicates that in general they forestalled criticism by ensuring that their reputations were beyond reproach. That is, what may have been viewed as undesirable behavior was preempted by the normally withdrawn lifestyles of these eccentrics, as well as by their exceptional ability to contribute positively to social harmony. If dissent was ever intended, it was executed under the generally benign pretense of strangeness or play.

It is clear that the emergence of aesthetic eccentricity in eighteenth-century Japan followed the innovations of certain outstanding individuals. But it is also clear that, as the copious *kijinden* appearing from the end of the century demonstrate, strangeness was a phenomenon that transcended class and occupation. These developments must now be contextualized within the intellectual landscape wherein these individuals prospered.

CHAPTER 4

Strange Thoughts

A Confluence of Intellectual Heterodoxies

> *The wackier the better, just so long as one*
> *isn't the same as everybody else.*
>
> —Hiraga Gennai (1728–1779)

The second half of the eighteenth century was beset by a sense of decline, an "autumn," as Takahashi Hiromi phrases it.[1] In part, such sentiments crystallized around the perceived disintegration of political authority. The shogun, Tokugawa Ieharu (1737–1786), was a tragicomic figure popularly viewed, according to one Dutch observer, as "a lazy, lustful, stupid man."[2] Described by Timon Screech as one who slept late, ate much, and accomplished little, Ieharu was a laughing stock throughout his rule. The reign began in 1760 with the worst of portents—a major fire that destroyed much of Edo, and later witnessed natural disasters, famines, and a culture of excess that weakened the *bakufu* and incited civil unrest. At this time, Chief Councilor Matsudaira Sadanobu reported widespread public convictions that the *bakufu* had succumbed to corruption, lost the ability to rule, and was close to collapse.[3]

The same era, however, also witnessed a flurry of cultural activity by an abundance of exceptional scholars. This dichotomy between sociopolitical weakening and cultural energy framed and nourished unprecedented intellectual innovation. Less interested in doctrinal consistency than in making sense of human experience, by this time both samurai and commoner thinkers were picking and choosing from a variety of disparate, even antagonistic intellectual traditions. The aesthetic strangeness being developed and popularized by first- and second-generation *bunjin,* therefore, paralleled an array of emergent heterodoxies. Lending intellectual validation to aesthetic and behavioral strangeness, collectively they generated a cultural milieu favorably disposed to *ki* and *kyō,* the aesthetics of eccentricity that would become ubiquitous by century's end.

This chapter discusses an assortment of intellectual credos that fortified individual agency. After problematizing Zhu Xi Neo-Confucianism as a true orthodoxy in the Tokugawa period, it introduces Confucianism's "mad" side—its doctrinal defense of *kyō.* We then revisit the Daoist roots of the *ki* aesthetic via its synergy with the Wang Yangming School (Yōmeigaku or Ōyōmeigaku) and National Learning (Kokugaku). Each of these traditions proved useful to eccentric thinkers like Hattori Somon (1724–1769) and Shidōken (1680?–1765), whose respective heresies advanced new ontological interpretations. The propagation of such thinkers suggests that a diverse and dynamic intellectual culture was becoming increasingly tolerant of strange people with strange thoughts. It was within this milieu that *kijin* maneuvered to find their place.

NEO-CONFUCIANISM: A REASSESSMENT

Maruyama Masao has argued that within the classical Confucian canon the term "heterodoxy" (*itan*) describes mistaken thinking, broadly construed, or thoughts oppositional to the Way. The fact that *itan* had always existed and, as Confucius and Mencius observed, ran rampant through society, Maruyama avers, naturally validated ideological enforcement of orthodoxy (*seitō*): the Way.[4] In early modern Japan this notion was reinforced by even those scholars who challenged Zhu Xi thought. Ancient Learning thinker Itō Jinsai noted that *itan* consisted of all that violated the original Way of the sages and that self-regulation was necessary to suppress it. When Song period Confucians began studying Buddhism and Daoism, he continued, their thought became *itan.* Jinsai's contemporary Yamaga Sokō (1622–1685) also attacked heterodoxy, attributing its recent proliferation to declining interest in the sages' teachings. But, he warned, simply attacking it was futile, for *itan* would yield to the proper Way only if people devoted themselves to righteousness. Ogyū Sorai's philological studies demonstrating how language differed from later and contemporary usages also exposed misinterpretations and inconsistencies in Neo-Confucian writings. Sorai found many instances of heterodoxy within the *Analects* and the *Kongzi jiayu* (Confucius' words at home), acknowledging that it fostered treacherous or rebellious thoughts and thereby defied the Way. But, like Jinsai, his philological work also concluded that *itan* characterized the myriad Confucians whose writings were based on Zhu Xi.[5]

This succession of damaging challenges eroded the legitimacy of Zhu Xi-ism's alleged orthodoxy within academic spheres, Maruyama maintains. But its position was never threatened within public and official spheres. Official initiatives like the Prohibition of Heterodox Studies (*Kansei igaku no kin,* 1790) continually reinforced sharp distinctions between the Confucian classics and *itan* works by, for example, Ogyū Sorai. Nonetheless, from the mid-eighteenth century Sorai's teachings (Soraigaku) and their historicist approach to understanding the world had became pillars of learning. Buttressing the popularity of *kanshi* and Chinese aesthetics, as well as the nativist backlash against Chinese studies, its near universal applicability rendered it a common denominator for members of disparate schools who were challenging inherited social knowledge.[6] But as Meiji philosopher Nishi Amane's (1829–1897) autobiography reveals, although Sorai's writings had become a cornerstone of early modern thought, they continued to be perceived as heterodoxical. At age twenty Nishi fell ill and was confined to his bed. During his convalescence, he writes, he felt that it would be disrespectful to read Zhu Xi while lying down but permissible to read a heretical work, and so he read Ogyū Sorai's *Rongo.*[7] This confession reveals a gap in Tokugawa thought between the normative as prescribed and the normative as practiced.

Like the bulk of postwar scholarship, Maruyama's writings make sense of Tokugawa intellectual history through a pair of binaries: one between Neo-Confucian "orthodoxy" (Zhu Xi-ism) and the various "heterodoxies," and one between Neo-Confucianism and modernity. Consequently, Neo-Confucianism has been reviled, first as an intolerant and oppressive ideology, and second as antithetical to the promise of modernization. Subsequent scholarship has qualified these assertions and refined our use of the terms orthodoxy and heterodoxy. In doing so it has also corrected the view that the crystallization of intellectual strangeness (heterodoxy) emerged simply as a reaction to an oppressive orthodoxy. While acknowledging the importance of Maruyama's work, for instance, Wm. T. DeBary has pointed out that Zhu Xi-ism engendered a dynamic intellectual milieu that embraced rationalism, humanism, ethnocentrism, and historical-mindedness, all of which moved Tokugawa thought in the direction of modernity.[8] Tetsuo Najita has also refined the Maruyama thesis, arguing that Tokugawa society did not necessarily subscribe to orthodoxy as an a priori set of structures, but rather used it to explain extant beliefs. It was, he contends, a philosophy useful to Japanese thinkers for its ability to make sense of practical and political realities.[9] Ancient Learning, including Soraigaku, moved closer to these realities by elevating the tangible influences of time and place over Zhu Xi's rigid devotion to Principle (*ri*) and material force (*ki*). Rather than changing the intellectual character of its time, Neo-Confucian thinkers "provided scriptural and classical authority to what the Japanese already believed to be good and true."[10]

Kurozumi Makoto levels a more damaging attack on Maruyama, arguing that Neo-Confucianism played a critical role in Japan's modernization. Not only did it never amount to a true orthodoxy, Kurozumi contends, it actually engendered important strands of heterodox thought—Ancient Learning and Kokugaku in particular—which did demonstrate modern-like principles.[11] Most heterodox pioneers, in fact, were Zhu Xi scholars who found no contradiction or antagonism between it and other philosophies. Arguing against Maruyama's attempt to identify and codify differences between the various philosophical traditions, Kurozumi posits that Zhu Xi Confucianism was not static and inflexible but rather underwent its process of modernization in conjunction with Ancient Learning and other intellectual movements. It did not experience gradual erosion over the course of the Tokugawa period, but neither did it ever constitute an absolute orthodoxy. Rather, it was slowly accepted as an ideological feature of the social mainstream due to its gradual opening to and convergence with Western learning and Kokugaku.[12] Zhu Xi-ism remained an ideological overlay, however, never infiltrating to the level of ceremony, ritual, or social practice. It was largely through its ability to integrate with and exist syncretically with other doctrines by providing them with certain "theories, concepts, and ethics," that Neo-Confucianism was able to promote itself and infiltrate public consciousness.[13]

Neo-Confucianism's adaptations to *kinsei* life are also manifest in its gradual acceptance of individual differences. By the mid-eighteenth century, several generations of Ancient Learning thinkers had formulated arguments favoring differentiation and pluralism in human nature. Herman Ooms, looking for the roots of an intellectual discourse on metaphysical difference within human nature, makes several important points. One is that the particularism of human nature had been recognized and debated as a philosophical issue from the seventeenth century. Ancient Learning scholars challenged the universality of original nature (*honzen no sei*) and human nature (*jinsei*) by shifting their attention to the distinctiveness of human character, ultimately finding metaphysical justification for articulations of difference between humans. In direct opposition to the universalism underlying Zhu Xi Confucianism's prioritization of original nature and human nature, Kumazawa Banzan, Yamaga Sokō, Itō Jinsai, and Ogyū Sorai all recognized an altogether separate endowment as more representative of human character—namely, pluralism. Banzan stressed the importance of preserving differences between people; Jinsai and Sokō both explained that, although individuals share Heaven as a common origin, after birth this commonality is nullified by their individual destinies. Moreover, by celebrating rather than bemoaning humanity's diversity, their conclusion that pluralism was a necessary and desirable reality of human society gradually eroded the viability of universalism.[14]

This positive appraisal of particularism in Tokugawa thought was consistent with the rational universalism endorsed by Zhu Xi. Human differentiation was not a philosophically subversive proposition; it was emblematic of Neo-Confucianism's tolerance for metaphysical strangeness. Charlotte Furth points out that Chinese cosmology does not categorically sanction abnormal phenomena but rather recognizes them as part of the heavenly Way. Regularity and irregularity are distinguishable within the Confucian Way, and the appearance of the latter affirms rather than subverts the former. "While patterns are seen as temporal processes, regularities are probabilities, not absolutes, and the 'strange' as a unique event, like snow in summer, will—as the philosopher Zhu Xi put it in the Song Dynasty—occasionally intrude in the scene without undermining the intelligibility of the whole."[15] Although by the seventeenth century Ancient Learning thinkers questioned whether strange phenomena were being accurately represented by traditional Confucian cosmology, their skepticism was directed toward the capacities of human understanding, not the cosmology itself.[16] Metaphysical strangeness continued to be accepted as a part of the cosmological pattern rather than rejected as aberrant or wicked. In the end, therefore, it was the rationalizing effects of Neo-Confucianism that had boomeranged to subvert the orthodox ideology of universalism and the importance it attached to civic responsibility and obedience.

These arguments invalidate the assumption of top-down oppression that has guided scholarship influenced by modernization theories. They also problematize modernist views of eccentricity (heterodoxy) as political dissent against an oppressive orthodoxy. Japanese and Western scholarship on the aesthetics of eccentricity in the Tokugawa period—represented most notably by Tsuji Nobuo's *Kisō no keifu* (Genealogies of eccentrics, 1968) and John Rosenfield's three-volume *Extraordinary Persons: Works by Eccentric, Nonconformist Japanese Artists of the Early Modern Era (1580–1868) in the Collection of Kimiko and John Powers* (1998)—have established a narrative claiming that *ki* constituted a revolt against a formidable, monolithic Neo-Confucian structure that had inhibited self-determination and self-expression. Viewed from above, the ascendance of strangeness would indeed appear a threatening and destabilizing political movement, but within coteries devoted to the cultivation and enjoyment of *haikai, waka, nanga,* and *sencha,* fascination with strangeness was more of a negotiation (or positioning) for apolitical space. The crystallization of intellectual eccentricity, likewise, cannot be explained entirely as a reaction against the oppressive nature of intellectual "orthodoxy." While it is true that *kijin* gravitated toward alternative philosophies of various forms, historical documents reveal no evidence that either discursive eccentricity or *kijin* themselves acknowledged any decisive binary dividing heterodoxy and orthodoxy. To note that Neo-Confucianism was not necessarily hostile or doctrinally intolerant toward alternate philosophies, and that it even fueled inquiry into Ancient Learning, Kokugaku, Wang Yangming, and Daoism, therefore, invites revised explanations for the mid-eighteenth century's budding culture of strangeness. Further, it recasts the cultural field as a negotiated space formed more from the diverse interests of its residents than by any pervasive ideology. Zhu Xi-ism's coexistence within a constellation of doctrinally compelling alternatives was aided by its recognition of the social value of strangeness, and particularly of madness (*kyō*).

A GENEALOGY OF *KYŌ* IN THE CONFUCIAN TRADITION

Kyōjin or *kyōsha* (mad person)[17] were universally recognized terms—certainly more familiar in print culture than the term *kijin*—and played an increasingly important role in literary currents during the second half of the eighteenth century. This was a time when, stirred by increasing interest in Wang Yangming and Daoist thought, certain irreverent writers employed an aesthetic of madness to generate edgy, comic, and emotionally expressive literature (*kyōsha no bun,* or *kyōbun*). The writings of Hiraga Gennai and Ōta Nanpo, for example, combined slang and popular colloquialisms with lowbrow topics to produce comic, irreverent social critiques. *Kyōbun* brought to prose the satirical spirit of comic Nō farce (*kyōgen*) and comic *tanka* (*kyōka*).[18]

Kyō was not only a recognized literary trope, it was commonly associated with eccentricity, and thus seen as a willful expression of resistance. This has obscured the fact that, from Confucius through Wang Yangming, Confucian thinkers consistently expressed guarded admiration for the mad persons of their time. Just as Zhuangzi aligned strangeness with Heaven, so Confucian writers have taken a positive, though qualified, position on the deviant individual. Thus, as *ki* is the aesthetic term advanced by Daoism, *kyō* is that under which the Confucian discourse has advanced its own perspective.

The discourse on *kyō* exists within the context of human character, potential, and proximity to the ideal Middle Way of the Confucian gentleman. For Confucius and his interpreters, those who occupy the extreme margins are closer to the Middle Way than those masses that occupy no particular position at all. One such extreme is *kyō;* the other is *ken* 狷 or *kan* 簡—being fastidious, self-contained, and aloof from politics and material pursuits. The respective talents and ambitions of *kyō* and *ken/kan* are not intrinsically subversive; they merely lack the regulation and guidance to be constructive. The extremism of deviance, then, is a wasted resource for which the Confucian answer is regulation. Confucius has the following to say on the matter: "If you cannot manage to find a person of perfectly balanced conduct to associate with, I suppose you must settle for the wild [*kyō*] or the fastidious [*ken*]. In their pursuit of the Way, the wild plunge right in, while the fastidious are always careful not to get their hands dirty" (*Analects* 13:20).[19] Here Confucius asserts that those overcome by either impetuousness or caution are preferable to those lacking such qualities. Even a gentleman who follows the Middle Way is easily corrupted by the world's disorder, but the wild and fastidious follow their own principles with the ambition of gentlemen. While they cannot conform to the orderliness of society and are consequently relegated to its margins, their intentions nonetheless support a potentiality for virtue.

A passage in the *Mencius* extends this sentiment, introducing a graded view of human worth based on actual and potential proximity to the Middle Way. The gentleman is closest, followed, again, by the wild and fastidious. Mencius lays out the rationale of this hierarchy in VII:B:37, cited here, which refers to and elaborates on passage 5:22 in the *Analects*.

Wang Chang asked, saying, "Confucius, when he was in Chan, said: 'Let me return [to Lu]. The scholars of my school are wild [*kyō*], but fastidious [*ken*]. They are for advancing and seizing their object, but cannot forget their early ways.' Why did Confucius, when he was in Chan, think of the wild scholars of Lu?"

Mencius replied, "Confucius, not getting men pursuing the true medium to whom he might communicate his instructions, determined to take the wild and the fastidious. The wild would advance to seize their object; the fastidious would keep themselves from certain things. It is not to be thought that Confucius did not wish to get men pursuing the true medium, but being unable to assure himself of finding such, he therefore thought of the next class."

"I venture to ask what sort of men they were who could be styled 'The wild?'"

"Such," replied Mencius, "as Ch'in Chang, Tsang Hsi, and Mu Pei, were those whom Confucius styled 'wild.'"

"Why were they styled 'wild?'"

The reply was, "Their aim led them to talk magniloquently, saying 'The ancients!' 'The ancients!' But their actions, where we fairly compare them with their words, did not correspond with them.

"When he [Confucius] found also that he could not get such as were thus wild, he wanted to get scholars who would consider anything impure as beneath them. Those were the fastidious—a class next to the former."

The wild and fastidious are at the extremes, furthest from the Middle, but their ambition carries within it a potentiality lacking among a third group. This third and final grade consists of the common lot, the "good careful people of the villages," whom Mencius calls "the thieves of virtue." "Confucius said, 'I hate a semblance which is not the reality. . . . I hate your good careful men of the villages, lest they be confounded with the truly virtuous.'"[20] Extending Confucius' hopeful view of the wild and fastidious and elaborating on precisely what separates them from the common lot, Mencius here redeems madness and clarifies the dependent relationship between the deviant identity and the Way.

Zhu Xi (1130–1200) also takes up this discourse on the wild and fastidious, expanding on Mencius' graded view of human virtue. In his *Zhuzi sishu youlei,* a commentary on the Four Books, he suggests that although the wild and fastidious are distinct from and inferior to the sage, they at least complete their endeavors thoroughly, either achieving their ambitions or withdrawing to maintain their integrity. This conscientiousness allows them to be regulated by the sage and, potentially, to return to the middle course.[21] Adherence to regulation has been central all along. Confucius had spoken of his desire to provide guidance for the mad persons of Lu, implying a potentiality lacking among others to recover the Middle Way. Those treading this middle course, Zhu Xi had concurred, are rare because they have the motivation of the wild but behave more cautiously; they also possess integrity or the capacity for self-regulation so as to avoid becoming overly detached.[22] As Brooks has noted, "as long as they are sincere, the [wild] are not only tolerable, they are educable."[23]

As noted in Chapter 2, Wang Yangming was far from silent on the matter of *kyō,* and his followers in China and Japan made important contributions to the eclectic opposition against Neo-Confucianism and its support of moderation and self-regulation. Wang's declaration, "There is *kyō* within me. Don't run and hide from my words," and his successor Wang Longxi's (1498–1583) assertion that "[t]he path to sagehood lies in the hands of *kyōsha,*" encapsulated the views held by the progressive faction of Wang Yangming that positioned *kyōjin* closest to the way of the sages.[24] It also maintained that *kyō* and *kyōjin* are unfettered by internal conflict and are therefore more advanced, progressive, and socially useful. Represented by an irascible group of *kyōsha* such as Wang Longxi and Li Zuowu, this faction defended human freedoms and gender equality by derailing tradition and ethical doctrine. Li Zuowu especially, Okada writes, "took up a madman's heresy" in that he "raised the standard of antiestablishmentarianism . . . , remonstrated and rebuked the government officials of the day, grew terrible in his anger at the society of that time, [and] performed many outrageous acts without regard to what others would think or say."[25]

While Wang, Li, and others of this school held *kyōsha* to be the most sagely of beings and *kyō* to be a doorway to sagehood, mainstream Tokugawa thought denied any relation between *kyō* and correctness. Yet Wang's declaration that "[t]he path to sagehood lies in the hands of *kyōsha*" exemplified the sorts of sentiments that inspired Edo period heterodox thinkers like Kinryū Keiyū, who penned the preface for *Hōsa kyōshaden* (Biographies of Nagoya madmen, 1778).[26] Though *Hōsa kyōshaden* contains little direct reference to Wang's thought or writings, the work signals an affirmation of such values as direct action and self-reflection. "For those who perceived dangers in defying Confucian ethics," Nakano notes, "deploying Wang

Yangming thought was a most effective means of doing so. Its internalization of the Way gave precedence to the individual's interiority, constitut-
ing an implicit affirmation of the autonomous self."[27] Such ideas proved
inspirational to literati disillusioned with the limitations of Zhu Xi-ism.
Hattori Somon, discussed at length below, switched his allegiance from the
Sorai School to Wang Yangming, referring to himself specifically as a *kyōsha*.
Bunjin like Akutagawa Tankyū (1710–1785) and Ike no Taiga, along with
others labeled as *kijin,* also subscribed to the principles of Wang Yangming
thought. The annals of Confucian doctrine, therefore, lent no shortage of
intellectual support for an aesthetics of madness. The esteem it had long
received among progressive Chinese thinkers disposed their Japanese counterparts to take it up with relative peace of mind.[28]

Heterodoxical Convergence: Daoism, Wang Yangming, and Kokugaku

Confucianism's qualified endorsement of eccentric identities dovetailed
with that of other philosophical traditions. As we have seen, Daoist archetypes inspired and supported identities of difference in myriad ways within
premodern Chinese and Japanese aesthetics. The irreverence exhibited
by prototypical eccentrics like the Seven Sages of the Bamboo Grove and
Tao Qian personified Laozi's and Zhuangzi's association of Heaven with
detached, carefree living. Subsequently, a Daoist inspiration for *ippin* painting, already discussed, became prevalent from the mid-Tang dynasty. This
spontaneous, transcendental artistic style was repeatedly rediscovered and
rearticulated through the Ming period,when it was integrated into literati
painting and subsequently emulated by Edo period artists.[29]

Daoist aesthetics were familiar and inspirational resources for seventeenth-century Japanese writers, as well. As Peipei Qiu has shown, the
Teimon, Danrin, and Shōmon Schools of *haikai* all found philosophical
inspiration in the *Zhuangzi* as well as in later Chinese interpretations of that
text. It was largely in an effort to legitimize itself, Qiu notes, that *haikai*
looked to a text that had long occupied a position of authority for generations of Chinese literati. Seventeenth-century *haikai,* then, "was not the
creation of an oppositional culture that attempted . . . to invert the social
and literary hierarchy, but rather a commoner culture that existed largely
within and sometimes became indistinguishable from the cultural orthodoxy."[30] Any serious *bunjin* had studied the text and was able to recognize

and use Zhuangzian references and iconography to add an iconoclastic loftiness to their painting, prose, and poetry. Examples abound. Poetry produced by Bashō, Baisaō, and other leaders of *bunjin* culture includes clear references to Zhuangzi; *Kinsei kijinden* collaborator Rikunyo (1734–1801) used Zhuangzi's words to describe Taiga as a recluse; and the monk Daiten (1719–1801) quotes Zhuangzi in his description of Itō Jakuchū.[31]

As eighteenth-century scholars interested in reading beyond the Neo-Confucian canon found Daoist texts readily available, Daoism became regularly invoked as more thinkers attempted to reconcile these two traditions. Ogyū Sorai's philological work charged that Zhu Xi Confucianism was actually based on Daoist terms that it had misinterpreted in its commentaries on the classics. The characters *ri* (Principle) and *ki* (material force), Sorai asserts, were first used by the Daoists.[32] Sorai's students Hattori Nankaku (1683–1759) and Dazai Shundai (1680–1747) studied and wrote on the *Laozi* and the *Zhuangzi,* further contributing to their popularity. Sorai also must have found Daoist irrationalism personally attractive, for his self-reference as "a madman who spent twenty days of the month groaning and the other ten laughing" is couched in characteristically Zhuangzian language.[33] Scholars also would have found that Daoism's articulation of a Way that was morally good and that resided in the forces of nature had clear parallels with the Neo-Confucian view of the cosmos as composed of morally good Principle (*ri*). Though the Neo-Confucian tenet of *kei* (seriousness and reverence for the purpose of reconnecting with *ri*) calls for purposive action as opposed to the Daoist precept of nonaction, both philosophies advocate self-cultivation as a means of reconnecting with moral beneficence residing in the natural world.

Daoist naturalism was also closely aligned with the rituals and myths Japan had claimed as foundational to its native philosophical beliefs. Within Daoist texts, Nativist scholars found literary precedent and philosophical support for the merits of Japan's uncontrived, spontaneous Ancient Way (*kodō*). Kamo no Mabuchi, who became something of an eccentric recluse late in life, regarded the *Laozi* as the only "correct work" produced by China, noting "numerous points of agreement between Laozi and our own ancient thought."[34] Mabuchi understood the Daoist Way as a social model that he envisioned as ascendant in ancient Japan. Daoist texts also articulated Mabuchi's own view of how the world had subsequently come to be held hostage by the contrivances of human intentionality. What was attractive to Mabuchi was the nonmoral, nonpurposive approach to living that both Laozi and Zhuangzi had used in their respective attacks on

Confucianism, views that became the basis of the Nativist argument against Neo-Confucianism.[35]

In theory and in practice, therefore, early modern thinkers would find Daoism to exhibit ontological parallels with Neo-Confucianism, as well as to share naturalist proclivities with Kokugaku. As such, it is no surprise that Daoist thought was plainly visible in the interstices of Neo-Confucian doctrine and that it came to hold an enduring attraction as an alternative philosophical resource.

Wang Yangming was equally influential in guiding and lending philosophical justification for eccentric self-making. Because it was neither institutionalized nor institutionally endorsed, scholars did not claim it as a primary philosophical affiliation. In fact, the nation's most prestigious academy and its archetype of Neo-Confucian orthodoxy, the Shōheikō, did not include Wang Yangming in its curriculum until 1838.[36] Yet Wang Yangming's advocacy of human intuition, action, and agency made it inspirational to generations of thinkers. His unification of thought and action was standard learning for all samurai. Writes Najita: "virtually every samurai, regardless of ultimate intellectual identification . . . went through an 'Ōyōmei [Wang Yangming] phase' and incorporated its message."[37] But it was also a philosophy of the masses. Early Wang Yangming proponents Nakae Tōju (1608–1648) and his student Kumazawa Banzan (1619–1691) became cultural heroes among commoners for expressing political disillusionment and resisting sociopolitical injustice. Its endorsement of intuition and individual action, particularly, validated a philosophical and behavioral diversity that placed the normative and the strange on an equal footing.

Wang Yangming was particularly well suited as a complement to Kokugaku. The experientialist approach of Hirata Atsutane's (1776–1843) school of Kokugaku resembled his activism and subjectivity. Hirata would find common ground with Wang Yangming by taking Kokugaku in the direction of action and intuition that enabled a unified intellectual foundation for political activism.[38] Like Wang's thought, Kokugaku also provided commoners with intellectual opportunities and venues of apolitical empowerment. Kokugaku thinkers who articulated connections between aesthetics and an apolitical national tradition made aesthetics a means for the disempowered masses to conceptualize the state and to view themselves as actors within that tradition. In other words, by learning classical art and literature, commoners could recover a sense of involvement in the nation and its cultural traditions.[39] Kokugaku's popularization of *waka*, for example, led to the formation of more commoner-centered literary salons and study groups, many of which welcomed the participation of women.

In the context of early modern Japanese thought, then, the mental and emotional emancipation validated by Daoism's principles of *ki* and *wu-wei* (effortless action), classical Confucianism's and Wang Yangming's advancement of *kyō,* and Kokugaku's pursuit of the uncontrived, instinctive sentiments of Japan's Ancient Way corresponded with the experimentations in art already discussed. Their mutual reinforcement enabled innovative thinkers to advance new interpretations of social knowledge.

STRANGE THOUGHT IN PRACTICE: SOMON AND SHIDŌKEN

Intellectual histories of early modern Japan have focused on the work of professional scholars, those who either received posts from *bakufu* and domainal authorities or who subsisted on revenue from teaching. This focus on the themes and individuals that charted the course of the intellectual mainstream has codified an intellectual trajectory—proceeding roughly from Zhu Xi-ism, to Ancient Learning, to historicism, to Kokugaku—propelled largely by individuals from the samurai class. Modern historiography's tendency to recover early Tokugawa intellectual history by drawing connections between the work of a core group of professional scholars does not deny the existence or historical validity of more heretical voices, but neither has it adequately recognized the latter's contributions to the field. For, while the *bakufu* endeavored to stave off intellectual liberalization through prohibitions and censorship, even indiscreet eccentric thinkers like Hattori Somon and Fukai Shidōken encountered little difficulty in inhabiting new discursive spaces.

The brash Tominaga Nakamoto (1715–1746) was an exception. Tetsuo Najita's study of Nakamoto and the Kaitokudō, a private academy for merchants in Osaka, examines class-consciousness and theoretical efforts to justify individual action within everyday commoner practice. For expounding historicist and dangerously heterodox theories, in 1730 the young Nakamoto was expelled from the Kaitokudō and his writings destroyed. Nakamoto had taken Neo-Confucian humanism several steps beyond its mandate of moral cultivation via the "investigations of things" (*kakubutsu*) and quiet self-reflection (*mokuza chōshin*). Echoing Sorai, he argued that virtue and ethics could not be learned from either history or historical texts. Individuals must learn to embody morality for its own sake. Only the experience of living measures moral virtue, Nakamoto asserted, and one seeking virtue need do no more than to practice discretion, care, filiality, humility, honesty, reverence, and responsibility in one's social interactions and relationships.

This form of moral self-cultivation need not be modeled after traditional practice or the pages of ancient texts, Nakamoto continued, but simply after what one knows intuitively to be reasonable and right. Further, ancient texts offer no more than "practical guidelines" for moral behavior and must be stricken from education to allow for personal reflection on virtue. Metaphysical and eschatological questions bring us no closer to the moral common sense required of social beings and so must also be eliminated from the study of ethics. Self-cultivation consists, first, in practical reflection on what is good and necessary and then in putting that into practice. Second, it requires the development of innate talents through the pursuit of an art. Enjoying artistic pursuits puts morality into practice, providing a channel to actualize the individual's innate virtue. Nakamoto, therefore, denied that moral truth resides either in Neo-Confucianism's various cosmological elements—*ten* (Heaven), *ri, ki*—or within the words of the sages as transmitted through the Confucian classics. Rather, he locates the source of moral virtue within individuals. As Najita notes, this proposition challenges social knowledge by locating the origin of virtue within rather than outside the individual.[40] Nakamoto's validation of individual intuition completed through action, clearly, had borrowed liberally from Wang Yangming thought.

Although Nakamoto's expulsion from the Kaitokudō in 1730 indicates that the mores of commoner society were as yet intolerant of his degree of intellectual eccentricity, his scholarship encapsulates the very sort of secular humanism that the academy was to embrace for the remainder of the eighteenth century. Under the leadership of Goi Ranju (1697–1762) the academy formulated and perpetuated an epistemological view of the commoner individual as adept at conceptualizing the "truth" of the world and making rational choices about how to organize and maneuver within it.[41] This secular celebration of individual agency and self-determinism better suited the interests of commoners seeking autonomy and advancement within the Tokugawa order. To this extent, Ranju, the figure guiding the academy's intellectual course during the mid-eighteenth century, owed a clear debt to Nakamoto. He supported an empirical, pragmatic approach to knowledge and, like Nakamoto, constructed a heterodox epistemology around practical concerns deriving from everyday experience.[42]

Najita concludes that intellectual eccentricity from the mid-eighteenth century was far from a tangential subculture. It was fostered by some of the period's most lucid and ambitious thinkers, who anticipated sociopolitical themes that were, a century later, to flourish and energize the political dissent that would catalyze the Restoration. As early as the mid-eighteenth century, Najita posits, active political dissent was much more prevalent than historians have acknowledged.[43] Intellectual eccentrics disgusted with the political system and willing to risk punishment by openly expressing contrary views were so widespread, in fact, that Najita estimates that 30 to 40 percent of aristocrats who traveled to Edo chose to remain there in order to become independent scholars. This emergent class of classless scholars, physicians, and *bunjin* voluntarily disinherited from official service "romanticized their freedom as entering the world of eccentric play and dreams, which meant leaving the universe of bureaucratic rule . . . custom and accumulated habit."[44]

This mass divergence from intellectual orthodoxy had been informed in part by the philological discoveries of Ancient Learning scholarship, Sorai's in particular. His historicism created new intellectual space by unlocking methodological and interpretive approaches to Confucian texts, authorizing an array of radical challenges to orthodoxy. New historical and philosophical inquiry carried in various directions Sorai's assertions about the necessity of placing the words and deeds of the ancients in proper historical perspective. They shared a common conclusion, however: that contemporary Buddhist and Confucian practices were flawed, the political state that sanctioned them was flawed, and social knowledge generally was flawed. The shock waves triggered by this reassessment of Neo-Confucian knowledge produced a generation of outspoken offspring. Hattori Somon can be included among these.

Because Somon suffered neither persecution nor societal backlash, less is known of him than of Nakamoto or contemporaries like Andō Shōeki (1703–1762) and Yamagata Daini (1725–1767), who were treated as heretics for extending Sorai's criticisms into the political arena.[45] The fact that his startlingly heretical writings were more philosophical and less political made him less noticeable to authorities and afforded him a comparatively uncontroversial life. Scant biographical information leaves much about him unknown. Although only a single biography (Tōjō Kindai's *Sentetsu sōdan gohen* [Stories of ancient philosophers, final volume], 1829) attempts an extensive examination of Somon's life, it is partially complemented by records of his social interactions and intellectual collaborations. Despite his obscurity today, Somon's inclusion in the first edition of *Heian jinbutsushi* (1768) is ample evidence of his notoriety in Kyoto during his own life.

Somon was from Kyoto's Nishijin district, where his family operated a weaving and textile business, the industry for which that area was known. He was beset by illness throughout his life. As a teenager he inherited the family business, but his weak constitution rendered him unable to give commercial affairs the attention they required. Years earlier he had already decided to entrust the family business to others, devote himself to study, and make his mark in the world as a Confucian scholar. Academia in Kyoto remained comparatively conservative during Somon's childhood. Whereas Soraigaku had won over intellectual circles in Edo in the 1710s, in Kyoto few studied it seriously until after Sorai's death (1728). It was not until the late 1730s that it penetrated Kyoto's academic echelons, a movement to which Somon initially contributed.[46] When he took over the Kanjizaidō private academy at age twenty-five, he complemented his lectures on orthodox Confucianism and Mahayana Buddhism with material on Soraigaku. Not all were quick to accept Soraigaku uncritically, however. The Kogidō academy, founded by the Ancient Learning scholar Itō Jinsai in 1662 and headed by his heir Itō Tōgai (1670–1738), included Soraigaku in its curriculum but did not highlight it. Perhaps consequently, a core group of Kogidō graduates formed a scholarly vanguard in Kyoto that rejected Sorai. This small anti-Sorai clique included the Chinese studies scholar Akutagawa Tankyū (1710–1785); Takeda Bairyū (1716–1766); Kimura Hōrai (1716–1766), who had studied under Sorai as a child; and Yoshino Kain (1699–1770).[47] Although there is no evidence that Somon attended the Kogidō, his associations with this cohort caused his devotion to Soraigaku to wane.

For over two decades Somon remained the master of Kanjizaidō and a pillar of the city's Confucian establishment, but his recurring illness forced him to spend increasing periods of time studying alone indoors. He developed interests in Buddhism and Daoism, which he gradually promoted alongside Confucianism. His semireclusive lifestyle further connected him to the sort of withdrawal associated with Buddhists and Daoists. Invoking China's iconic recluses, Tōjō's *Sentetsu sōdan gohen* describes Somon as one who hid in the mountains, immersed in fortune-telling and plucking his one-stringed koto.[48] Though an obvious misrepresentation of his actual life, the comparison surely gratified Somon, who actively cultivated this image by shaving his head and taking the sobriquets Master of the Three Teachings (*Sankyō shujin*) and Madman of the Mountains (*Sanjin kyōsha*).[49]

Somon was no mountain recluse, of course. He not only operated his own academy, he attended *kyōka* gatherings, published *kyōka* collections, and was otherwise active within a society of like-minded *bunjin*. In addition to the associates already listed, his literary collaborators included Chinese studies scholars Nagata Kanga (1738–1792), Emura Hokkai (1713–1788), and the omnipresent monk Rikunyo.[50] It was precisely his rejection of reclusion that reoriented him philosophically. His turn against Soraigaku, then, resulted from several influences: exposure to Tominaga Nakamoto's writings, discussions with Tankyū about Chinese literature, and his discovery of the radical left wing of Wang Yangming thought. First, Somon admitted that the analysis of Chinese writings in Tominaga Nakamoto's *Shutsujō kōgo* (Emerging from meditation, 1745) had influenced him deeply.[51] In a series of Sorai-esque assertions, Nakamoto had concluded that subjectivity and personal opinion are products of historical context. For this reason words had become incrementally detached from their original semantics. Given that Mahayana Buddhism was not based on Siddhārtha Gautama's original teachings, it could not be considered authentic.[52] Nakamoto then transferred this critique to Confucianism and Daoism, denouncing their applicability to modern life and advocating his Way of Sincerity (*makoto no michi*) as a modern moral.

Somon did not share Nakamoto's fiery disposition, but, Nakano asserts, he was the most conspicuous proponent of the latter's mission.[53] He extended Nakamoto's position by asserting that the Buddha's death forced his disciples to preserve and transmit textually ideas that the master had passed on orally. It was they who developed and codified Buddhism by selecting, embellishing, and perfecting his teachings within a set of scriptures. Concepts like predestination, original awakening, and bodhisattvas, Somon wrote, all appeared afterward as core features of Mahayana. Because what is called Buddhism was constructed five centuries after the Buddha's death, Somon reasoned, it carried little credibility.[54]

Song and Ming period colloquial literature exerted a second influence on Somon. Through discussions with Tankyū, he saw how literature produced as commercial entertainment rather than for explicitly didactic purposes enabled a smooth, secularized blending of disparate philosophical values. Whereas thinkers like Li Zhi and Ogyū Sorai had agreed that the virtues of literature should be separated from the virtues of Confucianism and Buddhism, authors like Wang Shi-zhen (1526–1590) had long produced popular literature that unified the moral philosophies of both endeavors.[55]

Such literature offered Somon a concrete model of how to integrate the philological study of sutras, history, and moral virtue.

Wang Yangming, finally, particularly the radical "left wing" (*sayoku*) branch as advanced by Li Zhi, provided Somon with a paradigm that bridged doctrine and practice. All teachings about the Way—whether the Confucian, Buddhist, or Daoist Way—were implicitly limiting in their dualistic thinking about correct and incorrect. Somon wished to eliminate these boundaries dividing rights and wrongs, benefits and detriments. He found it problematic to assert that right and wrong existed. Yet because scholarly discussions are based on right and wrong, a scholar that rejects them on a personal level must allow them as topics for debate. Somon's admiration for the sort of unrestrained action and emotion validated by Wang Yangming is also apparent in his *kyōka* collection *Gika saitanshū* (Collection of playful New Year's verses, 1763). Here, his literary collaborators Kinryū Keiyū and the Jōdō monk Daiga Kyōkan (Daiga the Mad but Perfunctory, 1709–1782) are depicted as madmen whose words and deeds evoke the radical left-wing proponent Li Zhi.

By the mid-1760s, Somon must have felt that he had misspent his time in conventional thought, for his writings confess a need to discard all restraints and express his true convictions. Now that he had mastered the three teachings, he felt himself to be a true *kyōsha* who could publicly reveal that the core of his beliefs derived from left-wing Wang Yangming thought.[56] It was at this time that he wrote his two primary works: *Sekirara* (Naked truth; published posthumously in 1785), in which he takes up Nakamoto's question of whether Mahayana should be considered true Buddhism, and *Nensairoku* (A record of clarity, 1769), a condemnation of Soraigaku. In both he examines from various angles the advantages and disadvantages of the unification of the three teachings.[57]

Sekirara asserts that contemporary Buddhist practices—studying the sutras, meditation, and oral transmission of knowledge from master to disciple—all aimed at grasping the incomprehensible as comprehensible truths. People are caught in concepts like the five stages of existence and the cycle of life and death, he lamented, but intellectualizing of this sort obstructs true understanding. Even the promise of enlightenment itself becomes a distraction. Enlightenment is not such a wondrous thing, Somon writes, "it emits less light than a firefly's buttocks. It does not bestow supernatural abilities like the shape-shifting powers of foxes and *tanuki;* it simply makes one free of delusions and obsessions. Treasures of gold and silver come to appear worthless, and beautiful women become no more appealing than rocks and trees."[58] Somon directed his attack on Buddhism at the external only, its teachings and pretenses rather than its essential ontology. It was the Buddhist monks that were fakes and the Mahayana sutras that were fabricated. The essence of the interior aspects of Buddhism, he felt, was about forgetting good and bad, existence and nonexistence. This was a return to the individual spiritual side left unadulterated by institutionalized Buddhism.

As Somon cautioned his readers against becoming enslaved by institutionalized religion, he also believed that orthodox thought should not be used to justify state policy. His critique of Confucianism in *Nensairoku,* therefore, paralleled his critique of Buddhism. The contradictions evident in the *Analects,* he felt, exposed discrepancies in Confucius' teachings that disqualified it as a trustworthy text. The Five Books and other Confucian classics he likewise considered to be soulless remnants of the ancient sages, lacking historical relevance and misguiding modern readers. For this reason, those who used Confucianism to camouflage political ambition were the greatest violators of Confucian ideals. Emperor Wu Wang (d. 1043 B.C.E.) and the Zhou kings were not saints, and the revered minister Li Si (280–208 B.C.E.), who had burnt piles of books and persecuted Confucian scholars, should be viewed as a great sinner.[59] "The Way is not something to be incinerated . . . and yet Confucian histories have constructed Li Si as a saint," Somon writes. "This makes the Confucian classics untrustworthy and ahistorical."[60]

Clearly, Ogyū Sorai's historicism—his deployment of philological evidence to deny newer interpretations of ancient language—was a doorway for Nakamoto and Somon. Both took Sorai's findings into the context of commoner life and combined them with Wang Yangming's celebration of human intuition and action. And although Somon was a revisionist who recognized that contemporary thought was rife with anachronisms, he escaped the persecution suffered by Tominaga and others by avoiding accusations of being anti-Confucian, anti-Buddhist, or anti-*bakufu.*

As a public figure, Fukai Shidōken (1680?–1765) shared nothing with Somon. And while the two embody dissimilar models of intellectual eccentricity, as thinkers they emerged from and responded to identical theoretical problems. Shidōken became a Shingon monk at age twelve and studied at several temples, where he grew increasingly impatient with the philosophical restrictions imposed by institutional Buddhism. In 1716 he set up a dais at Asakusa Kannon temple in Edo and for the next half-century supported himself as a street orator, preacher, and storyteller. He harangued onlookers about the fallacies of the three teachings and lectured on China's and Japan's ancient philosophical traditions. He was particularly famous for banging a phallus-shaped stick on a table as he delivered his sharp critiques (Fig. 4.1). By the 1750s Shidōken had acquired considerable notoriety. His "mad sermons" (*kyōkō*) were advertised in several publications; his portraits were circulated as well. Shidōken's fame, Nakano claims, rivaled that of Ichikawa Danjūrō II as the most recognized attraction around Edo, and in 1763 he was finally immortalized as the model and namesake for Hiraga Gennai's satirical *Fūryū Shidōken-den* (The modern life of Shidōken).[61]

Shidōken's preface to his tract *Motonashigusa* (Rootless weeds, 1748) explains the purpose of his lectures as penetrating the truth of the three teachings, which "for the ignorant is just tall tales and a source of merriment, but for the wise expounds the Law and the Way."[62] Advancing a

FIGURE 4.1   Shidōken. Katsushika Hokusai, *Kijin hyakunin isshu.* Tokyo Gakugei University Library.

non-dualist ontology evocative of Zen and Daoist thought, he continues by explaining the creation of Heaven and Earth in terms of sexual intercourse. After a titillating description of the union of male and female genitalia, he argues that sexual union was the process through which Creation originated. It is for this reason, he observes, that the character for Heaven (天) is written with the two ideographs for couple (二人).[63]

Shidōken rejected allegiance to all schools of institutionalized thought on the ground that none spoke to human experience. It is believed that the Law originated with the Buddha and Confucius, he asserts in *Motonashigusa,* but these teachings cannot fathom the *kokoro* (heart/mind). In fact, Buddhism refutes the *kokoro,* he lamented; the Tendai master Myōraku Daishi advocates making the *kokoro* the direct origin of things;[64] Shingon explains the need for purifying the *kokoro* through self-cultivation; and Confucianism calls moderation the highest virtue. None of these know the true essence of human nature, which changes along with everything else in nature. With these essentializing statements, Shidōken reduced a spectrum of disparate teachings to their fundamental principles and judged them on their applicability to human experience.

Further advancing his non-dualistic approach to living in *Kashōana monogatari bendan* (On tales of laughable orifices, 1761), Shidōken elaborates on his unified, nonsectarian view of the three teachings. Using paradoxical language to clarify the limitations of faith in a singular philosophy, he reduces metaphysics to the physicality of genitalia:

> Following one path will cause one to lose one's way and fall into a hole. . . . Over-reliance on expedients (*hōben*) creates a hole, but discarding expedients causes the hole to widen. Likewise, when one becomes ensnared by the emptiness of the Way one discards humanity. . . . Within the Way humanity is concealed, and within humanity the Way is concealed. . . . Truly, love is the beginning of feeling, lust is the source of compassion, the vagina is the root of formlessness, and in the center is the eight-leafed lotus blossom whose whiteness is the womb of diversity. Such is non-dual Mahayanic reality (*funi makamon*).[65]

Neither Buddhist expedients nor the Daoist Way are sufficient measures to evade the pitfalls of human experience, he avers. Overreliance on one is as deficient as nonreliance and ultimately leads to the same end. Rather, it is natural human emotion, and lust particularly, that nourishes the diversity of individual needs. Shidōken encapsulates these sentiments in the following verse:

kōkō no	the rigors of
shugyō wo mite	religious training
hate ireba	in the end
nakanaka moto no	return one to
bonpu narikeri	original mediocrity[66]

Shidōken's celebration of emotion (lust) over doctrine responded to the prevalent perception that the political and metaphysical worlds had plunged into decline. It was also representative of the conclusions drawn by a cohort of contemporary ideologues who were reinterpreting Neo-Confucian metaphysics to explain the relativity and plurality of human experience. It is significant, not only that this cohort was permitted to publicize counter-ideological ideas, but that it was publicly lauded for doing so. Clearly, a piecemeal, unsystematic integration of ideas drawn from Wang Yangming, Daoism, and Kokugaku resonated with people's experiences more closely than the standard moralistic dogma being taught at Confucian academies. Emotion was one point of resonance, and continuing attraction to these heterodoxies indicated a growing need to justify it philosophically. The so-called cult of *qing* (emotion) previously discussed as a literary trope celebrated emotion for transporting the subject to a liminal reality. Emotion infused the worldly with otherworldliness by imbuing reality with fiction and fantasy.[67] For a growing number of Japanese thinkers as well, it functioned as a strategy of detachment from systemic oppression, as a vehicle of transcendence that enabled self-expression and agency, those potentialities perceived as muted by a "cult of reason."

Wang Yangming, Daoism, and Kokugaku not only shared an affinity for emotion but also collectively endorsed individual agency and, by extension, the diversity that nurtured eccentricity. The distillation of emotion from these disparate teachings, therefore, was also a distillation of strangeness. From the intellectual milieu of the mid-eighteenth century, both emotion and eccentricity thus emerged as related self-making potentialities, a progressive phenomenon that Maruyama has called the "discovery of man." It is within this context, he writes, that for the first time "man began to be conscious of his autonomy . . . [and able to live] freely according to his own will and ideas."[68] The experiences of Nakamoto, Somon, and Shidōken indicate that correlations between intellectual freedom and emotional freedom were indeed expanding the boundaries of human action.

Their experiences also illustrate that intellectual and aesthetic strangeness stimulated and informed each other. Nakamoto, Somon, Shidōken, as well as rebels like Yamagata Daini, Andō Shōeki, and Hiraga Gennai, all were reinventing knowledge at precisely the time that Hakuin, Ike no Taiga, Itō Jakuchū, and Soga Shōhaku were reinventing art. Nor is the sudden emergence of *ki* at this moment coincidental. As classical Confucianism and Wang Yangming lent doctrinal support for *kyō* as a potentiality that drew the individual closer to Heaven, they also invoked the intuitive spontaneity extolled in *Laozi* and *Zhuangzi*. Following the Kyōhō period (1716–1736), references to and studies of these Daoist texts became more ubiquitous, bringing the idea of *ki* as defined by Zhuangzi alongside that of *kyō*. Nakano holds that what the former had called *kyō* the latter were calling *ki*, and that the two became united in public discourse.[69] *Kyō* indeed permeated the biographical discourse on *ki*. *Kinsei kijinden*, for example, includes entries for the mad monk (*kyōsō*) Dankai, Bashō's crazed (*kyōsu*) student Hirose Izen, and the madwoman (*kyōjo*) Fumihiroge.

Ultimately, the philosophical legitimacy carried by both *ki* and *kyō* proved critical to embedding strangeness within late eighteenth-century life. Supported by favorable views of difference within the three teachings, the designations *kyōsha* and *kijin* grew more sanctified. Their migration from intellectual and aesthetic circles to print and popular culture would be advanced largely by biography, the subject of Chapter 5.

CHAPTER 5

Eccentrics of Recent Times and Social Value

Biography Reinvents the Eccentric

Prior to the mid-Meiji period, Marvin Marcus writes, biography amounted to "an encyclopedic compilation of short narratives, a sequence of episodes—often apocryphal—that together come to define a given collectivity. Indeed, the concise, formulaic account of one's pedigree and accomplishments, enlivened by a representative anecdote or two (historical verifiability being quite beside the point), may be said to represent the norm of biographical writing in the Tokugawa period."[1] Marcus is quite correct in stating that early modern biography—following portraiture, landscape painting, and other representational arts—concerned itself less with objective realism and more with reinventing its subjects as embodiments of certain desirable traits. Paying tribute to notable individuals entailed recasting them as moral exemplars worthy of emulation. In this sense, Tokugawa biography was an ideological exercise that served to manifest the social value of its subjects, value that could then be extended to and claimed by the publication itself. Such was indeed the case for Ban Kōkei's *Kinsei kijinden* (Eccentrics of recent times, 1790), which preserved traditional biographic style while creating *kijinden* as a new subgenre.[2]

Assessment of social value, of course, is relative. For the Confucian, the value of ideas and cultural forms resides within sociopolitical utility and demonstrable public benefit; for the mercantilist, cultural forms must exhibit market value; and for amateur literati, value resides within enjoyment of autonomous culture (culture for its own sake). As an anthology of eccentrics, *Kinsei kijinden* (hereafter *KKD*) put a new face on social value by creating the *kijin* as a viable social commodity and a repository of virtue (*tokkō*). Individuals that came to bear the label of *kijin* found that the term augmented their cultural currency, and it was not long before eccentricity, the quality to which the book ascribed utilitarian value, was attracting market value as well.

Although one must credit Kōkei for creating the vehicle by which the term *kijin* 畸人 made its literary debut and for lending credibility to eccentric behavior, one must also recognize that his text was only one product of a broad preexisting attraction to an array of extraordinary or outstanding personalities.[3] As an umbrella term, *kijin* 畸人 incorporated the talented—the *ijin* (偉人; distinguished persons) and the *saijin* (才人; talented persons), with the reclusive—the *inja* (隠者) and the *itsujin* (逸人), with the strange and mad—the *kijin* (奇人) and the *kyōjin* (狂人) from generations earlier.

Despite the book's historical importance, therefore, Kōkei's celebration of the detached, antisocial individualism connoted by this Zhuangzian term was only the latest manifestation of an enduring interest in aesthetics of strangeness. Though the term *kijin* itself had yet to infiltrate either print culture or intellectual parlance, the notion of strangeness as aligned with Heaven echoed Bashō's devotion to *fūkyō* and reiterated Nankai's and Kien's convictions that strangeness (奇) was a component necessary to the aesthetic life. Given the plurality of forms and philosophical traditions informing eccentric identities, moreover, it is curious that subsequent *kijinden* writers invoking *KKD* note only its reference to *Zhuangzi*. This pattern of connecting eccentricity to Daoism is so dominant as to have eclipsed any recognition that (as we have seen) Buddhism and Confucianism claim equally developed traditions of articulating and celebrating deviant behavior.

With primary focus on *KKD*, this chapter will examine shifting representations of social value through biographies that engage with eccentric identities and aesthetic strangeness. Kōkei himself sought to update biography writing, as his preface to *KKD* explicitly juxtaposes his text with Gensei's (1623–1668) *Fusō in'itsuden* (Biographies of Japanese recluses, 1664) and Hayashi Dokkōsai's (1625–1661) *Honchō tonshi* (Histories of Japanese recluses, 1664), texts from over a century earlier. But given that these earlier works anthologized disparate historical figures for their Buddhistic piety or their poetic accomplishments and shared little literary or ideological ground with *KKD*, the comparison yields limited interest. Below we contextualize *KKD* by comparing it with two nearly contemporaneous predecessors: *Hōsa kyōshaden* (Biographies of Nagoya madmen, 1778) and *Ochiguri monogatari* (Fallen chestnut tales, 1780s).[4] After examining how extraordinary individuals were constructed in these two works, we return to *KKD* for an analysis of that text's formulation of *kijin* and how it reinvented eccentricity as a repository of social value.

BIOGRAPHIES OF NAGOYA MADMEN

Hōsa kyōshaden[5] (Biographies of Nagoya madmen, hereafter *HKD*) was completed in 1778 by the Owari samurai Hotta Kōzan (1709–1791) under the sobriquet Rikurin, and the following year a preface was added by Kinryū Keiyū.[6] From a purely literary standpoint, *HKD* is a shorter, less ambitiously compiled precursor to *Kinsei kijinden*. It assembles accounts of twenty-five eighteenth-century individuals occupying the social margins, all of whom the author claims to have observed. Its philosophical orientation, however, makes it a historic work from two angles: it deposes *KKD* as Japan's first biographical compilation of eccentrics (rather than recluses), and it forces a reinterpretation of early modern eccentricity as a byproduct of Daoist thought.

Consideration of this text returns us to Chapter 4's discussion of *kyō* as a discursive fixture within Confucian thought. Following Confucius, Mencius, Zhu Xi, and Wang Yangming, a number of Song and Ming Dynasty authors also wrote on the social value of *kyō*. It was further extended, for example, by Song Dynasty hermit and literatus Wan Shi (d. 1157) in his hundred-chapter book *Kuangjian ji* (Collection of the wild and the fastidious).[7] In his preface, Wan Shi accepts personal responsibility for transmitting Confucius' teachings to later generations, thereby identifying himself as a Confucian instructor and equating himself with the mad subjects of his book.[8] The ten-volume *Kuangjuan caizhong* (Regulating the wild and the fastidious in the Middle Course) by Ming scholar Yang Shijuan also contributes to the *kyō* discourse. This work records Yang's deliberations on loyal, filial, and righteous people from the Warring States period to the Yuan dynasty. The preface warns that taking an undeserved reputation and making bold claims is inferior to behaving in a manner consistent to one's nature. Therefore, none are more wild or fastidious (*kyōken*) than those who are ambitious, humane, loyal, and filial. Even if the gist of Confucius' and Mencius' instructions is incomprehensible, Yang asserts, one is not far off if one employs self-regulation and ardently pursues personal endeavors.[9] The three-volume

Kuangfu zhiyen (Words of a madman) and its two-volume sequel written by the Ming scholar Chen Jiru (1558–1639), a compilation and commentary on strange individuals, further contributes to the Confucian discourse on *kyō* within the genre of biographical writing on eccentrics.[10]

Although only a sampling of such works, the above indicates that a mature and distinguished literature on *kyō* erected by an eminent lineage of Confucian thinkers was available to Hotta Rikurin before he wrote *Hōsa kyōshaden*. Though it is unclear if and to what extent Rikurin knew of the various minor works contributing to this discourse, his references to the *Analects* and the *Mencius* reflect considerable familiarity with *kyō*'s connection to moral virtue. Kinryū Keiyū's preface displays this Confucian orientation most directly, revisiting "the wild and the fastidious" from both Confucian classics: "These individuals have admirable intentions but their deeds do not correspond to their words," he recounts. "Some move ahead with their plans; others hide and protect themselves against intrusive outsiders. Yet the world looks down on them and only Confucius has been disposed to see their worth." Keiyū goes on to describe Rikurin's role as more than that of follower, but as Confucius' surrogate in his willingness to step forward and redeem local *kyōsha*. Continuing, Keiyū combines the words of Confucius and Mencius to resurrect their sentiments within his own historical context, stating that the world is in decline and that numbers of gentlemen and madmen have dwindled due to widespread involvement in corrupt mundane affairs. As Keiyū admits to extreme, uncontrolled emotions, thereby comparing himself to a madman, his preface advances an estimation of *kyōsha* as morally superior beings. By invoking a classical discourse on *kyō,* Keiyū also presents an ostensibly popular work as a philosophical treatise.

The work's literary reorientation of high and low is matched by an identical thematic reorientation. Collectively, its various subjects—the recluse, the depraved, the deformed, the crippled, the alcoholic, the idiot, the prophet—embody a set of themes that, separately or jointly, indicate madness. Sōsuke, for instance, is a crazed, mendicant monk who, via a poetic reference to Zhuangzi's famous butterfly dream, is compared to a Daoist adept; Ishimawari is a simpleton whose actions, described as "swift and effortless, as if he were riding on the wind," evoke the image of Daoist immortals. Kume, "with his hair tied up in back, pointing toward Heaven like Zhili Shu's, drifted around from village to village," is to be viewed as a Japanese incarnation of this Zhuangzian icon, whose uselessness is the very source of his transcendence. These recurrent indicators of madness accompany the very tools of play long recognized in the Daoist sage: drinking, singing, dancing, poetry composition and recitation, wandering, world rejection, and appreciation of nature. They also evoke the tradition of nonconformist aestheticism famously represented by an esteemed collective of Chinese and Japanese recluses.

It is fitting that Rikurin uses allusions to Zhuangzi and known Daoist tropes to flesh out his own subjects. But it is equally fitting that these entries are interspersed with deviant behavior read in Confucian terms. Temperamentally, the *kyōsha* in this work evoke a Zhuangzian nonconformity while demonstrating the lofty ambitions and intentions of Confucius' "wild and fastidious." Ogosa, the work's first entry about a dim-witted local whose buffoonery and grandiose pronouncements become a source of amusement, is not to be chastised for divulging his delusional fantasies. "For him," Rikurin assures us, "doing so is superior to those foolish, errant thoughts of common men." Likewise, the stone seller of Yadamura "loitering around the public square . . . would preach from memory about the fleeting vicissitudes of human life, the strange twists of karmic fate, the biddings of Heaven and Hell, and . . . the teachings of the five Confucian virtues." It is at the lowest social strata, therefore, that we encounter the voices of wisdom and the exemplars of moral virtue that synthesize multiple philosophical traditions.

It is natural that identifying traits of the quintessentially Daoist *kijin* can parallel those of representative Confucians. An anecdote from *KKD*, for instance, relates that as a young painter the literatus Ike no Taiga traveled through Ōmi, Minō, and Owari to sell his painted fans. The pictures were too strange to be sellable, however, so upon his return to Kyoto he stopped on the Seta Bridge and tossed them into the water as an offering to the dragon king. Though the strangeness of his Chinese-style pictures is misunderstood and unpopular, Taiga embraces this and finds personal contentment in it. The stone seller of Yadamura from *HKD*, who each day discards his unsold cache, is an easy comparison. From such anecdotes the modern interpreter is apt to tease out Daoist morals—Zhuangzi's assertion regarding "the use of uselessness," for instance. But one can glean an equally viable interpretation from the Confucian canon. In the *Analects* (9:6), Confucius says to his disciple Zigong: "In my youth, I was of humble status, so I became proficient in many menial tasks. Is the gentleman broadly skilled in trivial matters? No, he is not."[11] The young Taiga, similarly, knew himself to be a lowly man and recognized that as such he had acquired a variety of lowly skills. But he also recognized that success lay beyond perfecting worldly abilities.[12]

Hōsa kyōshaden, therefore, challenges the binary of Neo-Confucian "orthodoxy" and Daoist subversion, the latter being the only framework that recent historiography has offered for the appearance and proliferation of eccentrics at this time. Its subjects straddle the mundane and the heavenly: as Daoist eccentrics they move "in accord with Heaven," and as Confucian *kyōsha* they "lay hold of truth." The fact that Confucian orthodoxy and Zhuangzian heterodoxy share such views indicates that Daoism was neither the sole nor even the prevailing intellectual and aesthetic inspiration for eccentricity in the late eighteenth century.

FALLEN CHESTNUT TALES

Like *HKD, Ochiguri monogatari* (Fallen chestnut tales; hereafter *OM*) predates *KKD.* Though its initial publication bears the date 1823, the work was originally produced and circulated two generations earlier. Following its eighty-first and final entry, the text states that the writer (*hissha*) of the entire book is Matsui Narinori (1731–1786), a samurai of the Ōinomikado house in Kyoto. With the exception of a single episode from 1792, the chronology of events related in the text concludes with a sutra recitation at Ninnaji Temple in 1780, suggesting that the original was compiled by Narinori sometime between 1780 and his death in 1786. The single later episode, as well as the epilogue, could only have been added by Fujiwara Ietaka (1747–1799), also of the Ōinomikado house, who was credited as author on the cover. We can assume with relative confidence, then, that *OM* was produced in the early 1780s by Narinori and transcribed—and nominally expanded—later by Ietaka. Tajihi Ikuo has asserted that although it was not published until four decades later, at least ten copies of the manuscript circulated in the interim.[13]

Importantly, Tajihi also suggests that the work was produced within the context of Iwagaki Ryūkei's (1741–1806) Kyoto poetry circle, whose members collaborated on various painting and poetry projects with Ike no Taiga, Gyokuran, Maruyama Ōkyo, Akutagawa Tankyū, and others whose biographies would appear in the text.[14] Like *HKD,* certainly, it was produced by and for a local readership. Heavily stacked with Kyoto residents of local celebrity, it complemented such works as *Heian jinbutsushi* (published periodically from 1768) as a pseudo-hagiographic compilation of urban icons.[15] Given that most of its entries are short and offer only a moderate degree of biographical detail, *OM* is an unremarkable example of mid-Edo biography if viewed out of context. Read as a precursor to *KKD*, however, it illuminates precisely how Kōkei was able to capitalize on current commercial appetites for strangeness by reintroducing some of *OM*'s subjects through the discursive identity of *kijin*.

Given that copies of *OM* were circulating during the 1780s, and particularly that members of Iwagaki Ryūkei's poetry circle are known to have interacted with Ban Kōkei, Mikuma Katen, and Rikunyo, the three collaborating authors of *Kinsei kijinden* and *Zoku kinsei kijinden* (*ZKKD*), it is unlikely that the latter were unaware of *OM*. Kōkei and Rikunyo, we know, were friends with Ike no Taiga, Tan Bunchū (1732–1790), and Gen Tadamoto (1738–1792), all entries in both collections. And indeed, *OM*'s stylistic similarity to the biographies of hermits mentioned by Kōkei in his preface further illuminates Kōkei's wish to eulogize local icons through the new interpretive lens of *kijin*.

Considering the contemporaneity of the two texts and the fact that both were produced by and about Kyoto locals, one would expect considerable overlap in their selection and treatment of these celebrities. It is striking, therefore, that among *OM*'s eighty-one entries and of the roughly 168 entries from *KKD* and *ZKKD*, only eight individuals share inclusion in both texts. Equally striking is how differently these eight are represented. *OM*, following the form of earlier Chinese biographies of hermits, delivers biographical details—family names, origins, occupations, and truncated anecdotes—while giving due credit to accomplishment in Chinese learning and aesthetics. *KKD* also follows this format, but enlivens biographical details with more anecdotal evidence of extraordinary and exemplary behavior. It expresses an interest neither in associating eccentricity with Chinese learning nor in denying that association, its objective being to celebrate worthy individuals for the ways in which they connected an aesthetics of strangeness with moral uprightness. Its deemphasis of ideological partisanship and its positioning of Keichū, Kada no Azumamaro, and Kamo no Mabuchi, Japan's major Kokugaku thinkers, alongside Confucians like Nakae Tōju and Kaibara Ekken marks it as a revisionist response to Chinese patterns of biography writing. Given that these two texts shared no ideological or commercial objectives, it is clear that the eight individuals who were included in both works—Ike no Taiga, Baisaō, Kinoshita Chōshōshi, Ishikawa Jōzan, Mochizuki Chōkō, Yōren, Gen Tadamoto (Nagata Kanga), and Tan

Bunchū—had earned broad respect around Kyoto. Here I shall compare how six of these were represented in *OM* and *KKD* with the objective of clarifying their respective agendas and demonstrating how Kōkei's advancement of the *kijinden* genre advanced Edo period biography.[16]

In his preface to *KKD*, Kōkei singles out Taiga and Baisaō as individuals whose behaviors exemplify the *kijin* ideal. His entries for both include anecdotes meant to illustrate an association between righteousness and idiosyncratic character. The following excerpt is representative:

> Taiga takes little notice of flattery or insults. He remains unobtrusive and avoids being diverted from what he's doing. He is disheveled on the outside but disciplined on the inside, and in his dealings with people he is humble but not obsequious. His manners are simple. When he is supposed to go he does not; when supposed to reply he does not, and this is the code of behavior that he lives by. He is blessed with talent but does not want more; he is governed by propriety and does not break with that; and he shows no interest in profits or losses. He also surprises people by dabbling in all sorts of different things, and this is why he is a *kijin*.[17]

The remainder of the entry showcases Taiga's idiosyncrasies, humility, Buddhist devotion, and Daoist untrammeledness.

In form and content, Kōkei's entry appears to have borrowed liberally from a eulogy for Taiga written by Tangai Jikujō in 1777.[18] It reiterates the character traits identified by the earlier *OM,* which begins its passage on Taiga as follows:

> He was called Taiga Dōjin and from childhood he loved painting. He roamed broadly to see the country's celebrated spots, and having climbed Mount Fuji, Hakusan, and Tateyama numerous times gave himself the sobriquet Pilgrim of the Three Peaks (*Sangaku dōja*). Once he completed a series of twelve paintings of Mount Fuji as seen in the rain, mist, clouds, snow, moonlight, and such, each with its distinctive expressiveness. . . . By nature he had few desires, and so to treasure-seekers asking for paintings he replied that he wielded his brush only to express what lay in his heart. Only to the needy would he donate his paintings, which always brought them tremendous economic benefit.[19]

In this markedly shorter entry for Taiga, *OM* also details an aesthetic, if not spiritual, connection to China that is omitted in *KKD:*

During the Meiwa period (1764–1772), Taihō (C. Ta Peng, 1691–1774), a priest from the Manpukuji Temple in Uji who had come from China [in 1722], summoned Taiga and asked him to paint Lake Xi Hu [in Huangzhou] on a ten-foot square screen. With Taihō alongside, Taiga took his brush and starting sketching, and when the priest witnessed the mountain taking form, he exclaimed: "Oh, that's extraordinary! This looks just like Mount Feilai Feng.[20] I was born in that place and have traveled all around it. I didn't think a place could be reproduced so perfectly, and I certainly don't understand how a person from this country could have drawn it so!"[21]

By highlighting both Taiga's lifelong relationship with Manpukuji, the headquarters of Ōbaku Zen in Japan and a center of Chinese learning, and his uncanny connection with Chinese iconography, this entry depicts him as an exemplar of the Sinophilia that grounded *bunjin* aesthetics.[22] Although *KKD*'s entry does not deny the depth of Chinese influence on Taiga, relating that while young he studied Chin and Tang dynasty painting methods, Kōkei's own literary and aesthetic interests leaned in the opposite direction, toward nativism. Kōkei authored studies on the *Man'yōshū* as well as native Japanese poetry and prose. He also promoted *wabun,* prose in Japanese that endeavored to capture the emotional authenticity of the native language while eliminating all possible forms of Chinese influence.[23] It is fitting, then, that *KKD*'s entry understates Taiga's debt to Chinese tastes.

Baisaō's entries in these two works also reveal Kōkei's tendency to downplay the Sinophilia that pervaded *bunjin* culture. Both *OM* and *KKD* begin by establishing that Baisaō's individuality and untrammeledness made him a beloved icon of the Kyoto streets. With his brazier and baskets of teaware, *OM* proclaims, Baisaō was a local landmark "loved by one and all."[24] That text then turns to Baisaō's piety as an Ōbaku Zen monk and the fact that, considering himself unworthy of the honor, he declined to inherit the abbotship at Ryūshinji temple from his master, Keirin. We are to understand that it was Baisaō's devotion to Keirin and his continuing fealty to the principles of this Chinese sect that compelled him to reject this administrative position for a lifestyle more closely aligned with the sect's original teachings.

This information is overlooked in *KKD,* which focuses on Baisaō's retired years and tea utensils. He left the priesthood, it suggests, in order to devote himself entirely to his way of *sencha,* the simple act of consuming tea. This, Baisaō claimed, not only expresssed his resistance to what he saw as the degeneracy of monastic practice but also transcended worldly and monastic affairs. *KKD* relates that he sold his *sencha* on the street at various historic and popular sites around the city and charged customers only what they wished to pay. And while people called his habits odd, the modest simplicity of peddling *sencha* afforded him unprecedented fulfillment. Baisaō explains by comparing himself to a strange head priest from long ago who had given up preaching Buddhist dogma. Contemplating those esoteric teachings, the priest had said, "is too much like jabbing a needle at your eye. Lose your head for just a moment and you'll end up blinding yourself. Instead, isn't it better to turn one's energies to learning and self-cultivation?"[25] The rejection of Ōbaku Zen in Kōkei's entry not only dismisses what *OM* claims to have been Baisaō's sole spiritual affiliation, it also distances this font of Chinese learning from *bunjin* culture.

The urban recluses Kinoshita Chōshōshi and Ishikawa Jōzan (discussed in Chapter 2) appear side by side in *OM* but are positioned first and last, as bookends, in *Zoku-kinsei kijinden* (*ZKKD*). Regardless, as contemporaries who emulated Tao Qian and Bo Juyi by rejecting official service, they stand as important early Tokugawa archetypes whose reclusion resulted from political events. The fact that they appear in *ZKKD* rather than the earlier *KKD* suggests that Kōkei either found their political dissent to be morally suspect or their Sinophilic aesthetics distasteful. Chōshōshi's brief entry in *OM* omits mention of his discharge from service to Ieyasu and focuses on his retirement and turn to aestheticism. It states, simply, that he was talented in Japanese and Chinese studies and that, following his withdrawal to a residence in nearby Ryōzen, he enjoyed interacting with others who shared his fondness for poetry.[26] Kōkei's biography is more extensive. It explains that as an in-law of Ieyasu and the nephew of Toyotomi Hideyoshi, Chōshōshi was beset by conflicting loyalties during the battle of Sekigahara and fled to Kyoto, leaving the castle at Fushimi unprotected. The remainder of the entry emphasizes his rejection of society and love of the arts. He lived in a small hermitage and was unable to support himself, it continues, but spent his years there cheerfully preparing for death without resenting his poverty and low standing. *Waka* like this one accentuate his rusticity:

ikuru hi no	smoke from the hut
yado no kemuri zo	where I live my days
mazu tayuru	when it ceases
tsuhi no takigi no	will leave behind only
mi wa nokoredomo[27]	my body of firewood

In fact, Chōshōshi was far from indigent. He retained a family fortune that allowed him to live in comfort without an income and even to amass a library of some fifteen hundred Chinese volumes.[28] For Kōkei it was more important to connect Chōshōshi to aesthetic reclusion as a literary trope than to produce an accurate biography, and inserting reclusion poems as factual served his purpose. By embracing the literary as literal, Kōkei's biography magnifies Chōshōshi's eccentricity while making sense of him as a historical figure.

OM affords Ishikawa Jōzan somewhat more space than it does Chōshōshi:

Ishikawa Shigeyuki [Jōzan] was a samurai from the Minamoto clan. He possessed broad learning, was a skilled poet, and received high praise for his prowess as a warrior. When the shogun attacked Nanba Castle [in Osaka in 1615], he led the attack and fought brilliantly, taking heads. But Jōzan was accused of disobeying orders and not rewarded. In shame he resigned his position and erected a hut near Ichijōji-mura north of the capital, changed his name to Jōzan, and lived in reclusion. Once he was summoned by the shogun but declined to go, citing old age as an excuse. . . . He brushed verses by the thirty-six immortal Chinese poets and added them to portraits [by Kanō Tanyū] that he hung in his dwelling, the Shisendō (Hall of the Immortal Poets). Jōzan received a koto that had been owned by the Ming scholar Chen Meigong (1558–1639) and often strummed it while reciting his original verses. The hut exists now as a temple, and retired Emperor Gomizunoo, while on excursion in 1729, heard of Jōzan and visited it.[29]

karauta no	that saint of Chinese songs
hijiri wo amata	and countless paintings
utsushi ga mo	his name,
sono na mo tomo ni	like his hut,
kuchinu io kana	will never perish

Reizei Chūnagon Tamehisa (1686–1741)

. . . Upon seeing the koto, the Emperor declared: "This was owned by a great man. I will take good care of it for posterity," whereupon he wrapped it in brocade and took it with him.[30]

Jōzan's rejection of a shogunal summons evokes a pattern of antiauthoritarianism among noted Chinese recluses, most famously Tao Qian. The rejection also served to align Jōzan with the imperial institution, whose authority had also been nullified by the *bakufu,* in implicit opposition to the Tokugawa. Emphasizing the Sinophilia of both Jōzan and Chōshōshi allowed *OM* to avoid examining them as controversial political figures. *ZKKD,* however, claims that the summons Jōzan disobeyed was issued by the retired emperor Gomizunoo (1596–1680), not by the shogun. This discrepancy, certainly, furthers the agendas pushed by both texts: it helps *OM* construct Jōzan as an unrepentant subject wronged by the Tokugawa regime who eventually finds comfort in Chinese culture, and it helps *ZKKD* reassert Jōzan's eccentricity while shielding it from suspicion as an anti-*bakufu* text.

With Jōzan, Kōkei again goes to lengths to construct a righteous eccentricity that is unverifiable as biographical fact. He writes: "[Jōzan] was sharper than most. He remembered events that had occurred when he was two years old; at age four he walked like an adult; at sixteen he was given a post; at thirty he exemplified filiality by retiring to care for his mother; and at forty he realized his aspirations by retreating into reclusion."[31] Such statements align Jōzan with the two primary qualities of the *kijin* as defined by Kōkei: extraordinary talent and notable Confucian virtue.

A recluse and a contemporary of Chōshōshi and Jōzan, Mochizuki (Hirosawa) Chōkō (1619–1681) allows for further comparisons of *OM* and *KKD.* Once again, *OM* shows comparatively more interest in Chōkō's devotion to Chinese learning. It relates that he enjoyed poetry and fashioned a small hut on the shore of Lake Hirosawa near Kyoto, "making only the moon and blossoms his friends," and then situates this living space within Chinese contexts. "This Sinophile [*karabito;* lit. Chinese; foreigner]," it continues reverently, "reminds one of the attempt to acquire the jewel located beneath the chin of the Black Dragon as related in 'Past scenery in Nanjing (*Jinling huai gu*).'"[32] *KKD*'s account of Chōkō, in contrast, omits all of the above references to Chinese learning, emphasizing only his notoriety around Kyoto as a recluse, *waka* poet, and former teacher of influential *haikai* poet Matsunaga Teitoku (1571–1653).

Although the biographical data contained in *OM* is generally consistent with that in *KKD,* the latter text often takes deliberate pains to convert it into evidence of eccentricity. Such is the case with the monk Yōren (1719–1774). *OM*'s entry depicts Yōren as a recluse and poet but focuses entirely on Reizei Tamemura's (1712–1774) attempt to track down Yōren at his hermitage in Saga. After several attempts to find the dwelling, it relates, Tamemura is directed to a forest hut. The hut is cramped, has a brushwood door, sagging eaves, and is furnished only with a hearth, pot, tea implements, and writing utensils. The floor is strewn with books and poetry collections but otherwise vacant, and Tamemura waits in vain, ultimately resolving to leave a poem and return home.[33] *KKD*'s entry, in contrast, tells of Yōren coming to Kyoto in disguise and living secretly in a watchman's hut. "He moved constantly and never saved a thing his whole life," Kōkei says. "Though a man of considerable talent, he gave no thought to appearance and looked like a madman as he walked around (*kyō shitaru yao nite ariki*). . . . He had a formidable memory, able to memorize long passages of the *Daichidoron* (Discourses on the Great Wisdom Sutra) at a glance and later transcribe them upon request."[34] Here, Kōkei eulogizes Yōren as an eccentric wanderer with a powerful mind and a carefree spirit. And, by including a dozen of Yōren's *waka*, which Yōren sang on the street between *nenbutsu* recitations, Kōkei showcases his aesthetic talents while accentuating the strangeness of his chosen lifestyle.

Illustrations also magnify *KKD*'s strangeness while further compromising its historical accuracy. As the subjects of all *KKD* entries were deceased, Mikuma Katen's illustrations could not have been drawn from recent personal observation. More likely they were products of Katen's imagination or gleaned from secondhand information. Katen's illustration of Taiga and Gyokuran (Fig. 5.1) may be the most often reproduced and circulated of the book's illustrations, and has become the face of Taiga as a *kijin*. While Katen had surely known Taiga, who had died in 1776, there is good reason to believe that he did not base this drawing on firsthand observation of Taiga's home. More likely he based it on a drawing by Taiga's friend and student, Kimura Kenkadō (1736–1802), who had visited Taiga's home numerous times. Kenkadō's own portrait (Fig. 5.2) should be considered more historically accurate. He depicts Taiga holding a shamisen and surrounded by books, papers, and brushes. Behind him Gyokuran is painting fans, most certainly to sell, for as a celebrated artist in her own right Gyokuran's labors did contribute to the household's income. Such a pragmatic depiction would not suit *KKD*'s purposes, and Katen likely chose to omit any reference to moneymaking by having Gyokuran playing the *koto*, accompanying Taiga on the *biwa*. Katen's illustration also shows a statue of a standing Kannon atop a stack of books on a table in front of the seated Taiga instead of in its proper place inside the family altar (*butsudan*). This out-of-place icon produces a strange effect, as does the visage of a cheerful but unkempt Taiga, unshaven and with his robe hanging open. It is likely, then, that Katen took certain liberties in order to construct the sort of personae that he and Kōkei wished to promote.[35]

Of the *OM* entries mentioned here—those destined to become anthologized in *KKD* as *kijin*—most are recluses (Chōshōshi, Jōzan, Chōkō) or monks (Baisaō, Yōren), and all are Kyoto residents who demonstrated exceptional talent for poetry, calligraphy, or painting. The text attaches Taiga, Baisaō, Chōshōshi, Jōzan, and Chōkō to Chinese learning, either through their connections with Manpukuji or for emulating the aesthetics of noted Chinese *wenren*. For the author Narinori, such was the preferred context for cultural notoriety and merit. Kōkei's work deemphasized Chinese learning while accentuating strangeness.

From all of this it is also clear that *KKD* was not the first biography to engage with extraordinary people and present them as paragons of moral

FIGURE 5.1   Taiga and Gyokuran. Ban Kōkei and Mikuma Katen, *Kinsei kijinden.* International Research Center for Japanese Studies Library.

virtue. *HKD* and *OM* also accomplished this through their respective ideological agendas. *KKD*'s integration of virtue and strangeness, however, was distinctive.

ECCENTRICS OF RECENT TIMES AND THE VIRTUE OF STRANGENESS

Kōkei's active participation in Kyoto's art and literary circles and his friendships with the day's accomplished *bunjin* had considerable bearing on *Kinsei kijinden*'s final form. A subset of his associations included fellow members

FIGURE 5.2   Kimura Kenkadō, Taiga, and Gyokuran.
Courtesy of Tomioka Pediatric Clinic.

of a salon associated with Imperial Prince Shinninhō (1768–1805) that, Kameya projects, "arguably represented the cutting edge of Kyoto artistic activity at that time."[36] The fact that members of this prestigious group aided Kōkei in researching, preparing, and proofreading *KKD* and *ZKKD* helps to explain why these texts constructed *kijin* as paragons of virtue rather than solely as oddballs, and why the finished product reinforced high ethical and behavioral standards.[37]

Allegedly, Kōkei gathered his material by affixing "*Kijin* Wanted" posters at inns around Kyoto.[38] These drew many responses—genuine and fraudulent, documented and oral—that helped Kōkei compile his entries. Though Kōkei took precautions to verify these accounts, it is clear that he left his personal fingerprints on the completed works. Several of Kōkei's friends who assisted him in compiling the original volume (1790) died soon thereafter, and Kōkei eulogized them in the sequel (1798) as tribute to their participation in the project. *KKD* illustrator Mikuma Katen (d. 1794) appears, with his portrait, in the sequel, as well as Kanzawa Tokō (d. 1795); Gen'a Chōmu (d. 1795); Tan Bunchū (d. 1790); and Nagata Kanga (d. 1792), who transcribed Rikunyo's *kanbun* foreword for *KKD*. Certain puzzling omissions also indicate bias. Soga Shōhaku's absence is a case in point.

Shōhaku, widely known as a gifted painter, transient, and madman, was one of the most conspicuous examples of aesthetic eccentricity of his day and surely an obvious choice for Kōkei. A likely explanation for *KKD*'s omission of Shōhaku lies in Kōkei's friendship with Shōhaku's rival, Maruyama Ōkyo (1733–1795). Shōhaku and Ōkyo had openly criticized each other's painting, and given that Ōkyo was the most highly regarded painter of his day (ranked first in *Heian jinbutsushi*) as well as a fellow member of Prince Shinninhō's group, their animosity surely disingratiated Shōhaku from Kyoto's art world.

Hiraga Gennai (1728–1779), an exceptionally gifted intellectual and social critic, was also passed over. A student of numerous sciences, an inventor, writer, painter, and Kokugaku and Rangaku scholar, Gennai was clearly one of the more brilliant and eccentric men of his age. One explanation for his omission from *KKD* is the fact that he lived much of his adult life in Edo. More likely, his erratic temperament—he killed a disciple in anger and died in jail—and scathing social critiques disqualified him from consideration. Why Kōkei overlooked Matsuo Bashō, who arguably contributed more to eccentric *bunjin* culture than any other individual, and Yosa

Buson (1716–1783), another monumental presence in *bunjin* networks, is unclear. Omissions of this sort, as well as Kōkei's decision to include only the deceased whose lives could be evaluated in their entirety, not only made his work less current but suggest a nativistic denial of the present.

Despite their biases, as Japan's earliest compilations of *kijin* biographies Kōkei's books established philosophical and literary precedents for the numerous *kijinden* that followed. Specifically, it was Kōkei's preface (1788) that became the most commonly invoked definition of the term *kijin* and that provided the philosophical orientation that gave the term its contemporary moral context. By unifying Zhuangzian and Confucian ethics into a hybrid of strangeness and goodness, and then attaching his diverse collection of eccentrics to it, Kōkei's preface established an indelible precedent for later *kijinden* authors:[39]

> When some associates saw a draft of this work they said, "the *kijin* appearing in *Zhuangzi* are themselves one kind of *kijin*. But this book begins with [Nakae] Tōju and [Kaibara] Ekken and then continues on with more virtuous individuals. These should not be viewed as *kijin,* for don't they follow the Way that the rest of us should aspire to? Please explain."
>
> "You are correct," I said, "but the meaning of what I have written here is slightly different than what you are thinking. Consider it in broader terms. Of the individuals listed here, those like Baisaō and Taigadō are one type of *kijin*. But elders who employ humanity and righteousness, or youths who embrace loyalty and filiality are also considered strange when compared to others [who are neither humane nor righteous]. When a group of friends is drinking late into the night and loses all track of time, the one who remains clearheaded would be the eccentric. This is why, from my own drunken perspective, those who follow the Way appear eccentric and, for those like myself, can be of some small benefit."[40]

Kōkei thus identifies two types of eccentric: the freakishly talented and the extraordinarily virtuous. These two qualities could hardly seem more dissimilar, yet he shows no inclination to distinguish between them as moral exemplars or offers any justification for conflating them so effortlessly under a single term. For readers, the label of *kijin* alone should be sufficient to merit admiration.[41] Following these remarks, Kōkei posits *KKD* as a serious work. Each record, the reader is assured, is based on facts yielded by solid research. He disavows inclusion of individuals on the basis of mere fame or singular talents and denounces those "fake" *kijin* who cultivate the visage of oddballs in order to garner attention and personal gain. Finally, Kōkei avers, the book aspires to "be of some small benefit" to its readers.

Such statements set a standard and a literary tenor for later *kijinden* writers. *Kijin* (畸人) were to be essentially distinctive and superior in natural endowment to *kijin* (奇人). Kōkei's deployment of 畸 is all the more noteworthy when we recall that it originally carried negative connotations and "more sinister overtones of aberrant behavior rather than amusing nonconformism," as Melinda Takeuchi puts it.[42] Though Kōkei did not provide a clear distinction between 畸 and 奇, Rikunyo's preface does note an essential difference:

> What is 畸? It is said that 畸 is 奇. In the past there have been 奇人 among Confucians, and 奇人 among Zen Buddhists. There have been 奇人 samurai, 奇人 physicians, 奇人 poets, writers, painters, and 奇人 of the various arts. They have been known as such for their singular talents in one area, but those who have been called 畸人 are those for whom the location of this sort of natural talent is not discernable.[43]

The 奇人, who has acquired notoriety through accomplishment for a singular art, talent, or discipline, Rikunyo suggests, is thus intrinsically distinct from the 畸人, who possesses an inherent endowment that cannot be studied or learned.

These two prefaces, then, served multiple functions: they explained the origin of the term *ki* as a Daoist endowment signifying accord with Heaven; they placed *kijin* inside the pale of Confucian merit by equating them with social value; and they underscored the sense of strangeness craved by Kōkei's readership. That the philosophical incongruence between Kōkei's two types of *kijin*—Zhuangzian figures like Taiga and Baisaō and what might be called Kōkei's Confucian *kijin*, represented by Nakae Tōju and Kaibara Ekken—evoked no sense of contradiction reflects the intellectual diversity in place at the end of the eighteenth century. It is also noteworthy that during the heightened vigilance surrounding Matsudaira Sadanobu's Kansei Reforms (1787–1793) and Prohibition of Heterodox Studies (1790), readers found nothing antisocial in Kōkei's deployment of the *Zhuangzi*, which historically had been treated as a counterideological text. Kōkei's work thus leaves two legacies of interest. Already noted has been the book's distinction as the progenitor of a genre of biography writing and the literary monument by which that genre identified itself. Equally important is the role the work played in locating the formerly eccentric Daoist principles of effortless action (*wu-wei*), spontaneity, and strangeness within a mainstream discourse on social value.

As discussed earlier, the content of the entries themselves provides an abundance of evidence that Kōkei sought, in a qualified way, to reinforce the core Confucian tenet of virtue. As the foremost proponent of Wang Yangming, Nakae Tōju's teachings lent potential validity to all sorts of eccentric behaviors, but Kōkei strips him of all controversy and idiosyncrasy by showcasing his filiality, self-sacrifice, and generosity. The entry tells of Tōju secretly teaching himself the Four Books but later embracing free will and intuition after his exposure to Wang Yangming thought. Contrary to what the Four Books claimed, Tōju professed that thought and action were indistinguishable and codependent. A student challenged this point by asking about madmen: "But what of madmen (*kyōsha*)? Even if their thoughts are lofty their actions are surely corrupted. And then there are those frauds that toady before others. Their actions appear to be saintly but their hearts are defiled. In such cases, surely, thoughts and actions are divergent." In response, Kōkei has Tōju justify the unification of thought and action using language reminiscent of mainstream Confucian thought.

> Strictly speaking, madmen cannot be included among ordinary folks and so must be excluded from such discussions. Actions taken by frauds are schemes that succeed only by currying the favor of others and so cannot be counted as virtuous. It is a mistake to say that something is good because it appears so on the surface. Frauds have minds filled only with ambition and greed. Because thought and action are indistinguishable . . . thieves would not be greedy if they did not live as thieves.[44]

It is noteworthy that *kyōsha* here are socially harmful individuals likened to frauds and thieves and that Tōju ends up defending a Middle Way. As a result, this advocate of free will is reinvented by *KKD* as a spokesman for Confucian ethics.

Kaibara Ekken's entry, which follows Tōju's, is equally sober and reaffirms the book's claim as a serious work for moral edification. It closes, however, as follows: "I [Kōkei] have started the [first volume of this work] on virtue (*tokkō*) with Tōju and Ekken, and the next entries on the two priests Tōsui and Munō follow their example. I have no intention of handpicking some and dismissing others [to suit my purposes]."[45] But Kōkei does hand-pick specific material to suit his purposes. The Pure Land monk Munō's (1683–1719) entry, as is commonly the case in *KKD,* does not attempt to recapture his life accomplishments, but rather uses an allegory to deliver a moral lesson. Once, when the itinerant Munō had been offered lodgings by a family, it begins, a daughter entered his room and embraced him. Munō remained motionless and continued reciting the *nenbutsu* for the rest of the evening. At dawn the daughter, suffering from the humiliation of rejection, started ranting like a madwoman. Munō gives her a Buddhist name, a karmic connection, whereupon she gradually regains her sanity and devotes the rest of her life to Buddhism.[46]

The centrality of virtue in *KKD* indicates that Kōkei never intended the *kijin* as either a literary or social identity to make any countercultural statement that would challenge the ideological mainstream. However, by placing side-by-side individuals from all classes and occupations, it dismisses as irrelevant the class system's association of virtue with class or its assumption of graded standards of virtue as determined by class. As we saw in Kōkei's treatment of Yanagisawa Kien and Ike no Taiga, entries on *bunjin* are composed to manifest subjects' goodness rather than their more obvious contributions to the arts. Patti Kameya, moreover, has found that the prostitutes (*yūjo*) included in *KKD* exemplify moral rectitude rather than qualities like physical beauty that were traditionally associated with their profession.[47] *KKD,* then, replaces class with a new, egalitarian view of individual worth contingent on accomplishment, ability, and natural endowment. Such a project was both cynical and idealistic: cynical in its implication that true virtue was sufficiently uncommon to warrant the signifier *ki;* and idealistic in its effort to recover and publicize eccentricity as a vehicle for social merit rather than eccentricity for its own sake.

Kōkei's view was a secular, humanist composite of multiple philosophical traditions that possessed the visage of asocial strangeness but embodied the essence of incorruptible moral virtue. Zhuangzi had espoused the opposite intention of targeting Confucianism, and particularly its view of virtue, by exposing it as artificial and socially corrupting. This lends more irony to the fact that later readers and interpreters uncritically read Kōkei's and Rikunyo's reference to Zhuangzi as evidence of strong philosophical continuity between the two. Kōkei himself made no such claims. Indeed, by instructing the confused colleagues who had questioned his inclusion of Confucians Nakae Tōju and Kaibara Ekken to "consider it in broader terms," he confesses to be taking this in a new direction. Placing Confucians beside Buddhists and Nativists, and scholars alongside artists, warriors, prostitutes, and monks, and then connecting all of them to a generalized view of virtue, *KKD* effectively universalizes and secularizes the *kijin*.

KKD's unification of eccentricity and goodness through a humanized, nontranscendent persona, however, generalized 畸 and had the effect of lowering it to an approximation of 奇. Ishikawa Jun has noted that originally 畸 人 had been posited as angels fallen from Heaven, intermediaries between disparate worlds, and essentially superior to common folk.[48] His observation reiterates Zhuangzi's original definition of *kijin* as transcendent beings, as well as Rikunyo's own assertion of such. As apostles who rectify ignorance, Ishikawa continues, *kijin* are not merely reclusive individualists or persons who act strangely. *KKD*'s deployment of the talented and strange as paragons of virtue, he concludes, amounts to a conscious misinterpretation.

Kōkei, surely, was not the first to misappropriate this term. Misinterpretations of Zhuangzi's *kijin* may have reached Japan from China via Matteo Ricci's *Jiren shipian* (J. *Kijin jippen* [Ten chapters on eccentrics], 1608), a record of Catholic proselytizers who, like Ricci, strove to bring salvation to humanity by acting as intermediaries between this world and the divine.[49] While deploying the Zhuangzian *kijin* as a foil for these missionaries, the preface frames the work with distinctly Confucian language. It classifies its subjects as *kijin* for neither marrying nor accepting official posts, and for devoting themselves to harmonizing the human world with Heaven. *Kijin*, the work continues, follow individual will rather than the paths of others, and though their words are humble their actions are bold. They are frugal, reject fame, and benefit the world by awakening the greedy and jealous to their own pettiness.[50]

Ricci's view of *kijin* is consistent with Zhuangzi's to the extent that his missionaries functioned as apostles who, it was hoped, would unify the human with the heavenly. Kōkei's conflation of two kinds of *kijin*—the moral and the odd—however, implies that *kijin* of any stripe possessed intrinsic virtue. This lowered them to the human level and placed them within a social context.[51] It also codified the *kijin* as a quantified social identity. Hereafter, any individual conforming to this construct qualified. Codification validated a socially accepted strangeness that spoke to human society and the human experience. By suggesting that strangeness was an aspect of human nature and human society, *KKD* both reinvented the *kijin*'s social role and reassessed what it meant to be a human being.[52] For this reason, Ishikawa asserts, Kōkei's *kijinden* was responsible for the appropriation and vulgarization of *kijin,* for bringing them to the level of plebian amusement and reducing these former apostles to the role of ideological tools. Hereafter, he concludes, true *kijin* died out in early modern Japan and the meaning of 畸 was conflated with the array of connotations—from strange to talented to detached—carried by 奇.[53]

Biography assumes that the content of its subject's life contains social value and that the merit gleaned from the subject's story will exceed the effort required to read about it. Within the roughly contemporaneous biographical collections examined herein we find three distinct efforts to discern social merit through the lens of idiosyncrasy. *HKD* combines Confucian and Daoist allusions to represent "mad" delinquents and dropouts as playful sages; *OM* follows Chinese biographical form while reflecting secular appreciations of Chinese learning and aesthetics; and *KKD* unites the genius and the virtuous under the rubric of *kijin.* Each of these collections also extends this notion of social value in a particular direction. *HKD* does so by proposing that madness can possess an innocence and incorruptibility consistent with Confucian sincerity and Daoist spontaneity. *OM* takes the more secular view that merit is demonstrable within individual talent, be it religious or artistic. *KKD*'s contribution to this discourse lies in its distinctive integration of *HKD*'s redemption of strangeness and *OM*'s redemption of secular humanism, the notion that social merit is manifested in eccentricity emanating from within—"personal potency," as Kameya puts it.[54]

Collectively, these works reveal a repositioning of biography in Edo period popular literature. Though embracing a newfound secular eclecticism, biography inserted itself into popular literature while preserving its traditionally didactic function. Its reinvention of the eccentric, moreover, was also a repositioning in the sense that it brought socially marginalized individuals directly into the public spotlight. The result was a literary turn toward production and consumption of strangeness for commercial purposes.

KKD, in part, was conceptualized in such terms. Knowing of extant works like *OM,* Kōkei altered Mikuma Katen's original idea of compiling a volume on recluses because he felt the topic to be no longer fresh.[55] Kōkei's friend Ueda Akinari had already famously used the term *kijin* self-referentially in his preface to *Ugetsu monogatari* (1776), and his fame and commercial popularity were auspicious indications to Kōkei that a literary exploration into the *kijin* identity would also fare well commercially. While *Kinsei kijinden* is a monumental work deserving of its popularity, its conception included a commercial dimension that compromised the integrity of the very aesthetics it celebrated. To an important extent, it was this business decision that altered the position that aesthetic detachment, reclusion, and behavioral deviance would thereafter assume within the cultural field. The aura of failure that came to permeate this commercialization of eccentricity will be examined in the next chapter.

PART III

Finishers and Failures of the Nineteenth Century

CHAPTER 6

Strangeness in the Early Nineteenth Century

Commercialism, Conservatism, and Diffusion

Sinophilic *bunjin* had long been Tokugawa society's primary custodians of aesthetic strangeness. It was largely through their efforts that *ki, kyō,* and *muyō* were validated and popularized as cultural topoi. From the late eighteenth century, however, aesthetic eccentricity diverged from its previous trajectory and moved in varying directions.

In urban centers this diffusion was catalyzed by a swelling appetite for spectacle. Increasingly, public life became typified by ostentation and performance. Whether in the licensed or unlicensed pleasure quarters, leisure centers like Ryōgoku Bridge, or temple precincts, such spaces afforded citizens opportunities to watch and be watched. The carnival of public life, where street artists, singers, dancers, acrobats, magicians, comedians, and peddlers of exotic wares all sought to capitalize on people's cravings for the extraordinary, accelerated the blending of high and low. To the chagrin of those who were partial to more traditional tastes, novelty trumped elegance. Even among the general public, attendance itself was a public performance, an opportunity to have one's attire and comportment displayed and scrutinized.[1]

Aesthetic strangeness at this time also confronted several new challenges. On one hand, *bunjin* arts like *nanga* fell victim to their own success as painters claiming a proprietary mastery of Chinese aesthetics codified the genre, suppressing originality. Patrons coveting originality, on the other hand, reified strangeness by affixing price tags to it. For others, the *baku-fu*'s ineffectual responses to domestic unrest and foreign threats called for strange countermeasures, including political activism. Thus appropriated and marketed by various interests, eccentricity assumed multiple capacities across the social spectrum.

Numerous factors and developments informed this divergence. I shall begin by examining the impact of Ban Kōkei's *Kinsei kijinden* on publishing and print culture, particularly how the signifiers *ki* and *kijin* became applied to an array of contexts, including political dissent. I then consider developments within *nanga* circles, wherein the familiarity of aesthetic strangeness caused painters to retreat from *ki*, a sentiment increasingly articulated in painting treatises (*garon*). This retrenchment formalized aesthetic rubrics, refining the genre in ways that limited its potential to create eccentric art. Finally, I examine three prominent cultural figures—Uragami Gyokudō, Kagawa Kageki, and Watanabe Kazan—who, despite the ongoing diffusion and commodification of strangeness, found personal meaning in eccentricity and established legacies that would redirect the course of Japan's cultural field.

KINSEI KIJINDEN AND THE *KIJIN* BOOM

Kōkei's preface to *Kinsei kijinden* contains language suggesting that he produced the book with philanthropic intentions or "from a desire to create a better future," as Patti Kameya proposes.[2] But the book was also intended as a social commentary and a source of income. Kōkei admits that he decided against publishing a volume on recluses because he was looking for a fresher market, and relates that illustrator Mikuma Katen had plans to compile a sequel to *KKD* even before publication of the first volume. Rikunyo's preface also states that when he saw a draft he wanted to see it printed immediately. From such statements it is clear that Kōkei and other contributors perceived the work as a commercial product. Its success as such triggered, not only a wave of publishing that redefined Edo period biography, but also an avalanche of other literary works that capitalized on *ki* and *kijin* as buzzwords by fitting them with an array of new meanings and applications. Most authors were ambivalent about Kōkei's efforts to make virtue a requisite feature of eccentricity, reading *KKD* simply as historical fact or as a biographical resource. Hara Tokusai (1800–1870), for example, cites it as a source for his *Zentetsu zōden* (Biographies of past sages, 1844), a chronicle of prominent Confucian thinkers. Okada Shinsen's (1737–1799) *Kijin'ei* (Compositions on *kijin,* 1798), whose preface is dated 1792, also pays tribute to *KKD* by choosing a poignant or admirable quality from each of Kōkei's entries and working it into a twenty-eight-character *kanshi.*

Dispensing with Kōkei's moralism altogether, many other *kijinden* writers took as their publishing strategy Hiraga Gennai's credo, "the wackier the better." Santō Kyōden's *Kinsei kisekikō* (Thoughts on eccentric deeds of recent times, 1804) falls into this category. Dismissing Kōkei's endeavor to wed aesthetic detachment and moral virtue, Kyōden's work is a miscellany of amusing or unusual historical events compiled primarily as a commercial product for a market thirsty for spectacle. And, though the Meiji period journalist Miyatake Gaikotsu (1867–1955) calls Kyōden a repentant eccentric writer, this label is derived largely from Kyōden's ability to select subject matter for its commercial appeal and for his earlier indictment by *bakufu* censors.[3] Okada Chōken's (1759–1824) *Kinsei itsujin gashi* (History of paintings by eccentrics of recent times, 1824) is a catalog of eccentric artists (e.g., Taiga and Enkū), though it also includes individuals not known for artistic accomplishments (e.g., the famous swordsman Miyamoto Musashi). Okada rejects Kōkei's insistence on *kijin* as moral exemplars and includes more notorious painters like Soga Shōhaku and Nakayama Kōyō (1717–1780), a *nanga* painter and *kanshi* poet who for unknown reasons became mentally deranged late in life. *Hyakka kikōden* (A miscellany of eccentricities, 1835) by the comic fiction (*gesaku*) writer Yajima Gogaku takes *ki* as a descriptor for a broad spectrum of idiosyncratic behaviors, from the compulsive Striped Kanjūrō (chap. 2) to the old cross-dressing dancer Tatsumiya Sōbei, whose celebrity derived only from his standing as a public laughingstock:

> Whenever and wherever, there was no festival at which he did not dance. On stage he donned a young woman's wig, wore a long-sleeved kimono of black cotton with a printed pattern on the long train, held a small parasol, and danced while nibbling on a sweet potato. After turning sixty he got around on horseback and when he dressed in his young woman's outfit he covered his wrinkled face with white makeup, making his dance even more hilarious. Everyone competed to get a peek.[4]

Often authors inserted the term *kijin* into a book's title to enhance the work's marketability, even if its content downplayed strangeness. *Haika kijindan* (Accounts of eccentric *haikai* poets, 1816) by Takeuchi Gengen'ichi

(1742–1804) and its sequel *Zoku-haika kijindan* (1833) include individuals that Kōkei had established as *kijin* (e.g., Taiga and Gyokuran), but neither Gabō Sanjin's preface nor Takeuchi's narrative acknowledges *ki* as a qualification for inclusion. Given that the book's objective is not to celebrate eccentricity per se but rather to memorialize worthy poets, the appearance of *kijin* in its title demonstrates a tendency to expand the lexical applications of the term. *Kijin hyakunin isshu* (One hundred verses from one hundred eccentrics, 1852) by the woodblock print celebrity Katsushika Hokusai (1760–1849) also positions itself within the *kijinden* genre, but its entries are brief, its illustrations uninspired, and its *waka* wholly conventional.

The *kijin* boom also extended to the world of theater. The kabuki actor Ichikawa Danjūrō VII (1791–1859) and print artist Kitao Shigemasa II (1777–1835) produced *Ryōyū kijin* (Manly heroes, 1827), an illustrated storybook of heroic deeds, and several years later *ukiyoe* artists Utei Enba II (1792–1862) and Utagawa Toyokuni III (1786–1864) produced *Yakusha kijinden* (Biographies of eccentric actors, 1833). Better known is *kyōgen* and kabuki playwright Hanagasa Bunkyō's (1784–1861) *Dainihon kijin gazō: Fūzoku kōmei ryakuden* (Eccentrics of Japan: Biographical sketches of noted public figures, 1845), illustrated by the flamboyant woodblock artist Utagawa Kuniyoshi (1797–1861). More a celebration of greatness than strangeness, the work anthologizes two hundred and twenty individuals of enduring importance and extraordinary ability. While Bunkyō includes the recognized *kijin* Baisaō, Saigyō, Ikkyū, Taiga, and Gyokuran, most of his subjects are historical figures from earlier eras: Ono no Komachi, Murasaki Shikibu, Yoshida Kenkō, Taira Kiyomori, and Miyamoto Musashi, for example, as well as fairy-tale icons like Urashima Tarō. The illustrations are arranged in seemingly random groupings and accompanied by brief explanatory narratives. The volume ends irreverently, with Kuniyoshi himself seated with his back to the viewer.

The popularization of *ki* culminated with *kijinden* produced as advertisements for public spectacle. *Shokoku kaikaku keisei kijinden* (Accounts of eccentrically beautiful women, 1851), for instance, includes illustrations and descriptions of attractive *yūjo* (prostitutes), complementing these with flashy scenes from the pleasure quarters and apocryphal accounts of romantic encounters between stylish men and coquettish women. More notably, *Suikyō kijinden* (Accounts of drunken hell-raisers, 1863) by *gesaku* writers Kanagaki Robun (1829–1894), Sansantei Arindō (1832–1902), and illustrator Utagawa Yoshiiku (1833–1904), depicts a cohort of men and women known locally in Edo for their bawdiness and devotion to comic storytelling (*rakugo*).[5] The work itself is likely a product of *sandai-banashi,* a *rakugo* improvisational skit that takes three disparate themes solicited from the audience and weaves them together into a comic narrative. *Suikyō*'s narrative consists of entries relating how excessive alcohol consumption leads each member to rambunctious adventures. Rife with literary perversions and puns, each sketch amounts to a self-promoting autobiography aimed at enhancing the author's celebrity. As such it represents a culmination of trends set by earlier *kijinden:* it converts eccentricity into capital, and it moves internal aestheticism toward external amusement and spectacle.[6]

Although publishing was predominantly an urban industry that catered to readerships in Edo, Osaka, and Kyoto, provincial publishers also joined this movement. During the first half of the nineteenth century, local *kijinden* were published in domains nationwide, including present-day Nagano, Hyōgo, Okayama, Echigo, Sado, Hiroshima, Tosa, Miyagi, and Kanagawa prefectures. The scope of this phenomenon reveals *KKD* as a tipping point that set in motion tendencies within print media that altered how strangeness was produced and consumed. Rendered definable, knowable entities, *kijin* were compelling, not for their uselessness, as Zhuangzi had originally proposed, but as celebrities. As an appetite for strangeness expanded over a wider consumer base, however, *ki* became overexposed and diluted as an all-purpose signifier.[7] Never before had strangeness paid for itself on such a scale. It had become an orthodoxy in its own right.

COMMERCIALIZATION, POLITICIZATION, AND THE TRANSFORMATION OF *KI*

By the Bunka-Bunsei era (1804–1830), broader participation in the cultural field was contributing to a qualified erosion of distinctions between "high" and "low" cultural practice. With greater numbers populating the print marketplace, amateur *bunjin* writers increasingly gravitated toward more professional projects that, while compromising their claims to literary autonomy, enhanced their commercial viability. Many early nineteenth-century writers, consequently, lost the sort of *bunjin* consciousness that had driven the literary innovations of the preceding century.[8] Forms of high culture such as *waka* and *kanshi* endured similar fates. Previously, the class system had helped shield such pursuits from *haikai, kyōka, gesaku* (comic) literature, and similar forms of low culture, leaving them in the hands of higher samurai and intellectuals. In the early nineteenth century, however, high culture lost its connection to studied aesthetic styles and became transposed by pleasure-seeking, nouveau riche commoners. Consequently, it "lost its vigor" and "expired."[9]

Artistic originality is particularly prone to the neutralizing effects of commercialization. Pierre Bourdieu uses it to define art itself, which he describes as "a sacred island systematically and ostentatiously opposed to the profane, everyday world of production, a sanctuary for gratuitous disinterested activity in a universe given over to money and self-interest."[10] This notion of originality as oppositional to market culture aligns it with our discussion of aesthetic eccentricity. Indeed, Katharine Burnett defines *ki* not as eccentricity or strangeness but as originality.[11] Within a commodified cultural field, however, originality is quickly rendered conventional. As commercial demand converts autonomous (original) artistic practice to heteronomous (market-driven) practice, it converts artistic value to market value. It makes Bourdieu's "sacred island" a source of income. Popularization, therefore, transforms originality into a commodity whose artistic forms are dictated by its consumers.

While commercial success was a boon to some, to others it was cause for lament. The popularity of strangeness within works like Kōkei's *KKD,* for instance, raised suspicions. Was this attraction driven by strange art or merely by strange personalities? Confucian scholar Murase Kōtei's (1746–1818) observation that "The behavior of those whose paintings exhibit strangeness (*ki*) will surely be strange as well" reflects the truism that personality and art are generally inseparable within the minds of an adoring public.[12] This made an eccentric public image commercially advantageous for many independent artists.[13] Maruyama Ōkyo (1733–1795), in contrast, was quick to recognize and then reject the commercial benefits of using strangeness to gild his reputation. Ōkyo enjoyed celebrity status in Kyoto, was ranked first among artists in the 1792 edition of *Heian jinbutsushi,* and his death in 1795 qualified him as an obvious candidate for inclusion in *Zoku-kinsei kijinden* (1798). His omission from that text, therefore, is noteworthy. In fact, Ōkyo did not wish to divert attention from his art by being viewed as a *kijin* and even warned his followers against circulating sensational stories about him.[14] His utterly unremarkable lifestyle, consequently, allowed his paintings to take center stage within the Ōkyo discourse.

Ōkyo's caution was prudent, for many continued to insist that good art remain commercially unsullied, a sentiment expressed by the hermit monk

Ryōkan (1758–1831): "There are three things that I detest: books written by writers, the poetry of poets, and food cooked by chefs."[15] All three, Ryōkan intoned, reek of commercial professionalism. Yet commercialization was irresistible for most nineteenth-century *bunjin,* a fact that only exacerbated their disillusionment with society at large. Murase Kōtei and *nanga* painter Tanomura Chikuden (1777–1835) penned such laments, and others revealed similar misgivings about the present.[16] In *Ora ga haru* (My spring, 1819), *haikai* poet Kobayashi Issa (1763–1827) wrote: "[Hirose] Izen (1646–1711) was a Genroku *kijin* 畸人 whereas I, Issa, am a modern day *kijin* 奇人."[17] Though Issa's comment is meant to describe his poetic kinship with Izen, his differentiation of characters for *ki* implies a reduced aesthetic potency and comparative illegitimacy of contemporary vis à vis past *kijin*. In *Tandai Shōshinroku* (A record of daring and prudence, 1808), similarly, the intractable Ueda Akinari writes bitterly about the declining aptitude of his peers, such as this condemnation of contemporary poetry: "Students of Chinese poetry may now be breeding like maggots, but there are no paragons. There are not likely to be any. This is because they are unable to acquire even half the virtuosity of their teachers, and those teachers in their turn seem to have had but half that of their own teachers. What causes this gradual degeneration I do not know."[18]

While Akinari here claims ignorance of the reasons for this decline, elsewhere in the text he attributes it to greed and the reification of cultural products. He comments, for example, on the rampant commodification of pictures and scrolls brushed by masters like Taiga, Buson, Keichū, and Bashō.[19] Though it is unclear whether his disgust is fueled by their commercialism or by envy of their popularity, his grumbling reveals how art and commercial value had become inseparable within many *bunjin* circles. Yet even Akinari could not help evaluating artists based on the monetary value of their paintings. Buson's works, he says, are regarded as valuable treasures; Taiga's easily fetch one thousand in cash; and those by Murase Kōtei are nearly worthless, as nobody will buy them. What is especially revealing is that Akinari equates this marketability of paintings with aesthetic merit. Taiga and Buson are men of exquisite tastefulness, he reports, while Murase is wholly unrefined (*fūryū no nai hito*).[20] Akinari's ruminations suggest, paradoxically, that the originality exhibited by certain prestigious *kijin* was becoming objectified in the eyes of his contemporaries for whom virtuosity was partially determined by commercial demand. Moreover, by assessing the works Taiga produced in unfettered poverty as priceless masterpieces,

Akinari seems to highlight the paradox that excellent art assumes great monetary value but is generated by impoverishment—that is, the fact that Taiga and Gyokuran had to paint fans for cash attested to their authenticity as artists.

The commercialization of strangeness is also central to *ukiyoe,* which Elizabeth Lillehoj calls "perhaps the most market-driven of all visual arts of the Edo period."[21] *Ukiyoe* has elicited ambivalent reactions from art and cultural historians for shamelessly capitalizing on public fascination with kabuki actors, geisha, and life in the pleasure quarters. In a 2003 exhibition catalog promoting *ukiyoe* as an early modern avant-garde movement, for instance, curator Yokota Yōichi describes the art as consciously foregoing originality and lacking the self-confidence to aspire to artistic importance. Securing the patronage of the masses, he maintains, was all that mattered.[22] In doing so, however, it joined other arts in embracing eccentricity, as is evident from the activities of Katsushika Hokusai and Utagawa Kuniyoshi, two of the genre's most influential artists.

Hokusai is commonly posited as one of nineteenth-century Japan's greatest *kijin,* and by all accounts he was indeed a bizarre fellow.[23] He moved residences ninety-three times in his life, and while this nomadism was partially necessitated by his filthy habits and distaste for cleaning, it also reveals the restless spirit of a discontented wanderer. Discontentment certainly fueled obsessions, even paranoia, about his work and economic standing, causing him to nurse rivalries with his competitors. It also drove his prolificacy (he is said to have produced thirty to forty thousand pictures).[24] Yet somehow, despite his commercial success and his receiving higher commissions than Takizawa Bakin and other contemporary celebrities, he often found himself in debt.[25]

Equally responsible for Hokusai's reputation as an eccentric was his continual self-representation as such. He was fond of pointing out that his birth year, the year of the dragon, conferred propensities for wildness, pride, and rebelliousness.[26] He also took the studio name *gakyōjin* (Madman of Pictures). On the title page of his *Ehon saishiki-tsū* (Picture book on coloring) his illustration of a painter—presumably himself—wielding paint brushes in his hands, feet, and mouth invokes the Buddhist scholar Kūkai (744–836), who legend holds was able to write with five brushes simultaneously. He also illustrated *Kijin hyakunin isshū.*[27] In addition to these overt moves to advertise his eccentricity, Hokusai sought to further boost his notoriety by staging public exhibitions. These included a painting contest with the eminent *bunjin* Tani Bunchō (1763–1840), an event conducted in the presence of the shogun Tokugawa Ienari. On other occasions he held public performances in which he composed immense paintings, one a 350-square-meter portrait of Bodhidharma executed with a broom and a cask of ink.[28] Cinzia Vandi sees such behavior as evidence of Hokusai's desire to exceed his standing as just another commercial artist. As we have seen in other cases, constructing a reputation for eccentricity enabled him to dismiss certain rules and social expectations that would otherwise have restricted him artistically.[29]

Within the context of an urban culture that tended to integrate spectacle, commerce, and art, however, Hokusai's antics struggle to hold their authenticity. His idiosyncratic behavior is best viewed as a commercial expedient rather than as evidence of the sort of tortured genius we might attribute to Shōhaku. It could even be interpreted as normative. Rosenfield affirms that "Hokusai's eccentricities as an artist fit into well-established patterns in the artistic and literary culture of Edo-period Japan," thereby protecting him from *bakufu* scrutiny.[30]

Scrutiny fluctuated, however, and the field periodically endured stricter regulations, particularly during the Tenpō Reforms (1841–1843). At such times, *ukiyoe* artists and others whose art relied on humor and satire found themselves straddling official intolerance and the public's thirst for sociopolitical critique. Utagawa Kuniyoshi gilded his reputation as an eccentric by crossing this line. As part of the Tenpō Reforms, an 1842 edict forbade artists from drawing caricatures of kabuki actors and courtesans. Not only did the prohibition increase demand for such representations, it provided Kuniyoshi with a means of adding another layer of irony to his works. After the edict, Kuniyoshi won celebrity for portraits of kabuki actors that he drew as graffiti on walls around Edo. Though sometimes disguising his caricatures as goldfish, turtles, or cats, he made them easily recognizable. He also produced portraits of twelfth-century heroes from the Genpei War (1180–1185), and his audience had little trouble finding in these works parodic jabs at the existing political system.[31] Games, riddles, puns, puzzles, intentional mistakes and deceptions, the personification of animals—for Kuniyoshi, all were means of parody. His 1843 triptych "Minamoto Raikō and the Earth Spider" depicted the famous warrior Minamoto Yorimitsu (948–1021) sick in bed, protected against hordes of monsters by his lieutenants the Four Heavenly Kings. There was little doubt that the scene actually portrayed the sick government, represented by notorious senior councilor Mizuno Tadakuni (1794–1851), being protected from the rebellious masses by his elder statesmen (*rōjū*).[32] Kuniyoshi was detained following accusations of the work's presumed political innuendo, but was later released when investigations failed to produce evidence. Though the printing blocks were seized, imitations quickly appeared and sold rapidly. Ten years later, Kuniyoshi was fined for political satire, this time for a print of the artist Iwasa Matabei (1578–1650).[33]

Like Hokusai, Kuniyoshi was also involved in the production of several illustrated *kijinden*. He generated a series of lavishly colored prints titled *Chūkō meiyo kijinden* (Lives of remarkable people renowned for loyalty and virtue, 1845–1846), which paid tribute to an array of historical figures, ranging from Miyamoto Musashi to Ikkyū's courtesan Jigoku (Hell) to Gyokuran's grandmother Kaji. Of particular interest is his *Dainihon kijin gazō: Fūzoku kōmei ryakuden* (already discussed), whose seemingly random groupings of figures from disparate eras and settings produce a strange, comic effect. The only discernable pattern within the otherwise arbitrary groups is an absence of figures associated with professional schools of art. For Kuniyoshi, apparently, an artist had to be antiestablishment to qualify as a *kijin*.[34] Hanagasa Bunkyō, the work's coauthor, relates the circumstances under which it was conceived.

> Books record facts for later generations. Portraits reproduce appearances but try to make them new in some way. That is why they come to be called *ukiyoe*. My friend, Ichiyūsai [Kuniyoshi], by skillfully painting the great ancients in today's visage, became known across the four seas. He illustrated brave heroes from far and wide, and, as his paintings were bold as well, was given the name Ichiyū [Brave One].
>
> This book originated long ago when Kuniyoshi made a playful sketch one evening. [Presently the book took shape,] but he did not publish it for a long time. A bookstore heard of its existence and, thinking it shameful not to circulate it, decided to issue the work in two volumes under the title *Yūbi kijinbutsu* [Eccentrics brave and beautiful]. The store had no means by which to promote it, so I was asked to write something. Kuniyoshi heard about the publication plans and so repainted his works with people of different ages interacting with one another. . . .
>
> Later, the bookstore arbitrarily changed two characters in the title, making it *Kuniyoshi kijinbutsu* [Kuniyoshi's eccentrics]. It did so, not

because Kuniyoshi wished to promote himself, but because it desired his famous name to increase its sales.[35]

In this statement we find clear parallels with Kōkei's *KKD*. Like Kōkei, Bunkyō selects the most extraordinary subjects for inclusion without regard for social class. Yet the work also reveals how the *kijin* as a literary and aesthetic embodiment of difference had changed in the past half-century. Bunkyō makes no attempt to hide the term's use as a marketing device. Furthermore, while Kuniyoshi's intentional dehistoricization of his subjects becomes a playful gimmick that makes for entertaining reading, it also compromises the actual qualities and accomplishments by which these individuals earned celebrity. In other words, Kuniyoshi's pictures are bold and expressive, but they do not attempt to illustrate actual eccentricity. *Kijin* earn their place here less for their strangeness than for their notoriety.

Within an array of artistic genres and contexts, therefore, eccentric practice was paying for itself by converting mystique to financial benefit. But the term *kijin* also acquired currency beyond the cultural realm. Kōkei had applied it to a wide range of individuals, and certainly *Kinsei kijin-den*'s inclusion of heterodox scholars—Nativist Kamo no Mabuchi, Wang Yangming advocate Nakae Tōju, and Shingaku (Heart Learning) popularizer Teshima Toan (1718–1786), for instance—justified extending the term's usage to ideological and political matters. Intellectual heterodoxy had expanded and diversified throughout the century and recently been energized by interest in Dutch studies. For the *bakufu,* it was this growing attention to ideological alterity and alternate (strange) approaches to statecraft that necessitated the Prohibition of Heterodox Studies that same year. Such intersections between cultural and ideological strangeness helped extend usage of the term *kijin* into previously unrelated capacities.

One noted contingent whose political activities also coincided with the appearance of *KKD* was the so-called *Kansei sankijin* (Three *kijin* of Kansei), consisting of Hayashi Shihei (1738–1793), Takayama Hikokurō (1747–1793), and Gamō Kunpei (1768–1813). Imperial loyalists who knew each other but acted independently, these ideologues publically criticized *bakufu* corruption and fiscal incompetence. They also saw the growing incidence of foreign incursions (both rumored and real) as evidence of Japan's naval inferiority and coastal vulnerability. Hayashi, whose family had lost samurai status following a crime committed by his father, advocated greater accessibility to education, the military occupation of Hokkaido, stronger national defenses, and mastery of Western military technologies. Soon after publishing *Kaikoku heidan* (On the military problems of a maritime nation, 1791), Hayashi was arrested and imprisoned for criticizing *bakufu* policy and inciting unrest. Copies of the book and its printing blocks were destroyed. Takayama, closely following Hayashi's cause, walked the length of Japan preaching loyalty to the emperor. He was detained in 1793 and, six days after Hayashi had died of illness, forced to commit ritual suicide. With the Kansei Reforms ending the same year, censorship and enforcement relaxed enough for Gamō to continue advocating a combination of royalism (*sonnō*) and exclusionism (*joi*). For the next twenty years he wrote studies of the imperial institution and indictments of the country's military unpreparedness.[36]

Although persecuted in their own lifetimes, Hayashi, Takayama, and Gamō proved inspirational to later activists and useful to the *bakufu*. Britain's victory over China in the Opium War (1840–1842) caused particular alarm over national security and magnified the visibility of political activists, many of whom resumed the very causes initiated by the *Kansei sankijin*. To the growing numbers of Nativists in the ranks of government, the *Kansei sankijin*'s xenophobic convervatism made sense, and before long some officials were responding accordingly. Mito (Ibaraki) domain instituted Hayashi's recommendations for its own coastal defenses and lobbied the *bakufu* to do likewise, and later the *bakufu* would use Hayashi's *Kaikoku heidan* in its reevaluation of shoreline defenses. Restoration loyalist Yoshida Shōin (1830–1859) was inspired by all three, particularly Takayama, who had most forcefully advocated Wang Yangming's unification of reason and action. For Yoshida and his students, the inadequacy of the *bakufu*'s response to foreign threats warranted precisely the sort of strange, wild acts of extremist rebellion initiated by Hayashi, Takayama, and Gamō.[37]

This trio had been dubbed *Kansei sankijin* as early as 1815, the term *kijin* here signifying not eccentricity but patriotic, self-sacrificial activism.[38] Subsequently, *ki* became a validation of political defiance. And while *ki* represented a challenge to political stability, some late-Tokugawa dissidents also applied it to the restoration of political stability. To this extent, for those engaged in political protest *ki* could be interpreted as moral righteousness or as inseparable from political reform itself.[39] *Ki* coursed through the spirit of *joi* (expel the barbarian), best represented by the Kiheitai, Chōshū's samurai-commoner army that formed in 1863 around Takasugi Shinsaku (1839–1867). As Takasugi noted, the Kiheitai's endeavors were not only *ki* in the sense of opposing the *bakufu,* but also included a healthy helping of madness (*kyō*).[40] Yoshida Shōin, from Chōshū, likewise implicated his own madness in *Kyōfu no gen* (Testimony of a madman, 1858), a manifesto petitioning the military mobilization of Chōshū. Indeed, recognizing the madness of their cause, both for its treasonous nature and for the impossibility of its success, a core group of revolutionary "men of high purpose" (*shishi*) took pseudonyms invoking *kyō*. Shōin's student and future prime minister Yamagata Aritomo (1836–1922), also from Chōshū, adopted the name Kyōsuke (Crazy Boy). The Chōshū samurai Takasugi Shinsaku, another of Yoshida's favored students, variously referred to himself as Tōyō Ikkyōshō (Crazy Man of Eastern Japan) and Seikai Ikkyōshō (Crazy Man of Western Japan). The Buddhist monk Gesshō (1817–1858), who collaborated closely with Saigo Takamori's (1828–1877) *sonnō jōi* activities in the 1850s, called himself Seikyō (Pure Madness). Gesshō died in an attempted double suicide with Saigo, who survived.[41] By the period's end, then, signifiers of strangeness (*ki*) and madness (*kyō*) had been appropriated by multiple interests and converted into signifiers of political opposition.

PAINTING TREATISES (*GARON*) AND AESTHETIC STANDARDIZATION

Politicization of the term *kijin* also corresponded to greater political involvement among previously apolitical *bunjin*. This is explained in part by the fact that greater numbers of samurai holding official posts were taking leadership roles within *bunjin* circles. Uragami Gyokudō (1745–1820), Tanomura Chikuden, Tani Bunchō (1763–1840), Rai San'yō (1780–1832), and Watanabe Kazan (1793–1841), all among the most influential painters of the early nineteenth century, held official posts either prior to or during their activities as artists. And despite their accountability to superiors and susceptibility to punishment, many developed critical views of Tokugawa governance. After the failed efforts of his forebears Sakai Hōitsu (1761–1828) and Kameda Bōsai (1752–1826), Chikuden submitted petitions opposing various domainal policies. He, along with Gyokudō, ultimately resigned his post.[42] Scholar-artist Rai Sanyō formulated an evolutionary view of history in his *Nihon gaishi* (An unofficial Japanese history, 1826), a dangerously irreverent work that Tetsuo Najita calls "the single most influential interpretive history of late Tokugawa," declaring that military usurpation of power from the imperial house had resulted in political incompetence and social depravity.[43] Such sentiments reveal new intersections forming between artistic practice and political awareness, as well as growing tendencies toward open dissent.

This generation of *bunjin* was also conflicted in matters of aesthetics. On the one hand, limited accessibility to Chinese manuals and paintings had encouraged innovations among earlier *nanga* artists that had helped free the genre from artistic correctness (*sei*). On the other hand, the accomplishments of those generations had brought to the *bunjin* arts increasing exposure and appeal, making later *bunjin* aware of themselves as custodians of an extraordinary lineage with its own rubrics of correctness. Taking this responsibility seriously, they approached art as a body of knowledge to be apprehended intellectually as a formal process. For many practitioners this involved writing treatises on painting (*garon*) that articulated aesthetic standards in terms of *sei,* thereby encapsulating these standards within an established framework. Sakazaki Shizuka finds that, among all *kinsei* period artistic treatises, twenty are on *nanga* painting, while only seven are from the Kanō professional school, three are on Western painting, two on *ukiyoe,* and one each from various other schools.[44]

In their prioritization of realism and the subjective content of painting, most of the twenty *nanga* works consciously aligned themselves with Chinese treatises.[45] Typically composed in Chinese, they closely emulated the technical and theoretical principles of continental writings. As Chineseness became tantamount to correctness, some took this Sinophilia to extremes. The Osaka saké brewer and *sencha* devotee Tanaka Kakuō (1782–1848) was so intent on making his *sencha* practice authentic that in 1832 he contacted Nagasaki merchants to place an order for imported Chinese water. A year later, three eighteen-liter bottles arrived. Kakuō's *sencha* cohort considered this treasure too valuable to consume themselves and so, in order to share its benefits with the entire city, emptied it upstream in the Yodo River, Osaka's source of drinking water.[46] Most painters, similarly, considered it a great compliment to be told that their works looked Chinese. Indeed, Tanomura Chikuden could receive no greater praise than to hear fellow painter Rai Sanyō's reaction to his work: "Chinese! Chinese! He's truly Chinese!"[47]

The Sinophilia endemic to early nineteenth-century *garon* also contributed to a petrification within the genre that stifled nonconformity and individualism, the very energies that had originally generated the literati subculture. Treatises by Chikuden and Kanai Ujū (1796–1857), for instance, advocated "inspired copying" rather than "imitative copying," maintaining that superior painters must grasp originality while honoring their predecessors. Innovation must thus remain wedded to tradition itself, while gratuitous displays of eccentricity or novelty were to be avoided.[48] While this mildly paradoxical mandate was open to interpretation, most *nanga* treatise writers sought to minimize strangeness in their collective pursuit of an authentic standard. Both in theory and in practice, therefore, the public nature and standardizing function of *garon* were antithetical to the inclinations of originality. Uragami Shunkin (1779–1846) also exhibited a devotion to conformity that inverted the individualism that had guided his father Gyokudō's generation. In *Rongashi* (On painting and poetry, 1842), he writes: "Learning painting is like practicing Zen: one can squander away many years sitting in meditation. Though one accumulates a mound of worn-out brushes it may all amount to nothing. . . . We must read, consult the old masters, forget the self, and follow the way of nature."[49] This is an instructive statement, not because it expresses anything particularly new, but because it reveals a divergence from earlier *nanga* practice. Shunkin's call to "forget the self" advocates retreat from overdeliberation and self-absorption. While coming close to invoking conformity, Shunkin's appeal nevertheless dutifully echoes treatises from Ming and Qing period China. His appeal to "consult the old masters" cites the standard laws by which *bunjin* defined themselves, and his reference to reading reiterates the Chinese literati credo to "read ten thousand books, travel ten thousand *ri*" espoused earlier by Chikuden and others in their own writings.[50] We thus find in Shunkin's statement a rejection of originality and a devotion to learned collective knowledge.[51]

Conservatism evident in treatise writing was also informed by the Confucian view of the arts as means of moral cultivation. In *Gadō kongōsho* (Vajra on the way of painting, 1801), Nakabayashi Chikutō (1776–1853) avers that the artist should speak and act in a noble manner, for "a painting carries quality if it carries the soul within it. . . . One makes it one's own by submitting to the Heavenly Way. One must submit to one's heart, which in turn must submit to the past."[52] Chikuden's *Sanchūjin jōzetsu* (Chatter of a mountain dweller, 1813) and Anzai Un'en's (1806–1852) *Kinsei meika shogadan* (Discussions on calligraphy and painting by distinguished families, 1844) later affirm that excellence in art is indistinguishable from the artist's moral constitution.[53] Painting well, then, emerges from personal character that, through study, refinement, and due deference for tradition, has acquired the requisite moral qualities.

Third-generation *bunjin* were thus torn by a paradoxical mandate. While aware of the artistic merits of strangeness and originality, they were equally committed to approaching art through formal mastery of technical conventions and Confucian moralism. Chikuden, for example, revered the eccentricity of earlier artists like Taiga and criticized his own generation for abandoning autonomy and bowing to the tastes of patrons.[54] "After Taiga's death, painters copied his untrammeled brushwork to hide their own clumsiness and win popular approval. These followers were numerous," Chikuden wrote.[55] His *Sanchūjin jōsetsu* openly and repeatedly extolled the ethos of reclusive aestheticism characteristic of other eighteenth-century painters, and in its successive accounts of worthy *bunjin* the work occasionally takes the tone of a *kijinden* itself. Repeatedly bemoaning the state of their genre and the abilities of themselves and their contemporaries, painters like Chikuden believed themselves to be living an aftermath. And without doubt theirs was an age that surrendered a spirit of individualism to a spirit of gatekeeping. Among them, the defiance of Shōhaku and zaniness of Kinkoku found no tangible legacy. Striving to recover *nanga*'s subcultural vision was an artificiality that yielded more of the same, and the best they could do was preserve an appreciation for Kien, Nankai, Taiga, and Buson. For Chikuden, however, preservation only affirmed himself as an anachronism. *Sanchūjin jōzetsu* voices the consensus of his contemporaries on this point:

> No one today can produce the calligraphy of [Ogyū] Sorai, [Itō] Tōgai, [Kitajima] Setsuzan, or [Hosoi] Kōtaku. Nor can anyone paint the works of Hyakusen, Kien, Taiga, or Buson. Why is this? It is only because vulgarity makes [modern men unable to do these things]. . . . I am eagerly awaiting the reappearance of [their] type of genius.
>
> One hundred years ago the laws of calligraphy and the theory of painting could not have been as complicated as those of the present time, which expend all possible efforts and are all-inclusive. Still, people today cannot reach the same level. The more detailed their endeavor becomes the more often it fails. The more skilled they become the more vulgar [the result]. It is for no other reason but that "in the past men studied to improve themselves, but today they study to impress others."[56]

Chikuden's self-condemnation underscored a pessimism toward his own times that was shared by *bunjin* representing a spectrum of ideological camps, including Nativists. The Nativist movement gathering momentum behind ideologues like Motoori Norinaga (1731–1801) and, later, Hirata Atsutane (1776–1843) included within its ranks numerous important writers and artists who mounted challenges against Chinese aesthetics. In most cases these did not include challenges to aesthetic standardization, however. Strangeness remained ideologically suspect. In *E no koto* (On painting, 1799), Norinaga himself offers a Nativist critique of aesthetic change:

> Painting well is making the subject look realistic. . . . When painting human subjects, one must make bandits appear lowly, the great appear great, and the virtuous appear virtuous. But painters these days don't think this way. It used to be that portraiture transmitted a level of virtue in accordance with the subject's rank. Now painters concern themselves only with the spirit of the brush, and as a result high, virtuous people appear humble and stupid. . . . Such ugly paintings are deplorable, for lovely people should not appear unsightly. Beautiful women should be painted as such, but nowadays they look ugly. Warriors look wrong, as well. They should be depicted as quiet and gentle to show their true nature, but these days they look more like demons. If we fill our books with such images, people from other countries will accept them as fact and think of all Japanese as demonic. Likewise, if foreigners see Japan's nobility looking vulgar and its beautiful women looking ugly they will accept it as true. When future generations of Japanese see these paintings they should see reflections of themselves.
>
> As a rule, Japanese paintings are rougher than Chinese, which contain more detail and precision. Therefore, even if a Japanese painting may be considered superior to a Chinese painting, the former will be defeated by the details—the fur of the animals, the feathers on the birds, the patterns on the leaves—of the latter. Chinese paintings look better, but in broad terms Chinese and Japanese painting both have points to admire and points to criticize, so one cannot conclude that one is superior to the other.[57]

Contrary to his stance on virtually all other foreign influences, Norinaga believed that Japanese artists could learn more from Chinese compositions. But this position also stressed painting as an ideological endeavor in its capacity to represent Japan and convey native morals. Art must not take liberties or violate the natural features of its subjects. Realism, he asserted, must be honored, but only a realism that in turn honored the virtues of the Japanese people, who, for Norinaga, were rightly represented by warriors, elites, and beautiful women. For Norinaga and his supporters, therefore, the desire for Japanese art to discover its own identity did not validate strangeness. Theirs was a conservative position aligned with mainstream *garon* on this point.

Against this unified front, a minority sought to recover native originality by denouncing uncritical adulation of foreign imports. Hiraga Gennai's well-known essay *Hōhiron* (On farting, 1774) derided intellectuals and literati who merely copied Chinese models without cultivating their own artistic visions. Regarding the popularity of Dutch studies, influential scholar Miura Baien (1723–1789) opined: "Westerners employ their minds in practical experiment. . . . In this way they uncover the finest detail. But there is natural principle (*jōri*) in heaven-and-earth, and as long as they still carry out their experimental observations without comprehending *jōri* they are still a long way from the truth."[58] Both opinions hold that blind devotion to the exotic compromises Japan's cultural integrity. The art critic Kuwayama Gyokushū contributed to this discourse in his *nanga* treatise *Gyokushū Gashu* (Collected works of Gyokushū, 1790), which argued against traveling to Nagasaki to learn from famous Chinese masters—a popular pilgrimage for curious literati. One could learn the secrets of Japan's local masters more quickly, he argued. Later, in *Kaiji higen* (Talks on rustic painting, 1799), Gyokushū held up the strange works of Taiga and Kumashiro Yūhi (1693–1772) as models of native artistic achievement.[59] Taiga and Yūhi are impassioned by their surroundings, giving them fresh perspectives, he asserts, and by embracing immediate experience and attuning their minds and senses to their surroundings they create paintings that are uniquely Japanese. "These artists fill their works with strange depictions of landscapes that amaze common people," he wrote supportively.[60] The joy of landscape painting lies in personal experience, in transcending Chinese theory and infusing art with a native personality.

The Third Generation

As we have seen, the nineteenth century's diversifying features—growing conservatism within the literati arts; the diffusion, commodification, and politicization of strangeness; and a growing sense of sociopolitical decline—created an array of outsiders and oddballs whose diversity problematizes classification as a unified generation. As a set of aesthetic topoi, *ki* also became more diffuse and generalized. First, its familiarity as a commercial phenomenon compromised its aesthetic potency. Second, conservatism in the field diminished potentials for innovation, relegating *ki* to the realm of spectacle. This section considers three eccentric aesthetes: Uragami Gyokudō (1745– 1820), Kagawa Kageki (1768–1843), and Watanabe Kazan (1793–1841), whose multiplicity will represent the diffuse forms of aesthetic eccentricity that emerged in the nineteenth century. All well-known contributors to late Tokugawa culture, collectively these controversial, sociopolitically marginal figures stood out as anomalies amidst the conservatism and conventionalism already discussed. They also exhibited uncompromising individuality that engendered important artistic achievements within an increasingly volatile cultural climate.

Gyokudō the Lawless

Uragami Gyokudō, an eclectic *bunjin* skilled at poetry, painting, and calligraphy, is best known as a master of the *kin* (C. *qin*), a Chinese seven-stringed zither (Fig. 6.1). He is also a transitional figure. On one hand he was individualistic, defiant, and exhibited the strong sense of independence that Ban

FIGURE 6.1 Uragami Shunkin, Uragami Gyokudō at age seventy. *Gyokudō shichijūsai juzō.* Hayashibara Museum of Art.

Kōkei had found so admirable in *kijin* like Hyōta and Baisaō. Yet he was also beset by a diminished capacity for detachment and a pessimism toward the state of the artistic field, both characteristics of nineteenth-century *bunjin* generally. While lauded as an authentic vestige of the *bunjin*'s "golden age," therefore, he also represented a more contemporary, less remarkable demographic.

Gyokudō was a middle-ranking samurai whose loyalty and diverse abilities propelled him into remarkably high positions. By the time he withdrew from official service at age fifty, he held the posts of Chief Inspector (*ōmetsuke*) and Administrator of Temples and Shrines (*jisha bugyō*) for Bizen (Okayama) domain. But occupational success did not mitigate his increasing disillusionment with *bakufu* policy, particularly senior councilor Matsudaira Sadanobu's crackdown on heterodox studies, and in 1794 he abandoned his residence, moved into his son Shunkin's house in Kyoto, and devoted himself to the arts. He passed his days in leisure, wandering about with his *kin* on his back, looking for a likely piece of ground to sit and strum. His playing often drew crowds of appreciative onlookers, this fact embarrassing Shunkin's wife enough to keep her at home. Sugimoto Shutarō guesses that, had Ban Kōkei produced his *kijinden* a few years later, Gyokudō's carefree wandering and scandalous behavior would have made a fitting entry.[61]

Others see Gyokudō's eccentricity as less behavioral and more aesthetic, but clearly both were fueled by his fondness for alcohol. Gyokudō's friend Chikuden relates that Gyokudō considered inebriation a requisite preparation for painting, and that he occasionally got drunk ten or more times before finishing a work. His work indeed exhibits a conspicuous recklessness, such as his habit of using overly wet brushes or scratching texture into paintings so as to cause the ink to pass through to the back—a recklessness that Chikuden commends.[62] While Umehara Takeshi calls his brash painting style reflective of true madness (*kyōki*) and the essence of *ki* (*ki no naka no ki*), it defies precise categorization.[63]

Gyokudō himself did not formally articulate his aesthetic sensibilities in writing. The closest he came to explicating his view of artistic virtuosity is commentary on what he took to be superior works. In *Jishiki Gyokudō kabe* (Gyokudō's wall, 1797) he comments at length on five Ming period landscape paintings that he had brought to an exhibition in Shikoku in 1793. Here Gyokudō concludes that contemporary artists could not reproduce such feats of technical excellence. What he found so genuine in these five "friends" is their depiction of pure human life from an utterly detached vantage point.[64] For example, he praises a painting by Chang Yuan-feng (early sixteenth c.) that sets a rustic hut and a cliff against an empty backdrop, inviting the viewer to imagine another world beyond the self. This embedded potentiality of transcendence, he laments, was absent in the sort of painting then being produced in Japan. Others at the exhibition saw and imitated these five paintings, but Gyokudō's own imitations—a kind of free interpretation informed by personal emotional outpourings—were utterly unique. In their rejection of craftsmanship and detail, they manifested his internal affectations and creative freedom at the moment of creation.[65]

In a number of compelling poems and statements, in fact, Gyokudō himself commented on his lifelong disinterest in formalized study of Chinese models. The most confessional was an introspective, semiautobiographical passage in *Jishiki Gyokudō kabe:*

> I, Gyokudō the *kin* player, was orphaned as a child. I started [Confucian] studies at age nine and also studied the *kin* for a long time, for I had no talent for anything else. Being dense, I had no knowledge of the arts of chess (*shōgi*) and fencing. By day I would sit in a small room, book in hand, but presently I would grow weary of study and begin plucking the *kin* and singing softly. I liked to read but did not understand the words of the ancients and so just closed my eyes. Clearly, I was unfit to be a scholar. I liked to play the *kin* but did not understand the pitches and so played merely for my own enjoyment. Clearly, I was unfit to be a *kin* master. I wrote essays but, lacking eloquence, wrote only to satisfy my own will. Clearly, I was unfit to be a literatus. When I wrote calligraphy it was without knowledge of the Eight Laws, writing only in ways that suited myself. Clearly, I was unfit as a calligrapher. I painted but, not knowing the Six Laws of Painting, was content to swipe my brush about aimlessly. Clearly, I was unfit to be a painter as well.[66]

On another occasion Gyokudō revealed his impatience with what he saw as an overintellectualization of painting: "When I approach composition all I can do is proceed by painting haphazardly. Deliberating on how best to craft an image puts me in a quandary. My mind becomes cluttered with pointless rules and techniques. When it comes to that, it is so much better to simply throw down the brush and gaze at a real landscape."[67] Elsewhere he wrote: "I never paint in ways that adhere to the Six Laws. I just paint randomly (*midari ni*)."[68] Such confessions reveal more than the typically self-effacing language expected of *bunjin*.[69] Gyokudō's impatience precluded any possibility of technical precision demanded by the Six Laws, and one gathers that this sort of personal failure was an inevitability he had learned to accept.

His self-declared "lawlessness" was by no means heretical, however. Indeed, such tributes to freedom and carelessness reveal a sound knowledge of Chinese art and literature. He articulated his fondness for nature, reclusiveness, and *kin* playing, for example, through the rhetoric of Tao Qian. And despite claims to the contrary, Gyokudo's painting and poetry reveal a dialogic relationship with Chinese sources, including variations on verses from Du Fu (712–770) and Su Shi (1036–1101).[70] This ode to utter uselessness, for example, closely invokes the tributes to aesthetic detachment ubiquitous in Chinese recluse poetry:

> When I feel tired I call for wine.
> After recovering I sometimes write poetry.
> Playing the *ch'in* is actually wearisome;
> To be idle is naturally best of all.[71]

And yet, despite Gyokudō's admiration for and thematic adherence to Chinese works, he was able to avoid drawing on them stylistically, a principal reason for his reputation as an eccentric. His originality was so strong that "he transmuted whatever influences he received" and drove off all potential followers.[72] More than any other artist discussed here, Gyokudō is distinctive for holding steadfastly to a personal artistic style despite close involvement with more conventional *bunjin* contemporaries.

Minagawa Kien's (1734–1807) comments provide one possible explanation for this artistic independence. Kien, who had guided Gyokudō's aesthetic development since childhood, wrote that as a painter Gyokudō possessed boundless talent and an unrestrained desire for self-expression. His poetry, Kien continued, drew on inspiration from his painting, and his painting drew on inspiration from his *kin* playing.[73] Gyokudō indeed considered himself a musician above all else, and it would be natural to assume that he utilized his sense of musical expression to ground his other artistic endeavors. Among *bunjin*, this is an attribute particular to Gyokudō and suggests how he was able to retain stylistic originality at a time when *nanga* practice was moving in the opposite direction.

Gyokudō's lawlessness, then, was a rejection of imitation. "Being addicted to habits of the past disallows anything different," he once protested, implying that those who copy others do not know themselves, whereas those who (after a taste of wine) develop their own style acquire greater self-awareness.[74] From there, and in full recognition of those who came before, one is then able to construct one's own laws. Herein lies Gyokudō's eccentricity, for among his contemporaries few deigned to reject artistic correctness. It was a rejection that trumpeted what others knew but feared to utter: that their skills served them well as imitators but not as true innovators.

Despite his independence, Gyokudō never sought isolation. Throughout his long retirement he lived in material comfort while maintaining a large circle of friends, patrons, and students, and his inclusion in the 1813 issue of *Heian jinbutsushi* lends testimony to his local celebrity. Especially during the last decade of his life, however, his paintings betrayed a "dark and brooding spirit" that reflected a lifetime of emotional turmoil. Art and music were sources of solace, particularly following the deaths of his wife (1792), only daughter (1796), and close mentor Kien (1807).[75] They were also an outlet for tensions deriving from the threat of official harassment due to his interest in Yōmeigaku. Gyokudō developed this interest through interactions with Kawamoto Ryūken (d. 1790), who taught it at a private academy in Bizen. When the Prohibition of Heterodox Studies proscribed such studies in 1790, Ryūken closed his academy and committed suicide. Gyokudō's own large library of Wang Yangming's writings was also closed after the prohibition. Addiss hints that Gyokudō may have fallen under official suspicion for his associations at this time, and Rosenfield suggests that this subjugation profoundly affected Gyokudō's estimation of *bakufu* statecraft.[76] Moreover, Yōmeigaku seems to have provided the intellectual impetus for him to pursue an "antisocial" calling of emotional indulgence over social respectability. Adherence to intuitive action as taught by Wang connected Gyokudō at a fundamental level to the subcultural energies from which literati art had originally emerged but which others of his generation were loath to imitate.[77]

Kageki the Reformer

As a pastime, *waka* was eclipsed by the popularity of *haikai,* its study and practice preserved mostly by scholars, Nativists, and those associated with the imperial court. In the late eighteenth century, the proprietary and exclusionary culture surrounding *waka* training loosened, however, allowing for less codified, more personalized practice. Accordingly, *waka* came to attract a broader, more plebian patronage that privileged personal affectation over formalized craftsmanship.[78] Though born a low-ranking samurai, Kagawa Kageki assumed leadership of a small commoner's movement challenging traditional *waka* poetics. A tall, gaunt, pallid figure with crooked teeth and a large nose, Kageki was a portrait of strangeness, and throughout his life he seemed to attract discord and controversy (Fig. 6.2). At twenty-six he eloped with a woman from his native Tottori domain to Kyoto, where he was adopted by the poet Kagawa Kagemoto (1745–1821). The free-thinking Kageki had difficulty studying under others, however, and he later parted ways with Kagemoto by mutual agreement. While maligned in Edo, for much of the early nineteenth century he was the foremost *waka* poet in Kyoto, where he evoked a mixture of revulsion and awe for the remainder of his career.

As Bashō had fought to imbue *haikai* with an affective sophistication worthy of high art, Kageki toiled to rescue *waka* from elitist traditionalism and convert it to a medium of human feeling. This involved wresting it from

Figure 6.2   Kagawa Kageki. Rinsen Shoten.

professional schools by renouncing their esoteric teachings. Kageki developed such ideas through his association with Ozawa Roan (1723–1801), who held that the essence of *waka* emanates not from study but from one's heart and mind. "If this country is to forge its own way of poetry," Roan insisted, "*waka* cannot be caught up in being witty, noble, humorous, gentle, or unusual"; it must be spontaneously natural.[79] Though Kageki received informal instruction from Ozawa, taking him as a formal teacher would have restricted his own poetic independence. He did, however, use Ozawa's views on poetry as a point of departure for his own. Following the notion that *waka* must "forge its own way," Kageki converted Ozawa's insistence on reason into an insistence on individuality, famously concluding that "A *waka* is not something reasoned, but something tuned."[80] His description of poetry as a "tuning" (*shirabe*) is roughly analogous to that of spirit consonance (*ki*), the most important of the Six Laws reiterated by centuries of painters. Both concepts refer to the artist's endeavor to achieve an interpenetration of subject and object. Traditional *waka* had sought to achieve ingenuity through the use of rhetorical devices like pivot words (*kakekotoba*), which Kageki felt hindered emotional spontaneity. *Shirabe,* on the other hand, redirected attention from pretense and form to genuine emotional depth. In *Kagaku teiyō* (Poetics, 1850), Kageki professed that pivot words neutralize the affective depth and thereby lower the quality of *waka*. One's singular objective had to be emotional sincerity.[81]

Kageki's attacks incited angry rejoinders, principally from Nativist schools in Edo disgusted by his *waka*'s crudeness. In their use of rustic imagery, colloquial language, and light humor, even his serious compositions drew criticism as *haikaika,* "eccentric verses" with *haikai*-like qualities.[82]

> *Haru no no no no ukaregokoro wa hate mo nashi tomare to iishi chō wa tomarinu*
> [My buoyant heart is as boundless as the field of this spring day—
> A butterfly stops to rest, just as I commanded it.][83]

This poem's first part is both playful in its alliterative use of "o" sounds and self-indulgent in its focus on personal joy. Even more shocking to his critics, the second half refers to a popular children's song. Overall its effect suggests the sort of light but mundane snapshot typically reserved for *haikai*. For traditionalists who opposed the modernization and popularization of *waka,* this alone was sufficient proof that Kageki was simply "ignorant." His poetry's "vulgar" and "perverted" propensity for self-reflection, they chided, amounted to nothing more than egotism.[84] "It is contemptible that anyone so arrogant could write such amateurish verse and consider it poetry," wrote Edo affiliates of the school founded by Kamo no Mabuchi.[85] Continuing, they remarked that Kageki's *waka* would never be socially accepted because, under the pretense of being new, it purported to say what should not be uttered. His "tuning" was laughable in its lack of principle (*ri*), they continued, and its inability to distinguish between good and evil did no more than incite social unrest.[86]

Kageki's *Niimanabi iken* (A divergent view of New Learning, 1815), a rebuttal of Kamo no Mabuchi's *Niimanabi* (New Learning, 1765), responded to Edo Nativists by opposing Kokugaku's traditionalism.[87] Mabuchi's view of language is mistaken, the essay maintains; meanings do not change, only the sounds and pronunciations change. Borrowing from Bashō's poetics, Kageki stressed that *waka* must be a product of the present time and place. "These days *waka* is not of the official sphere, nor is it about rewarding good and punishing evil. This attempt to systematize it with rules serves only to confuse people," he wrote.[88] Restricting oneself to archaic language which so many find unintelligible "is like hating oneself [as a modern person]."[89] Moreover, compositions about famous places, people, or objects beget an artificiality that degrades the art form. Instead, he explained, poetry must be an honest investigation of one's own feelings.

Maligned in Edo and controversial even in his home of Kyoto, Kageki confronted opposition for much of his career. In fact, the Kyoto literary establishment, including Ban Kōkei, generally approved of the aspersions coming from Edo, and in 1811 court poets attempted to put an end to his teaching activities.[90] Yet Kageki remained defiant in the face of all criticism. He had an especially dismissive view of Kōkei and other scribblers of prose, a craft that Kageki felt he had long since surpassed as a poet. "I am content even if my *waka* is flawed," he averred. "I am content, and wherever I go I am determined to explain to everyone the correct path. Even if I incur the wrath of Heaven I will not give up the ambitions of my youth. I will have no regrets and will continue blazing this trail even if it kills me!"[91]

Like Gyokudō's claim to lawlessness, this declaration must have neutralized any possibility for further dialogue. It is no coincidence that the unrepentant willfulness of such statements recalls the rhetoric echoed by Yōmeigaku proponents. At age twenty-eight (1795) Kageki had studied with Igai Keisho (1761–1845), a Confucian scholar and proponent of the Eclectic School's (*setchūgaku-ha*) integration of Zhu Xi, Ancient Learning, and Wang Yangming. Kageki professed that Wang's teachings were well suited to the study of poetry, and it is clear that his approach to *waka* was informed in part by Wang's defense of individual intuition.[92] Kageki's explanation of *shirabe* and sincerity (*makoto*), for example, share close parallels with Wang's rhetoric, and his unification of the two mimics Wang's unification of intuitive knowledge and action.[93]

Despite the controversy surrounding Kageki's newfangled poetics, we occasionally find an interesting unanimity in his reception by both critics and supporters. He was labeled a *daitengu* (great braggart) and a Christian by his enemies, and a *tengu* (an extraordinary talent) by his own disciples.[94] His is "a poetry of wildness" (*kyō*), quipped Ueda Akinari critically, but his verses were also so judged by his admirers. In *Fude no saga* (Evils of the brush, 1802), Murata Harumi (1746–1811) criticized Kageki as "a man in Kyoto who goes around boasting that he is the only one who can write poetry these days."[95] Yet it was this charismatic self-assurance that brought him success. Indeed, not only was his *waka* considered off-kilter, Kageki himself earned a reputation for madness around Kyoto. His student Kinoshita Takafumi (1779–1821) labeled him a genuine *kyōjin,* claiming that both his views and his verses violated common sense, and that while his intelligence made him an outstanding poet, he would be impossible to associate with were it not for his extraordinary magnanimity. Some years later Kinoshita overcame his aversion and became Kageki's student. Clearly, even Kageki's critics were drawn to his talent.[96]

Kageki attracted between 1,500 and 2,000 students, many of them women, and his Keien School of *waka* remained influential for the remainder of the Tokugawa period. Few could deny that he had challenged and successfully revised the Way of *waka*.[97] Such accomplishments were not products of an intentionally forged aesthetic strangeness. Kageki was called a *tengu,* a *kyōjin,* and his poems were deemed works of madness because his Way was born from an obstreperous personality and an extraordinary aesthetic sensibility. In this sense he represented an alternate form of aesthetic strangeness in the early nineteenth century.

Kazan the Defeated

As a samurai disenchanted with the *bakufu*'s ineffectuality and apathy toward Western learning, Watanabe Kazan recalls the progressive patriotism of the *Kansei sankijin.* His turning to art as a source of solace evokes Chikuden and Gyokudō. Kazan was not an activist, however, and he differed from Chikuden and Gyokudō in his inability to isolate his art from political scrutiny, a danger that earlier *nanga* painters had taken care to avoid. Kazan's intelligence fueled his downfall as both a political thinker and an artist, for while his loyalty garnered the esteem of his superiors, his independence, foresight, and study of the West alienated him politically.

Kazan served as an official in Edo for the Tahara domain, but as an avid student and advocate of Western learning he developed adversarial political views that prompted him to criticize the *bakufu*'s isolation policies and poor fiscal management. In 1837, the American ship SS *Morrison* entered Japanese waters in search of trade. When *bakufu* forces repelled it with cannon fire, Kazan wrote *Shinkiron* (A timely warning, 1838) criticizing this action as backward and self-defeating. Though he stopped short of calling for a repeal of the seclusion policy, it is clear that he viewed it as destructive to national interests. In fact, Kazan's was only one among a cacophony of voices then being raised against *bakufu* corruption and incompetence. The year of the *Morrison* incident witnessed a record number of uprisings by samurai and peasants alike, and even Tokugawa Nariaki (1800–1860), the daimyo of Mito, came forth with criticisms of the seclusion policy. Such outcry required redress, and the following year Kazan and Dutch Learning devotees were rounded up and imprisoned. Six months later Kazan was returned to his domain and placed under permanent house arrest. He committed ritual suicide in 1841.

As an artist Kazan demonstrated natural talent from a young age, and by his twenties he was earning commissions, organizing painting exhibitions, and running his own studio. His application of Western painting techniques such as shading and vanishing-point perspective, however, developed into an extraordinary realism that distinguished him among contemporary painters. Knowledge and talent, while inciting the suspicions of fellow bureaucrats, made him exotic to fellow painters. His house arrest only enhanced his celebrity, the numerous visitors to his home fueling the ire and resentment of his detractors. While variously viewed as a traitor, a martyr, or a prophet of national enlightenment (*kaika*), Kazan was no revolutionary. His study of the West opened him to perspectives that eluded his contemporaries, while his unusual integration of free thinking and stringent Confucian moralism confused some and inspired others. Kazan's peer, the Yōmeigaku follower and *sonnō jōi* proponent Ōhashi Totsuan (1816–1862), wrote of him:

Kazan's body is pure and tough, like the tone of a resonating bell. When he takes up a brush, words and pictures flow forth seemingly without thought or effort. He wears a long sword and short hakama, so that a stranger would think him a warrior. When he visits Mr. X he gazes at pictures and maps of Western lands from morning to night without taking either food or tea, complimenting them persistently. I also heard from his family that Kazan sits in his room and spends half the night reading. His family says that it is normal for him to laugh loudly at the funny places, as if he were discussing them with someone. He is a bona fide *kijin*.[98]

Although seen as a *kijin,* Kazan's approach to art reveals a calculated integration of strangeness and correctness rather than the sort of free-wheeling improvisation characteristic of Gyokudō. In a letter to his disciple Tsubaki Chinzan (1801–1854), he clarifies his own thinking on the subject by citing a treatise by Southern School painter Hun Nan-tien (1633–1690): "Where there is a brush and ink there is a painting. Where there is spirit resonance (*in*) and elegant taste (*omomuki*) there are brush and ink. Refined elegance is synonymous with *in*. When the strangeness of *ki* is complete and extended to its limit, this is *omomuki*."[99] Kazan explains that painted forms must possess "spirit resonance" and "taste" to avoid becoming mere imitations of the subject on paper. And while "resonance" holds potential for both refinement and vulgarity, without *ki* it achieves neither. As we know from Gion Nankai's similar testimonial nearly a century earlier, such statements were not unusual among *bunjin*. Of interest is how Kazan uses *ki* to inform his mastery of correctness. Here *ki* is perceived, not in terms of antisocial abandon, as it had for eighteenth-century *kijin,* but as studied originality.

In *Issō Hyakutai* (A clean sweep: One hundred aspects, 1818), Kazan's condemnation of gratuitously "mad" painting further elaborates his views on aesthetic strangeness. Here he notes that the lower classes had begun painting those highbrow subjects and themes previously reserved for professional painters. This is a valuable development, he maintains, in that it helps to preserve customs and history, and, to the extent that painting carries the potential to teach good and evil, it can contribute to widespread moral cultivation. However, Kazan continues, the new works are vulgar in their excessive sensuality, as well as ignorant of past masters and painting styles; they neither preserve history nor encourage good and chastise evil. These new painters do not embody the spirit of *nanga*. "Mad" painting, moreover, like Buson's "exaggerated and deformed figures," could never have artistic or social value.[100]

In such statements, Kazan emerges as a conservative who understood *ki* as a deliberate, thoughtful aesthetic to be applied in ways consistent with Confucian correctness. And yet Kazan's painting was unique. He has been called the Edo period's last great painter, who "attained a degree of corporeality and psychological expressiveness unequaled before or after in traditional Japanese painting."[101] Indeed, his development of a distinctive hybrid of Japanese and Western expression helped to guide the course of Japanese art in the nineteenth century. And while art offered him a means of escape, guilt and agitation disallowed him any possibility of solace. In fact, Kazan brought an affective intensity to both political and artistic matters that pulled him in opposing directions. "I want to see through to the deepest layers and experience a lasting impression," he wrote, but his emotional intensity only magnified his internal conflict.[102] Loyalty to family and lord, attraction to unfettered aestheticism, thirst for knowledge through the study of foreign science and art, and devotion to political action as a remedy for social injustice—these various impulses could not be reconciled.

Kazan's snarl of compulsions thus took an emotionally destabilizing toll. He viewed his arrest and confinement as evidence of failure, which drove him deeper into depression. Overcome with remorse for incommoding his lord, the daimyo of Tahara, and even for the inconvenience that would be caused by his impending suicide, in letters he described himself as "a born loser," "unfilial and disloyal," and on a separate occasion confessed to extreme madness.[103] Unable to extricate his personal convictions from his official duties, Kazan's was a fully politicized eccentricity, an enlightened mind doused by a benighted government.

Prior to Ban Kōkei's *KKD,* eccentrics and eccentric art had been predominantly bourgeois phenomena whose patently apolitical positioning avoided confrontation with the Tokugawa regime. From the late eighteenth century, as economic instability, the erosion of the class system, and heightened urgency surrounding national security fostered a sense of societal decline, aesthetics of strangeness forked and proceeded along inconsistent trajectories as predominantly mass phenomena. The *bunjin* arts lost vitality, and aesthetic change was carried out by strong, uncompromising personalities like Kageki's whose charismatic strangeness catalyzed reform. Meanwhile, as *kijin* and *kijinden* were being marketed as commercial phenomena, *ki* and *kyō* were informing countercultural energies and political dissidents. These ranged from the moderately outspoken—samurai *bunjin* like Gyokudō and

Kazan who were disillusioned with the *bakufu*'s antiquated policies—to more extremist royalist cells.

Such developments posed several challenges to individualism and aesthetic originality. First, commercialization rendered strangeness familiar and less artistically significant. Second, treatise writing within *bunjin* circles codified and institutionalized the literati arts, precluding their tolerance for strangeness. Meanwhile, the visibility afforded by popularization brought strange aesthetics (*ki, kyō*) into broader sociopolitical contexts. The political intolerance of late Edo society interpreted intellectual eccentricity as dissent to be exterminated, the very reprisal exacted upon the *Kansei sankijin* and Watanabe Kazan. Being strange within a society that increasingly saw eccentricity as either a gimmick, aesthetically incorrect, or politically dangerous was still possible, however. It could be actualized through disassociation, as was carried out by Chikuden and Gyokudō, or by incontrovertible talent, as was achieved by Kageki. As the next chapter discusses, it was largely the efforts of non-*bunjin* eccentric personae that propelled the diffusion of aesthetic strangeness during the period's final years.

CHAPTER 7

Reevaluating Strangeness in Late Tokugawa

In many cases, early modern Japan's aesthetics of strangeness was a success story. A number of its protagonists—Baisaō, Taiga, Jakuchū, Shōhaku, Kageki—achieved extraordinary notoriety during their own lives and continue to be recognized as the period's greatest talents. Even those who faced occasional hostility or punitive reprisals for their antics—Nankai, Kien, Rosetsu, Kageki, Kazan—generally lived as local celebrities free of public contempt. The explosion of *kijinden* and the appropriation of *ki* by disparate interests across the social spectrum also indicate an infiltration of strangeness into late Tokugawa society.

The following discussions take stock of the preceding chapters with a view toward revisiting and revising certain faulty assumptions that have surrounded eccentric art in the Edo period. One such assumption interprets aesthetic strangeness as a product of late Edo's "culture of play" and lacking cultural importance.[1] It perceives the breakdown of hierarchies and the theatrical nature of late Edo life as evidence that superficiality and spectacle were eclipsing genuine innovation. A second, related misperception posits Japanese eccentric artists as having been timid and therefore failing in their presumed attempts at revolution.

This chapter concludes our study by problematizing such interpretations. Doing so will entail revisiting structures (*ga* and *zoku*) that have generated historiographical biases against the playful nature of late Edo urban culture, as well as reevaluating vestiges of modernization theory— specifically, the view that eccentric art drives historical change. It finds, first, that *kijin* not only opened up liberated spaces in which the amateur arts could function separately from officialdom, but that they expanded public faith in and tolerance for strangeness, which in turn acquired considerable cultural capital. Second, it shows that strangeness, which had long occupied a niche in premodern Japanese culture, rejected wanton wildness in favor of shrewd—not timid—experimentation positioned between the acceptable and unacceptable. That is, aesthetic eccentricity tended to be an inwardly directed interrogation of self rather than an externalized form of sociopolitical dissent. Implementation of a prudent "best practice," then, fostered a discovery and celebration of strangeness that indeed exerted lasting impacts on Japanese culture. Finally, an examination of self-portraiture in the Edo period will serve as a retrospective, a means of reviewing some of the artists and themes showcased in this study.

Mass Culture and Failure

The cultural impact of aesthetic strangeness has been overlooked due to its associations with the failure of late Edo culture itself, which has been viewed as a disappointing byproduct of sociopolitical decline. As we have seen, this perspective was advanced even by that period's own representative thinkers. Kokugaku icon Motoori Norinaga's tract *E no kato* criticized Japanese painters for their inability both to master Chinese painterly techniques and to develop praiseworthy native forms. Ueda Akinari and Tanomura Chikuden likewise bemoaned their own generation's lack of talent. Also finding little commendable about this period, Meiji period ideologues like Okakura Tenshin (1862–1913) and Ernest Fenollosa (1853–1908) viewed Tokugawa plebian art as amateurish, weak, tentative, and localized—all faults that prevented it from surpassing the sophistication of the professional Kanō and Tosa schools. Their condemnation derived from the view that aesthetics connects art to the state and exerts either deleterious or beneficial influences on the political whole. Fenollosa attributed the destruction of the Ming Dynasty, for example, to a contagion of heretical arts in China. Then, he relates, when Ming refugees arrived on Japanese shores and formed communities in Nagasaki and Kyoto, their heresy infected the ignorant masses: "A great school of Japanese 'bunjinga' fanatics now grew up in Japan, whose style in following the most misshapen cows, gentlemen with trepanned skulls, and wriggly-worm branches of their masters shows even in its deliberate distortion a certain distinction. . . . And yet from any universal point of view their art is hardly more than an awkward joke."[2]

In apparent agreement, many modern studies evade the problem of late Edo by reducing early modern aesthetics to discussions of the Genroku period. Toshihiko and Toyo Izutsu's *The Theory of Beauty in the Classical Aesthetics of Japan* and Ueda Makoto's *Literary and Art Theories in Japan,* for instance, cannot find much worthy of discussion after Matsuo Bashō. Treatment of Japanese aesthetics in *Sources of Japanese Tradition,* the singular authority in Japanese documentary history for half a century, does not go beyond the Genroku period either, but is content to characterize the last century of Tokugawa history in terms of tension between Neo-Confucian rationalism and nativistic revivalism. Michael Marra's groundbreaking work on Japanese aesthetics jumps from the Medieval to the Meiji period. Whether these studies are unsure of how to treat late Edo culture or consider it unworthy of treatment, it is clear that they view it as the end point of a progressive decline.

In part, the perceived deterioration of late Edo culture resulted from the erosion of high and low as a basic aesthetic framework. More critically, it also paralleled the gradual disintegration of boundaries between economic status groups. Early in the eighteenth century, aesthetic terms such as *fūga* (wind-blown elegance), *sui* (sophistication), *tsū* (connoisseurship), and *iki* (refinement; stylishness) emerged as expressions of privilege, signifying leisurely ideals for the privileged classes. Class boundaries in both urban and rural areas were progressively eroded by commercial expansion, however, and as aspirations for class advancement were rendered irrelevant, the aesthetics of the elite became those of the masses, therein losing their original function. "Aspiring culture" became well within reach, and aesthetics that had once served as markers of class, *ga* and *zoku* particularly, lost their oppositional relationship and exclusivity. As Bashō raised *haikai,* traditionally considered a *zoku* poetic form, to the level of *ga,* many of his successors ceased thinking of the two in rigidly dualistic terms. Yosa Buson's *ga zoku* theory, Takebe Ayatari's (1719–1774) treatise *Kanga shinan* (Guide to Chinese painting, 1779), as well as most of the treatises produced by nineteenth-century *nanga* painters, all reiterated the importance of avoiding vulgarity by reinventing *zoku* in the form of *ga.*[3] Producing art thus involved acknowledging it as a dialectical entity consisting of opposing currents—as both a prescribed Way (*dō*) and a heterodoxical "back street" (*ridō*). It also required mastery of both. By the early 1800s, therefore, *zoku* and *ga* were being integrated into popularized literature and painting, while *fūga, sui, iki,* and *tsū* were reduced to simple "descriptions of certain kinds of behaviour."[4]

The assimilation of high and low was an aesthetic criterion in itself and, while drawing the scorn of some, was widely viewed as a natural correction of artificial hierarchies. Gabō Sanjin's preface to *Haika kijindan* (1816), for instance, advocated dispensing with high and low altogether. Predetermined assumptions about *ga* and *zoku* distorts people's view of poetry and harms their understanding of elegance and vulgarity, Gabō observed.[5] In *Kana sōsetsu* (Kana preface, 1825), Ōta Nanpo also maintained that the form and substance of both terms were not mutually exclusive, noting simply that "the refined person who sports with *zoku* is the master of *ga*."[6]

Hierarchies eroded, and high and low lost meaning as a mutually exclusive binary, creating a vacuum filled by more liberated forms of expression, including millennialist abandon and a carnivalesque playfulness.[7] Such expressions afforded escape from the mundane tedium of daily life. This emergent mass culture, what H. D. Harootunian has framed as a rupture between culture and politics, absorbed the studied strangeness that had heretofore been admired by *bunjin* as evidence of high-mindedness.[8] *Ki*, as we have seen, also moved from an elite aesthetic to a mass aesthetic, exemplifying the attrition suffered by high culture in general. These developments caused strangeness to be interpreted as a facet of play and a byproduct of the fissure between culture and politics.

Scholarship on the playful decadence of late Edo urban society is generally content to explain it as a simple reaction to political oppression or to equate it with a pattern of political change involving the low overcoming the high (*gekokujō*). Prohibitions imposed on art and literature deemed to be immoral, some have argued, restricted artistic freedom and starved society for the unconventional. Under such conditions, any expressions of originality, especially those that challenged such regulations, were instantly attractive. In this sense, eccentricity was the new heroism of its day.[9] Nakanishi Susumu's study of *kyō* in Japanese history likewise concludes that *kyō* embraced the freedoms afforded by a world going to ruin. Exhibiting *kyō* enabled one to extricate oneself from complicity in those ruinous processes.[10] Others concur that the *kijin* phenomenon was a reaction against the conformity imposed by state control. Oppression, it is claimed, triggered countercultural responses via the only means available: expressions of eccentricity.[11] All such interpretations read late Edo strangeness as a form of political resistance.

There is little debate on this position. And *kijin,* as products of a frivolous culture of play and symbols of subversion that ultimately failed to overthrow the high, are subsequently dismissed as failed and historically inconsequential. Moreover, historiography advances several dubious claims about the nature and social impact of *kijin*. John Rosenfield maintains that the attitudes of eccentric painters were hostile to the Tokugawa order and to the "obedience, selflessness, frugality, modesty and diligence" of Neo-Confucian orthodoxy.[12] Their hostility, he argues, was directed at the state's tight control over daily life, and yet as political activists *kijin* failed to operate outside Neo-Confucian parameters. Their attempts at subversion failed because strangeness, their weapon of dissent, was inadequate as a means of reform. Because their art was cautious and conformist, Rosenfield continues, they were chained to convention and unable to achieve a degree of subversion comparable to that attained by their Western counterparts.[13] The fact that *kijin* were admired and celebrated rather than socially alienated only accentuates their failure as subversives. Saeki Shōichi also compares *kijin* unfavorably to Western eccentrics. Whereas artistic eccentricity in England expressly opposed the puritanical influences of the Church, Saeki argues, the equivalent movement in Japan was moderate. *Kijin* failed to develop a sense of civil liberty and so were unable to employ *ki* as an expression of political rebellion.[14] Yoshimura Teiji affirms that Japan's eccentric artists did not use art to help acquire civil rights. Consequently, art became "narrow, impoverished, and irrelevant in a world that stank of hypocrisy."[15]

The commercialization of *ki* in late Edo has also drawn laments from literary critic Ishikawa Jun, who observes that by definition *kijin* were individuals aligned with heaven. As intermediaries between the heavenly and the human realms, *kijin* originally functioned as society's apostles. Ban Kōkei's *kijinden* vulgarized them, however, by reducing them to the level of plebian amusement. True *kijin* thus died out in early modern Japan, Ishikawa argues, because Kōkei's and subsequent publications confused the sacred with the bizarre.[16]

Not only did the propagation and urbanization of eccentricity cheapen the *kijin* as a social identity, historians claim, they denigrated aesthetic reclusion as a general practice. Eccentricity was also denigrated by the impoverished, passively withdrawn nature of typical Japanese recluses, they continue. Compared to their Chinese counterparts, who, as elites, did not experience hardships or practice celibacy, Japanese recluses lived poorer, more austere lives. Lacking the ability to compete, they lost the fight for social survival and retreated into isolation. Defeated individuals like the monk Zendayū, who carried a pine log on his shoulders from Kamakura to Edo to build a hut for himself, and the monk Tōsui (anthologized in *KKD*), who ate food left by a dead beggar, harbored no bitterness toward the world as Chinese recluses did. Lacking the wherewithal to enter society's struggle for survival and demonstrating no will to protest against it, they represent only weakness and defeat.[17] It is also argued that Japanese recluses tended to live in public settings, retain a sense of public service, and perform their duties without displays of open dissent. And because they adhered to communal mores and harbored no inclination toward protest, they ultimately served no social function or benefit.[18] Moreover, their so-called aestheticism consisted of little more than empty observances. As urban commoners became more active in the *bunjin* arts and relocated those arts within urban centers, their eventual appropriation of reclusion rendered it a meaningless façade.[19]

If strangeness failed to actualize either political dissent or genuine artistic innovation, others conclude, it is better explained as a commercial gimmick to capitalize on the playful, theatrical nature of the times. Theatrics were indeed a part of public life. Standardized arts like tea ceremony and flower arrangement, greetings and much of formal speech generally, the pageantry of official functions, and the alternate attendance processions to and from Edo were all layers of formulaic performance that obstructed original expression.[20] If public life was a kind of theater, those who produced and marketed it, including artists, of necessity took pains to showcase themselves. For them, eccentricity was a form of advertisement.

Kabuki, which lay at the center of the theatrics characterizing late Edo public life, will serve as an example. Kabuki had flourished as a wellspring of both strangeness and political subversion since the early 1600s. The term *kabuki odori* itself meant "tilted," eccentric dance. Early actors mixed outlandish performances with sexual innuendo, while gangs of street toughs (*kabukimono*) emulated their swagger and provocative fashions. The *bakufu*, quickly recognizing kabuki's complicity in fueling dangerous oppositional energies, imposed regulations mandating who could perform, who could attend, the subjects of its plays, and the numbers and locations of its theaters. Forbiddance, of course, only magnified kabuki's cultural allure. At one point authorities even attempted to eradicate the art altogether, an aim it soon recognized as unrealistic.[21] Within this restrictive climate, kabuki remained ostentatious and provocative. It developed elaborate costumes, sets, and technical devices to achieve maximally emotional and dramatic effects; its actors dazzled audiences with exhibitionism and fantasy; and its plays, their political content only thinly veiled, bespoke a pessimism toward contemporary society.

Kabuki's capacity for individual expressiveness suffered, however. By the eighteenth century it had become increasingly rigid and dominated by lineages of signature actors specializing in specific types of roles (*yakugara*) and proprietary styles inherited from their predecessors. Originality faded as each generation mastered, preserved, and only minimally reinterpreted their repertoire of performative forms (*kata*). In the worst cases, performances consisted of stylized conventions and gimmicks, while long-running productions were so well known that their theatrical interest hinged on a series of predetermined climactic moments.

As "eccentric dance," then, kabuki's strangeness came to reside in its separation from reality. This was a formalized strangeness well suited to the theatrical tenor of public life, but as a contrived, commercial art form driven by mass fanfare, it did not adhere to the aesthetic traditions of *ki* and *kyō*.[22] Rather, it used eccentricity to advertise itself.

Kabuki playwright Tsuruya Nanboku (1755–1829), author of the well-known *Tōkaidō Yotsuya Kaidan* (Tokaido Yotsuya ghost stories, 1825), is a case in point. Nanboku's rise to success from a humble background was noteworthy, but his identity as an eccentric derived mainly from the exaggerated belief that he was poorly educated and aesthetically unrefined. Nanboku famously misused Chinese characters in his compositions, most likely as an intentional ploy to advertise his lowly background and draw attention to the limited education he had received at a temple school (*terakoya*) in Edo. His plays, too, are distinctive for their explorations of the supernatural, grotesque, and macabre; for reveling in base human passions; and for delighting in the frightful, evil side of the human psyche. Nanboku's succession of plays about street thugs, prostitutes, villains, ghosts, and monsters sought to reflect the brutality, darkness, and violence of life with unprecedented realism. And while boldness gilded his image as a wild man lacking the polish and subtlety of a cultivated writer, Nanboku possessed deep literary knowledge and carefully tailored his themes to public tastes, leaving little doubt that his eccentric image was contrived as a means of professional advancement.[23] It is this culture of self-promotion—not merely in kabuki but also in the gimmicky, theatrical nature of urban mass culture generally—that has incurred disdain from critics and generated skepticism surrounding the strangeness that permeated late Edo life.

To review, historiography has claimed, first, that *kijin* were political and subversive but failures in this capacity compared to their Western counterparts because they failed to initiate change. Second, it posits that *kijin* were artistically inventive but not truly strange or innovative. Rather, as progenitors of a mass aesthetic associated with a frivolous, theatrical culture, some represented more of a commercial phenomenon than genuine artistic advancement. Their innovations as such neither endured nor meaningfully altered Japanese culture. They also lost their original function as society's apostles. Moreover, eccentrics were further degraded by their reclusive tendencies, which in Japan signified asocial escape rather than countercultural engagement. Arthur Waley's description of eccentrics as "the vagaries of a section of humanity which will, in any case, always be found troublesome and irritating," then, has continued to parallel views of Japanese outsiders as historically anomalous and inconsequential.[24]

STRANGE ART AND HISTORICAL CHANGE

There are problems with all these views. One is their assumption that *kijin* did not successfully actualize reform, that they did not drive historical change, as was their charge. Because its innovations are often enjoyed and subsequently absorbed by the mainstream, art, and strange art in particular, is perceived as a transformative social force. Artistic innovations, it is argued, push the field to evolve and progress more readily than do other institutions. This idea is embraced by thinkers as diverse as the statesman Ōkuma Shigenobu (1838–1922) and the Western psychoanalyst Carl Jung (1875–1961). In his preface to Motoyama Tekishū's *Meijin kijin* (Notables and eccentrics, 1926), Ōkuma writes: "The first *kijin* whose words and deeds appeared in newspapers and other media were artists. It was only later that other types of people came to take this label and that the strange lives of warriors, workers, and others were recorded and disseminated."[25] His statement suggests that strains of eccentricity begin within the arts and then filter into other social realms, an observation consistent with our findings that *ki* was first embraced by *bunjin* and only later espoused by others. Jung discusses this phenomenon in the context of modernity's interest in subjectivity, also concluding that art is the first to herald social changes. "Art has a way of anticipating future changes in man's fundamental outlook," he observes of the modern individual's attention to self, "and expressionist art has taken this subjective turn well in advance of the more general change."[26] Ōkuma's and Jung's statements represent a public discourse that identifies art as a font of subjective energies and thus an antecedent for the sorts of self-reinvention that actualize broader reform.[27]

Given the modern notion that outsider art anticipates change, claims that *kijin* did drive historical events are not surprising. Ishida Takao asserted that if *kijin* existed in accord with Heaven (the Zhuangzian premise regularly echoed by *kijinden* writers) then they epitomized the ultimate aspirations of mainstream society. By personifying social ideals, he maintained, *kijin* fueled the progression and directed the course of human society.[28] The booklet *Kansei sankijin no keifu* (Genealogy of the three *kijin* of Kansei, 1999) also concludes that *ki* is the engine that drives historical events (*jidai wo ugokasu gendōryoku*).[29] The eccentricities of this trio of imperial loyalists, it contends, precipitated the restorationist events of the nineteenth century. Sawada Fujiko's *Zokubutsu to kijin* (Fakes and eccentrics, 2005), similarly distinguishes between *kijin* and *zokubutsu* (fakes) by the formers' ability to catalyze reform.[30] Such statements generally fail to explain this process, however, perhaps content to accept the satirist Miyatake Gaikotsu's dictum that "often society progresses only through the sacrifice of certain victims."[31]

Debated at least since Georg Hegel posited historical change as the product of dialectical processes, the proposition that art and literature should propel society forward assumes a teleological view of history as progressive and linear. Neither new nor unique to the Japanese context, it was also advanced by Marxist leaders like Lenin and Mao Zedong. Mao stated that art and literature "ought to be on a higher level and of a greater power . . . , nearer the ideal, and therefore more universal than actual everyday life," and that they should stimulate the masses to rise up.[32] The field of psychology, a second mouthpiece of modernization theory, has echoed this belief. Freudian psychoanalysis had expressed this position even before Jung associated subjectivity with expressionist art. Freud's separation of human desires from social mores placed the individual at odds with modern civilization but situated the eccentric beyond the pale of civilized society. From his perspective, those who opt to indulge base instincts and give full rein to spontaneous impulses, even artistic ones, are opting out of civility.[33] Thus excluded, eccentrics are uniquely enabled as social critics; thus reviled, they are also the ones for whom change is most critical. For Freudian and Jungian psychoanalysis, then, the outsider (the antimodern) is ideally poised to challenge and propel social advancement.

Do our findings corroborate such propositions? By definition eccentrics, non-centrics, would seem to require obscurity to merit that label, and it is the case that pre-1970 Japanese historiography—and art historiography—pushed nonconformists into anonymity. In contrast, the history of

Western art is populated with, even defined by, such outsiders. Eccentrics like Goya, van Gogh, Picasso, Dalí, Toulouse-Lautrec, and Warhol occupy the core rather than the periphery of Western painting. Only since Tsuji Nobuo's *Kisō no keifu* (1968) has scholarship on Japanese art conceded that obscurity is not a requisite of eccentricity and recovered *kijin* as among the most talented and accomplished artists of their age. Indeed, many of the figures we have discussed were the giants of their respective callings. Hakuin was the Rinzai sect's most important leader and painter; Baisaō was the original popularizer of *sencha;* Taiga outshone other *nanga* painters for his innovations in true-view (*shinkeizu*) realism; Gyokudō's musical skills surpassed those of his contemporaries; Kuniyoshi and Hokusai were among the most important of woodblock print artists; and Kageki was the singular *waka* populist of his day. It would seem that those who possessed extraordinary talent and the strength of character to exert transformative pressures on their respective genres came to be styled eccentric.

As we deliberate on the role that strangeness has played in the development of artistic forms in Japan, we cannot dismiss interest in the proposition that it did impact the country's historical trajectory. Yet we must also recognize this notion as an intellectual byproduct of modernization that fails to explain how *ki* and *kyō* emerged and evolved. This study has found it more useful to examine how these markers of strangeness drew on multiple philosophical resources, earned and sustained social tolerance, and acquired cultural capital.

There is no denying that artists and writers tend to be among the first to herald changes in how subjectivity is perceived and expressed. Their activities, Pierre Bourdieu shows, derive from confrontation between the individual and the cultural field. More than any other field, he writes, art and literature entail a constant and uncertain clash with one's internal world.[34] Confrontation between the internal and the external compels the individual to engage with the problem of self, and it is art that articulates this confrontation. It is not the case, however, that changes in the external are unilaterally driven by internal changes, or vice versa. Significant transformations occur only when those occurring internally correspond with those occurring externally. Change is a product of this union. This applies to eccentrics as well, for any defiance of artistic norms will go unrecognized unless consumers are able to expand their appreciation of it along similar lines.[35] *Kijin,* in other words, will have little bearing on either art or society in general without a measure of public support. As the writer Nagai Kafū (1879–1959) observed: "If an author is going to struggle with the authorities for his rights, he must have sympathy derived from the general drift of society."[36] *Kijin* may indeed be barometers or antecedents of social rhythms, but they do not generate those rhythms alone.

Charges that *kijin* failed to actualize their intended reforms and thereby failed to drive history, then, misunderstand the primary objective of amateur art: namely, to establish itself as a singular liberated realm within an otherwise rigid ideological fortress. It was, as Jürgen Habermas defined art, "a sanctuary for the—perhaps merely cerebral—satisfaction of those needs which become quasi illegal in the material life process of bourgeois society."[37] Within poetry salons (*za*), study groups, and calligraphy and painting parties (*shogakai*), what Anne Walthall calls "literary public spheres" and "gender free zones," innovative men and women found means of self-reinvention, took new names, learned new skills, and formed new status-free relationships.[38]

Finally, we must not confuse assertions that eccentric artists were political entities with assumptions that they harbored political agendas. Despite exceptions like Kagawa Kageki's Keien school, literati art was a subjective, even private, exercise that endeavored to bypass rather than overturn the artistic establishment. Making comparisons with Western artists based on an assumed desire to engender an artistic revolution is to miss this point. Given that many important nineteenth-century *bunjin* held samurai status and worked as scholar-officials, political and artistic activities were generally kept separate. Doing so allowed *bunjin* of all status groups to share cultural spaces without discord. Any personal sense of defeat, therefore, more likely originated from their activities as bureaucrats rather than as literati. This, at least, would explain certain inner conflicts suffered by Hiraga Gennai, Kageki Kagawa, Nagasawa Rosetsu, Tanomura Chikuden, Uragami Gyokudō, and Watanabe Kazan—all samurai who either withdrew or were removed from their posts. Tanomura Chikuden's case is representative. As an Oka domain (Ōita prefecture) official, Chikuden understood that the ongoing peasant riots in Oka were justified reactions to the domain's exploitative tax laws, and in 1811 he submitted a written statement condemning the laws and criticizing the complacency and wastefulness rampant among the domain's samurai. Continuing riots the following year caused him to tender a second, more Confucian, statement calling for benevolence, mercy, and fiscal responsibility. He could hardly have been surprised when his petitions were ignored, but through these incidents he came to recognize the contradictions and weaknesses of the *bakufu*'s governance. Chikuden resigned and, although acquiring fame as a painter, never overcame this disappointment. He and others may have harbored a sense of hopelessness for their society's future, but this is not evidence of their personal failure as artists.[39]

ESTRANGEMENT AND BETWEENNESS

We must also address the argument that Edo Japan's eccentrics were moderate and timid compared to their European contemporaries. It is true that even the stylistic innovations of Ming Southern School painters—the forebears of Edo period *bunjin*—are not easily appreciated by Western audiences. John Canaday's observation that "the difference between orthodoxy and eccentricity in Chinese painting is never extreme" encapsulates a disappointment that also extends to Japan's eccentric artists.[40]

It is undeniable that aesthetic innovation in early modern Japan avoided stylistic anarchy and gratuitous wildness. Censorship posed one theoretical deterrent to wanton artistic controversy, though laws were inconsistently enforced and tended to hold samurai to higher moral standards than they did commoners. The samurai Ōta Nanpo was reprimanded for writing comic poetry, considered an altogether innocuous pastime for his commoner companions. Occasionally, however, townsmen celebrities were also targeted. Author and illustrator Santō Kyōden (1761–1816), for instance, was put under house arrest for fifty days, and Utagawa Kuniyoshi was indicted for political satire.

Invoking Tokugawa oppression to explain the alleged timidity of Japanese artists is tautological, however, affirming only a presumed timidity. Rather, it is necessary to recall that eccentric art gained currency by pursuing originality rather than idiosyncrasy for its own sake. One favored means of achieving originality was engagement with the irrational through the juxtaposition or negation of opposites, a technique that has long occupied an important niche in Japanese aesthetics. A range of poetic, theatrical, painterly, and other aesthetic forms embraced this practice by utilizing what has since been labeled estrangement. A literary technique articulated by the Russian formalist Viktor Shklovsky, estrangement begins with the assumption that we unconsciously structure what we perceive. The acts of seeing, hearing, and reading involve decoding and restructuring that information, accommodating it to our preexisting perceptual orientation. Estrangement through art expands perception by drawing attention to this process. It renders a formerly recognizable reality unrecognizable, making art, as a mode of representing reality, a source of freshness.[41] The function of art, Shklovsky asserted, "is to impart the sensation of things as they are perceived and not as they are known. The technique of art is to make objects 'unfamiliar,' to make forms difficult."[42] Intentional defamiliarization, then, recasts the constant as inconstant, distorted, or surreal.[43] By rendering the familiar enigmatic and alien, it causes a sharpening of senses and perceptions and induces the subject to experience the strangeness of life.[44]

Estrangement can be created through riddles, puzzles, metaphors, renaming, indecency, deceleration, or any other means of rejecting or denying the real, and Japanese artists have consistently experimented with such tactics.[45] Early aesthetes like *waka* poet Fujiwara Teika (1162–1241), Nō master Zeami Motokiyo (1363–1434), and *bunraku* playwright Chikamatsu Monzaemon (1653–1724) recognized that this distance was essential to imbuing art with the transcendental qualities that audiences craved. Excessive realism, they knew, upset this distance and compromised art's intended effect. In their respective treatises *Maigetsusho* (Monthly notes, 1219) and *Kakyō* (Mirror of the flower, 1424), Teika and Zeami both describe the pinnacle of aesthetic taste as a state beyond human reason and language. Zeami, in fact, turns to the irrational to depict the aesthetic pinnacle of Nō performance, which he describes only as "In Silla [Korea], in the dead of the night, the sun shines brightly."[46] By reducing the epitome of performative skill to a nonsensical contradiction, Zeami intimates that the accomplished actor exceeds the limitations of rational thought and language. Similarly, Teika uses literary devices such as emotional overtones (*yojō*) and mad verses (*darumauta*) to create effects that exceed the power of conventional language. Chikamatsu, likewise, explains this need for deviance in drama as follows:

> Art is that which occupies the narrow margin between the true and the false.
>
> . . . It participates in the false and yet is not false; it participates in the true and yet is not true; our pleasure is located between the two. . . . In any artistic representation
>
> . . . along with exact resemblance of the shape there will be some deviance, and after all that is why people like it. It is the same for the design of a play—within recognizable likeness there will be points of deviance . . . and since this is after all the nature of art, it is what constitutes the pleasure people take in it.[47]

The understanding that consumers of poetry and theater "expect and enjoy deviance" allowed those arts to reach their highest aesthetic potential.[48]

The forms of estrangement espoused by Teika, Zeami, and Chikamatsu are also theoretically consistent with Buddhist doctrines endorsing the dissolution of cognitive categories. Rinzai Zen endeavors to neutralize contradictions and distinctions by employing paradoxical riddles (*kōan*), shouting, and striking to induce a momentary, heightened sense of awareness free of rational thought. Tendai Buddhism's Middle Way within its Three Truths (*santai*) doctrine likewise recognizes non-dualistic relationships between concepts rather than the independent existence of those concepts.[49]

Zen's and Tendai's rejection of cognitive categories mirrors the juxtaposition and negation of opposites that were repeatedly discovered and deployed by writers, poets, actors, and painters throughout Japan's history. And though strangeness continued to perform its defamiliarizing function, it also adapted to changes in cultural forms themselves. From the late eighteenth century, it variously came to be manifested through *ki* and *kyō*. Thus we add *ki* and *kyō* to that category of aesthetics reserved for qualities—like *yūgen* (mysterious depths) and *yojō* (emotional overtones)—that exceed the logic of normative perception. Despite their diversity, the eccentrics who form the core of this study demonstrate an appreciation for the aesthetic value of estrangement, a cognizance that perception is clouded by habit and familiarity. They desire, in Watanabe Kazan's words, "to see through to the deepest layers and experience a lasting impression."[50] This desire to "see" and "experience" pertains to their activities as artists but is contingent upon achieving aesthetic distance. Detachment, it follows, is aesthetic empowerment.

As a praxis of detachment, aesthetic strangeness distances itself from the institution of art and in this way achieves autonomy. But therein lies its dilemma, for, theoretically, by positioning itself beyond the purview of professional art it makes itself oppositional. In its endeavor to defamiliarize and thereby draw attention to the "order" critical theory posits, strange art stands as an agent of entropy.[51] In the Edo period, however, rarely did authorities or audiences assume an oppositional agenda on the basis of aesthetic strangeness alone. They understood implicitly that an oppositional position did not necessarily signify an oppositional agenda. Moreover, eccentric art's potential for political disruption was weakened by the *bakufu*'s own hapless efforts to maximize order. That is, eccentricities are all the more destabilizing when systemic stability is being maintained and comparatively less noticeable when it is not.[52] In most cases, then, the sort of strangeness inspired by aesthetics like *ki* and *kyō* was understood as singularly artistic and therefore encountered few political obstacles.

Estrangement's rich history in traditional East Asian culture is thus to be understood as a subcultural mainstay. At no point did it attempt to compromise aesthetic integrity or embrace strangeness for its own sake. Even Ming painters affiliated with the countercultural Southern School cautioned that art must not strive for originality at the expense of aesthetic taste. Departing from "rules and reality" in pursuit of strangeness as a singular aesthetic criterion, they held, was equally misguided as producing nothing but imitations of past masters.[53] As a subcultural constant during the final century of the Edo period, *ki* achieved a proper degree of deviation, and we find an awareness of this notion among *kijinden* writers. In his preface to *KKD,* for instance, Kōkei distinguished between *kijin* and those one might call strange but who lived without restraint. While these latter individuals may provide us with comic relief, he declared, they lack filiality, loyalty, or sincerity, and so were excluded from his book.[54] Kuniyoshi likewise selected entries for his *Dainihon kijin gazō* from those dissidents who made the greatest positive contributions to Japan's history and culture. These and other *kijinden* tended to agree that difference is to be praised only when it is properly regulated and applied toward societal good.

It is especially important to realize that *kijin* themselves strove to embody these values by denying such absolute categories as difference (*i*) and correctness (*sei*). In accordance with Chikamatsu's dictum that "Art is that which occupies the narrow margin between the true and the false," and that human experience itself resides between categories and structures, many positioned their art between difference and imitation, new and old.[55] Eccentricity was not to be an exercise in self-abandon. On the nature of *haikai,* Yosa Buson observed that novelty itself is a matter of perspective: "It is, for example, like people running after one another along the circumference of a circle. Running ahead looks rather like following the person behind. We should not distinguish between the new and the old but only let our heart speak day by day."[56] We will recall that Hakuin's ruminations on No-Self, similarly, carried him beyond self-denial and reunited him with the thoughts and emotions of daily life. His enlightenment occurred by breaking through the dogmatic categories of correct and incorrect Zen practice. Like Buson and Hakuin, the *bunjin* Takebe Ayatari, who earned a lengthy entry in *Zoku kinsei kijinden,* found that strangeness returns to a qualified normalcy when carried to its ultimate conclusion. Though Ayatari had pursued individualism and originality for much of his life, he ultimately found them a trap. *Ki* led to a cycle of rejection that was just as enslaving as correctness. He wrote:

That which we call haikai . . . is uninteresting if it is straight. In haikai you engage in wordplay by taking something and warping it a bit here, or trimming it away there, or omitting something elsewhere. In so doing . . . you find a strange pleasure in rejecting the world around you. Then in your leisure relationships you reach the point at which you are lonely if you are not with the right group. Your feelings eventually get to the point where, if serious-minded, people seem repugnant; if well-mannered, they seem dense; if reserved, they seem backward; if they compose tanka, they seem hopelessly effeminate; if they compose Chinese verse, they seem difficult; if engaged in an occupation, they seem contemptible; if devoted to managing a good home, they seem stingy. All this comes about from composing in the haikai style, by which, through deep concentration, you end up rejecting the world in all its manifestations. Are there not people like that? I now look back on the time I was exactly like that, and feel strong pangs of remorse.[57]

By extending to its inevitable conclusion Gion Nankai's pioneering statement (Chapter 3) about the artistic necessity of *ki,* Ayatari discovers that an aestheticism of unqualified difference is destructive to self and society alike. We find, then, that aesthetics of difference cultivated by *kijin* actually reside between orthodoxy and heterodoxy, between correctness and difference. Moreover, if estrangement had always existed as a counterpart to correctness and therefore as a constant in the history of Japanese artistic practice, it would qualify as a form of aesthetic orthodoxy, a proposition that calls for reconsideration of exactly how different difference endeavored to be. Criticism that Japanese eccentrics are tame and moderate, therefore, is unjustified. Through estrangement they interrogated perceptual boundaries and conceptual categories within a clear context of originality.

Thus, one cannot judge eccentric artists in terms of success or failure, but rather as non-centric actors within an artistic field who helped redefine the boundaries of public tolerance. And rather than viewing them and their activities as modern-minded resistance, it is more accurate to view strangeness as a personal exercise aimed at winning emotional release and individualizing artistic expression. Victor Koschmann's description of Japanese resistance as expressive and symbolic rather than instrumental is applicable here. Patterns of Japanese protest, Koschmann posits, suggest that protesters "expect few results from their participation in politics, other than 'symbolic affirmation of their own principles.'"[58] Resistance is to be understood as a subject-centered exercise concerned more with self-affirmation than with achieving its professed objectives. It is an expression of moral freedom and artistic autonomy that is immaterial to tangible social change.

By now it is clear that assumptions of intended political activism misrepresent many *kijin,* and comparisons with more radical Western artists dehistoricize them. Eccentricity is relative to its society only. It cannot be measured by its degree of departure from the normative, only by its measure of departure given its objectives as such. *KKD*'s success, the publication of numerous subsequent *kijinden,* and the popularity that elevated eccentricity to aesthetic orthodoxy by the 1820s and 1830s all indicate a phenomenon with widespread and sustained allure. Indeed, strange art itself made few attempts to challenge hegemonic structures because it found more meaning by turning inward and interrogating the self.

SELF AND SELF-PORTRAITURE

This study has identified a correlation between eccentricity and unusually strong attention to self. Jakuchū and Hokusai adopted openly and publicly self-absorbed lifestyles that came to define them socially; the startling unpredictability of Shōhaku and Taiga was informed by an unassailable individuality; and the eccentric reputations of Hakuin, Yamazaki Hokka, and Yokoi Kinkoku were gilded by their narcissistic autobiographies. Revisiting instances of self-representation helps to illuminate this correlation. It also allows us to reemphasize a point in danger of becoming lost in the above analysis—namely that some eccentric artists, whether or not they consciously positioned themselves as social outsiders, were variously separated, alone, and misunderstood. In certain cases, self-absorption feeds alienation, which in turn leads to the withdrawn reclusiveness that has typified the "mad" artist. Evidence of the sort of neurotic soul-searching visible in Hakuin's, Hokka's, and Kinkoku's autobiographical ruminations is rare in the Edo period, as is pictorial self-representation. Nonetheless, examining the rare instances of self-portraiture helps identify cases where an unusually strong sense of self informs perceptions of strangeness.

Histories of Japanese painting normally trace self-portraiture to the turn of the twentieth century, when Meiji painters in the throes of an "inward turn" were producing tortured self-portraits similar to those being produced in the West. The misconception that this genre was a Western import, however, has led those looking at pre-Meiji Japan to conclude that Japanese self-portraiture began with Shiba Kōkan (1747–1818), among the first Japanese artists to experiment with Western oil painting.[59] This was not the case. While self-portraiture was rare among professional artists, from the Kamakura period (1185–1333) it was occasionally practiced by courtiers and amateurs alike. High-ranking Zen monks also produced self-portraits for pedagogical purposes. The image of a recognized person, they believed, helped disciples to grasp life's struggles and contradictions.[60] Such practices declined in the late medieval years even as outstanding individualist painters Sesshū Tōyō (1420–1506) and, later, Matsukadō Shōjō (1584–1639) and Iwasa Matabei (1578–1650), produced self-portraits.

The scarcity of self-portraiture makes the small body of such works by early modern *kijin* all the more noteworthy. In fact, nearly without exception those painters who produced self-portraits were considered eccentric. These works, it is true, are anomalies. Few are either highly expressive or showcase the emotional state of the artist, perhaps explaining why they have been overlooked as evidence of strong interiority. Ike no Taiga's self-portrait is representative (Fig. 7.1). Taiga, in profile, appears with his friend

FIGURE 7.1   Ike no Taiga, Taiga (*left*) with Mikami Kōken, 1763. University Art Museum, Tokyo University of the Arts.

Confucian scholar Mikami Kōken as the two celebrate Kōken's birthday. It bears a simple inscription: "To commemorate Kōken's fortieth birthday. . . . We have both sprouted white beards and ear hair, and before long we will both have welcomed forty. When we look at each other's faces now all we can do is laugh." Created solely to commemorate the occasion, the work is natural, spontaneous, and dispenses with symbolic, dignified poses. Here Taiga seeks simply to produce a snapshot of the emotions evoked by this enduring friendship.

Other cases of self-representation show more evidence of engagement with self. Hakuin, for instance, painted numerous animated self-portraits, most of them late in life (Fig. 7.2). Though these might be attributed to the practice among eminent Zen monks noted above, his are too expressive and charismatic to be considered merely pedagogical tools. Rather, they exhibit playful and experimental qualities that defy the tightening control over religious activities confronted by Hakuin during his lifetime.[61] The bold contrasts and exaggerated facial features showcase the emotional intensity that beset Hakuin throughout his life, while the facial expression itself depicts a man who is pious, contemplative, and without pretensions.

FIGURE 7.2   Hakuin, self-portrait, 1764. Eisei Bunko Museum.

The sculptor Enkū, anthologized in *KKD*, produced at least four self-representations. Though each is said to have been completed in a single session, their craftsmanship reveals close attention to detail. Figure 7.3 depicts Enkū smiling, an atypical expression in Japanese portraiture, and praying in peaceful repose. His head and face are carefully hewn, while the drapery of his robe is rendered with a simple pattern of abstract slashes.[62] The only other sculptor in the Tokugawa period widely regarded as an eccentric was Mokujiki (1718–1810) who, like Enkū, traveled throughout the country and carved a number of self-likenesses. Also smiling, in Figure 7.4 he sits with his begging bowl atop a gourd of saké.

For painters, to produce a single self-portrait was rare; for the eminent *bunjin* Okada Beisanjin (1744–1820), to generate three was exceptional. A talented but self-taught painter and a close friend of Uragami Gyokudō, Beisanjin shared Gyokudō's penchant for mixing art and alcohol. All three of his works were produced late in life and exhibit the playful good humor we see in Taiga's and Hakuin's self-portraits. Each also reveals joyful indulgence in saké, which may have indicated dissatisfaction with his position as an official for the Tōdō clan in Osaka.

FIGURE 7.3   Enkū, self-carving.
Courtesy of Shinmei Shrine.

FIGURE 7.4   Mokujiki, self-carving,
1801. Japan Folk Crafts Museum.

In the first (Fig. 7.5), painted at age fifty-seven, he strikes an immodest pose. Half disrobed, head bowed, eyes closed, and curled over a large saké cup, Beisanjin enjoys an intimate, besotted moment. The work proudly bears a seal that reads: "Having saké, I cannot fail" (*subete toku ni oite sake*).[63] Beisanjin's second self-portrait appears on his *Sansui jinbutsu kakizu* (Landscape with figures and blossoms) folding screen; he is the only known artist impudent enough to depict himself on such a scale (Fig. 7.6). After

FIGURE 7.5   Okada Beisanjin, self-portrait. Private Collection.

FIGURE 7.6   Okada Beisanjin, self-portrait. *Sansui jinbutsu kakizu,* folding screen (detail). Takaokayama Zuiryūji Temple.

sleeping off a round of drinking, the caption relates, Beisanjin awakes and calls for a boy to make tea, but the boy has since dropped off to sleep himself. Beisanjin, again looking disreputable, looks back at us with an impish laugh.[64] The final work (Fig. 7.7), rougher than the others, is also a portrait of impropriety. Painted at age seventy-five, it shows him in a drunken slumber, half collapsed, with his elbows draped precariously over a low table. His inscription extols the pleasures of inebriation and compares his inkstone to a field that never goes fallow.[65] In all three cases, the painter's subjectivity is reduced to the contentment he derives from indolence and dissipation.

Inoue Shirō (1742–1812), a physician and literatus from Nagoya, produced a most abstract self-portrait (Fig. 7.8). No more than a stooped, amorphous embryo with what appear to be whiskers hanging off the left side, it accompanies a *haikai* verse:

Iro mo ka mo	No color or scent
nakute hana miru	when flower-viewing—
kazahana kana	stuffy nose

Kazahana is written with the characters for "stuffy nose" but can also mean "snowflakes." Stephen Addiss offers a likely guess that, while Shirō's stuffy nose prevents him from appreciating the scent of the blossoms, it does not hamper his enjoyment of the blossom-like snowflakes, which are colorless and odorless.[66]

Watanabe Kazan, we will recall, was taken into custody in 1839 and committed ritual suicide (*seppuku*) two years later. Stripped of his rank during his years in confinement, Kazan assumed the status of a criminal, and sketches he produced documenting his hardship during captivity constitute an objective record of that new identity. One shows him with hands bound and without swords; in another, still under guard, he faces a coarse

FIGURE 7.7   Okada Beisanjin, self-portrait. Private Collection.

meal (Figs. 7.9, 7.10). We see here the sort of realism exhibited in Taiga's work, but for the first time can discern an intention to chronicle the internal anguish of a tortured mind. Idealization or stylization, commonplace in portraiture, is absent. His criminal status severed him from relations and responsibilities, leaving him free to dispense with the rules of drawing he had honed as a painter and Dutch studies scholar. Surely, knowledge of Western painting encouraged Kazan's experimentation in subjectivity, for not only are his sketches autobiographical, a pioneering development in

FIGURE 7.8   Inoue Shirō, self-portrait. Courtesy of Stephen Addiss.

Japanese art, they are also highly self-conscious. Their indulgence in the emotions of personal hardship, Satō Yasuhiro has suggested, is a distinctly "modern" expression unique in late Edo art.[67]

Yokoi Kinkoku; *ukiyoe* artist Miyakawa Chōshun (1682–1752); monk, recluse, and poet Ryōkan; *nanga* painter Tanomura Chikuden; nativist scholar Motoori Norinaga; Dutch studies scholar Shiba Kōkan; *Hōsa kyōshaden* preface writer Kinryū Keiyū; female Shōmon poet Tagami Kikusha (1753–1826); and *bunjin* Tani Bunchō (1763–1840) all produced self-portraits as well.[68] And at about the time that Utagawa Kuniyoshi

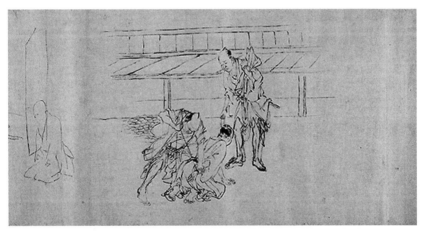

FIGURE 7.9 Watanabe Kazan in captivity, self-portrait. Tahara Municipal Museum.

FIGURE 7.10 Watanabe Kazan in captivity, self-portrait. Tahara Municipal Museum.

produced his own self-rendering (the final illustration in his *Dainihon kijin gazō*), Katsushika Hokusai also created at least two stylized sketches of himself as a recluse. In Figure 7.11 he strikes an unrestrained pose, gesticulating wildly and wearing a maniacal grin.[69]

Fascination with self at this time was unprecedented in Japanese art. Though self-representation was not a discernable tradition in any pre-Edo artistic genre, in the Edo period such works appeared with increasing

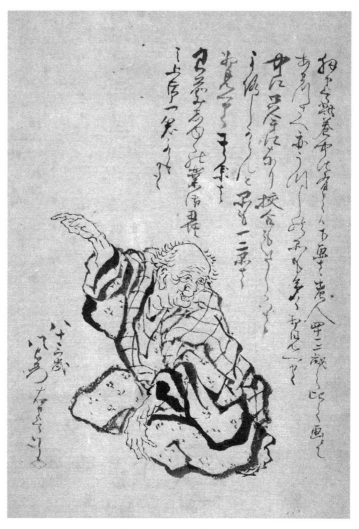

FIGURE 7.11   Katsushika Hokusai, self-portrait. Museum Volkenkunde, Leiden, RMV 3513–1496.

frequency from a diverse array of thoughtful individuals: monks (Hakuin, Ryōkan, Kinkoku); sculptors (Enkū, Mokujiki); Kokugaku thinkers (Motoori Norinaga); *bunjin* (Taiga, Chikuden, Beisanjin, Bunchō); *hai-kai* poets (Inoue, Tagami); Dutch studies devotees (Kōkan); *ukiyoe* artists (Miyakawa, Kuniyoshi, Hokusai); and dissident bureaucrats (Kazan). The intellectual and artistic eclecticism found here is instructive, for it shows that these individuals were all driven to transgress the conventions of their respective arts through creating overtly self-centered works. More interesting, those who produced these self-portraits were somehow exceptional, extraordinary, or otherwise eccentric. It is probable that egocentric displays like self-portraiture contributed to such reputations.

It will be no surprise that some equate the self-consciousness seen in these works as evidence of "modern" consciousness, as antecedents of the inward turn exhibited by mid-Meiji writers and artists. Without rejecting this position outright, we must recognize it as an extension of theorists' inclination to link self-consciousness with modernization. Undeniably, self-representation is a discourse with and an indulgence in self. It is a dialogue with self that raises the question of subjectivity. Which is the subject, after all, the painted or the painter? If a painting is an artist's rendition of a subject and carries the intention of re-creating that subject, then a self-portrait may be seen as the artist's attempt at self-invention.[70] Although early modern self-portraits do affirm the existence of an individual ego, they are fundamentally separate from modern works, which pursue an entirely different degree of realism.[71] Nonetheless, their existence does signal conspicuous cases of self-reflection—and publicity of that self-representation—long before the appearance of more modern forms of subjectivity. The autobiographies of Hakuin (*Itsumadegusa*) and Yokoi Kinkoku (*Ichidaiki*), the autobiographical confessions of Yamazaki Hokka and Watanabe Kazan, the egocentric, cathartic-sounding essays by Uragami Gyokudō, the self-absorbed declarations of Kageki, and other such documents all manifest an overt individualism that, "modern" or not, was instrumental to the identity construction of their authors as eccentrics. Rather than reflecting on their private lives, as was characteristic of the diaries produced by Heian court women, they elected to hold a mirror up to their lives as public figures.[72] In the cases of the several works introduced here that do not express their subject's inner state, their existence alone connotes self-awareness and, perhaps, a desire for public recognition. Rather than interpreting this form of self-consciousness as modern, it is more prudent to read it as evidence of growing self-indulgence and acknowledgment of qualified self-empowerment within a declining sociopolitical system.

Self became an acceptable theme in late Edo poetry as well. As we have seen, Kagawa Kageki had made self the requisite subject of *waka,* a license that followers like Ōkuma Kotomichi (1798–1868) took to extremes. Often composing more than one hundred *waka* daily, Kotomichi devoted himself to poetry to the exclusion of all else. This indifference to daily necessities may even have been responsible for his wife's premature death.[73] Only a deeply self-involved person, one imagines, would fixate on a solitary activity to the detriment of his family's welfare. Indeed, the ruminating self-obsession apparent in the following verse had only recently become poetically viable.

hin takaki	I long not for
koto mo negawazu	personal advancement
mata no yo wa	I want only
mata wagami ni zo	to be myself again
narite kinamashi	in the next life[74]

In this existential deliberation, Kotomichi is so attached to his personal thoughts and emotions that he cannot bear to part with them even in death.

Kotomichi's self-absorption was certainly loathsome to traditional *waka* poets, yet it was characteristic of the indulgent frivolity typifying popular and print culture that arose in the later Edo years. These cultural energies enabled the emergence of social spaces in which townspeople could engage in "interpretation," or critical contemplation of their own emotions and daily experiences. Katsuya Hirano has described the expansion of self-awareness within these spaces in much the way that Habermas posited the aggregation of public spheres in eighteenth-century Europe. The result, however, was not greater political participation but rather the consumption of a variety of popular and print cultural forms that enabled people to randomly and spontaneously transport themselves to "an entirely different world."[75]

Self-interests framed this alternate world. Returning to Gion Nankai's 1726 essay *Shōun sango,* in which he declares the necessity of *ki* in art, art historian Kanō Hiroyuki suggests reading between Nankai's lines by replacing the word *ki* in that essay with the word "self."[76] Doing so yields the following:

We should call people's attraction to self a kind of illness. Self stands in opposition to correctness and is what turns the ordinary into its opposite.

> . . . So while there is no question that people's attraction to self is a kind
> of illness, it is also true that where there is no self neither is there anything
> to taste.[77]

Kanō's is no fanciful proposition, for Nankai's attraction to eccentricity was surely informed by a longing for self-determination—to do, think, and say what he wished. Nankai was, after all, the samurai who had earlier been indicted and exiled for "dissipation and delinquency" (*hōtō burai*). The proposition speaks to the Confucian ideal of collective harmony achieved through sublimation of personal interests. In such a context, egotism would certainly be styled a social "illness." Nankai's statement, both the original and Kanō's revised one, indeed illuminates the frustrations endemic to such a credo, and to the awareness that the self-denial expected by Confucian ethics strips all flavor from human life. Such frustrations do suggest that the reclusive, erratic, or antisocial behaviors of eccentrics were attempts to engage with self and thereby secure a measure of freedom. They also enhanced the relevance of Yōmeigaku, whose validation of the individual became increasingly appealing, not just to political dissidents like the *Kansei sankijin,* but to aesthetes like Gyokudō, Kageki, and Kazan as well.

We find, then, that within a culture with no appreciable tradition of self-representation, a large percentage of artists deemed eccentric were engaging with self through autobiography, self-portraiture, and other means. Moreover, the members of this very contingent have earned celebrity as early modern Japan's most important artists precisely because their interrogation of self resonates with the egocentrism that has characterized modern life.

CONCLUSION

The preceding chapters have chronicled the emergence, expansion, and diffusion of eccentricity and madness as criteria for both aesthetics and self-making in Edo period culture. Contrary to how early modern Japan is commonly characterized—that is, as conformist, stolid, hostile to innovation, and "prohibitive to any form of unconventional, exceptional, peculiar or original behavior or attitude," we have found that Tokugawa society actually celebrated these qualities.[78] By the eighteenth century, society was already opening up to the observable differences between people and affirming the pluralism and diversity of human nature. Emotion and individualism as manifested in the arts were no longer reviled in either Confucian thought or daily practice; the strange and the normative, people discovered, need not be philosophically opposed. Such discoveries emerged from both "orthodox" and "heterodox" philosophical traditions. Readers found Hattori Sōmon's devotion to the radical branch of Yōmeigaku and *Kinsei kijinden*'s invocation of Zhuangzi no more profane than *Hōsa kyōshaden*'s invocation of Confucius. Ancient Learning's liberalization of Neo-Confucian thought lent validity to artistic innovation; iconoclastic artistic styles like *zoku* and *ippin* nurtured philosophical validations of strangeness; and interest in Yōmeigaku and other strands of intellectual heterodoxy informed a commercial literature that cast eccentrics as ideological exemplars. Innovations and expansions in thought, therefore, were quickly coopted by art, and vice versa, the two informing each other sufficiently to create a common trajectory.

Viewing the Edo period through the lens of strangeness—through aesthetics like *ki* and *kyō* in particular—highlights tensions between artistic correctness and strangeness, as well as the intellectual discourse surrounding those tensions. It reveals not only a broad spectrum of nonconforming, free-thinking individuals creating in nonstandard ways, but also reveals them as guiding how nonprofessionals came to appreciate and practice culture. Within Tokugawa's highly institutionalized, regulated society, these marginal figures collectively engendered important artistic innovations.

Long occupying an important niche in Japanese culture, attraction to the strange indeed ran wide and deep. It was during the Edo period, however, that conditions became favorable to realizing the full aesthetic potentials of eccentric art as well as its transformative contributions to mainstream Japanese culture. Learning from Chinese literati that unqualified difference is destructive to self and society alike, Japanese *kijin* did not confuse strangeness with wildness. They took a prudent, studied approach to art, cultivating an aesthetics that resided between the familiar and the heretical. Doing so imbued the literati arts with interest and longevity. In the nineteenth century, as those arts weakened, strangeness was handed off to non-*bunjin* eccentrics who took ownership of strange culture during the final decades of the Edo period. In the process, strangeness acquired economic and cultural power as a definitive feature of Tokugawa life.

These developments cannot be explained entirely as means of temporary escape from a highly regulated life. Had widespread interest in altering one's state of consciousness for such a purpose existed, means of doing so were readily available through alcohol and other substances.[79] And while it is true that the public found entertainment value in miscellaneous instances of behavioral peculiarity—in individuals like Striped Kanjūrō and Yamazaki Hokka, for example—the crystallization of aesthetic strangeness was neither an anomaly, a gimmick, nor a fad. On the contrary, it exerted lasting influences on Tokugawa culture. From early refugees (Chōshōshi, Jōzan) and Sinophiles (Nankai, Kien) to later painters (Taiga, Jakuchū, Shōhaku, Rosetsu, Beisanjin, Kazan), poets (Bashō, Hokka, Hyakuan, Kageki, Kotomichi), printers (Hokusai, Kuniyoshi), thinkers (Sōmon, Shidōken), and clerics (Hakuin, Enkū, Baisaō, Kinkoku), a taste for strangeness extended across the cultural spectrum. Eccentricity and madness did not drive history, but as aesthetic ideals they did animate the cultural field and inform the development of Tokugawa society itself.

NOTES

Chapter 1: Strange Interpretations

1 Nelson Wu, "The Toleration of Eccentrics," *Art News* 57, no. 3 (May 1956), p. 28.

2 *Kinsei kijinden* was written by Ban Kōkei (1733–1806), illustrated by Mikuma Katen (1730–1794), and published in Kyoto by Hayashi Bunkindō. In most cases, the term *kijin* was a laudatory attribution that precluded its usage in self-reference. In fact, self-referential use of the term was often enough evidence for later *kijinden* writers to indict such individuals as self-aggrandizing fakes and disqualify them as "true" *kijin*.

3 Marius Jansen, *Japan and Its World: Two Centuries of Change* (Princeton, NJ: Princeton University Press, 1995), pp. 7–8; Donald Keene, *The Japanese Discovery of Europe: Honda Toshiaki and Other Discoverers, 1720–1798* (New York: Grove Press, 1969), p. v.

4 Timon Screech, *The Shogun's Painted Culture: Fear and Creativity in the Japanese States 1760–1829* (London: Reaktion Books, 2000), p. 24.

5 Matthew P. McKelway et al., *Traditions Unbound: Groundbreaking Painters of Eighteenth Century Kyoto* (San Francisco, CA: Asian Art Museum, 2005), p. 11.

6 John M. Rosenfield in collaboration with Fumiko E. Cranston, *Extraordinary Persons: Works by Eccentric, Nonconformist Japanese Artists of the Early Modern Era (1580–1868)*, in the *Collection of Kimiko and John Powers*, ed. Naomi Noble Richard, 3 vols. (Cambridge, MA: Harvard University Art Museums, 1999), p. 36; Saeki Shōichi, "Images of Eccentrics: East and West," in *Biography East and West: Selected Conference Papers*, ed. Carol Ramelb (Honolulu: East–West Center and University of Hawaiʻi, 1989), p. 10.

7 Even chief shogunal councilor Matsudaira Sadanobu (1759–1829), despite his Prohibition of Heterodox Studies (1790), made extensive use of scientific, artistic, and historiographical innovations that would have been seen as heterodoxical only a generation earlier. See Screech 2000 for a full discussion.

8 Takahashi Hiromi, *Kyoto geien nettowaaku* (Perikansha, 1988), p. 151; Donald Keene, *Travelers of a Hundred Ages* (New York: Columbia University Press, 1999), p. 353.

9 The overwhelming majority will be men. Anna Beerens' exhaustive study of Edo period *bunjin* provides an apt gauge for this disparity: of the 173 included in her study, only five (2.8%) were women. Anna Beerens, *Friends, Acquaintances, Pupils, and Patrons: Japanese Intellectual Life in the Late*

Eighteenth Century: A Prosopographical Approach (Leiden: Leiden University Press, 2006).

10 Clifford A. Pickover, *Strange Brains and Genius: The Secret Lives of Eccentric Scientists and Madmen* (New York: Plenum Press, 1998), p. 259.

11 Smith, quoted in ibid., p. 261.

12 Ibid., pp. 261–262.

13 Ibid., p. 263.

14 Kay Redfield Jamison, "Manic-Depressive Illness and Creativity," *Scientific American* (February 1995): 62–67.

15 Patricia Waugh, "Creative Writers and Psychopathology: The Cultural Consolations of 'The Wound and the Bow' Thesis," in Corinne Saunders and Jane Macnaughton, eds., *Madness and Creativity in Literature and Culture* (Hampshire, UK: Palgrave, 2005), p. 177.

16 Quoted in Peter Bürger, *Theory of the Avant-Garde,* trans. Michael Shaw (Minneapolis: University of Minnesota Press, 1984), p. 25.

17 Al Alvarez, "The Myth of the Artist," in *Madness and Creativity in Literature and Culture,* ed. Corinne Saunders and Jane Macnaughton (Hampshire, UK: Palgrave, 2005), p. 199.

18 David Weeks and Jamie James, *Eccentrics: A Study of Sanity and Strangeness* (New York, Tokyo, and London: Kodansha, 1996).

19 Yajima Arata, Yamashita Yuji, and Tsuji Nobuo, *Nihon bijutsu no hakkenshatachi* (Tokyo daigaku shuppankai, 2003), p. 194.

20 Ibid., p. 199.

21 Michel Foucault, *Madness and Civilization: A History of Insanity in the Age of Reason* (New York: Pantheon Books, 1965), p. 13.

22 Shioda Junichi, *Japanese Outsider Art: Inhabitants of Another World* (Setagaya Art Museum, 1993), p. 38.

23 Robert M. Pirsig, *Zen and the Art of Motorcycle Maintenance: An Inquiry into Values* (New York: Bantam, 1984), p. 71.

24 Such realizations advance the necessity of experiencing the subject's "interior," affirming the sort of experiential methods able to penetrate the reflections of ourselves that too often guide our studies of others. Experiential methods have been advanced by Pierre Bourdieu's *Outline of a Theory of Practice* and Michel de Certeau's *The Practice of Everyday Life.*

25 Both Hakuin and Takebe Ayatari wrote autobiographical works, as did Yokoi Kinkoku, though Kinkoku's is replete with hyperbole and considered historically untenable. Other eccentrics did leave letters, essays, or miscellaneous statements revealing personal sentiments, but little that reflects on their own identities as eccentrics.

26 Thomas Hess, ed., *The Grand Eccentrics: Five Centuries of Artists Outside the Main Currents of Art History* (New York: The Macmillan Company, 1966), pp. 13–15.

27 Melinda Rinker Takeuchi, "Visions of a Wanderer: The True View Paintings of Ike no Taiga (1723–1776)" (Ph.D. diss., University of Michigan, 1979), p. 42.

28 Victor H. Mair, *Wandering on the Way: Early Taoist Tales and Parables of Chuang Tzu* (Honolulu: University of Hawai'i Press, 1994), p. 61. In this translation, "villain" should be understood as the antithesis of gentleman—namely, a lowly or petty person.

29 Zhuangzi points out that uselessness liberates one from the artificialities of human society, allowing one to reconnect with the Way.

30 Nakano Mitsutoshi, *Kinsei shinkijin-den* (Mainichi shinbunsha, 1977), pp. 7–8. See also Murakami Mamoru, *Ban Kōkei-sen autosaidaa 119-nin: Kinsei kijinden* (Kyōikusha, 1981), p. 20.

31 Dennis Washburn, "Ghostwriters and Literary Haunts: Subordinating Ethics to Art in Ugetsu Monogatari," *Monumenta Nipponica* 48, no. 1 (Spring 1990): 54.

32 Matsuda Osamu, *Edo itan bungaku nooto* (Seidōsha, 1993), p. 302. One account from the *Nihongi* explains the deformity as retribution for Izanami's transgression of speaking first and thereby breaking the law of male and female.

33 For more on *misemono,* see Andrew L. Markus, "The Carnival of Edo: *Misemono* Spectacles from Contemporary Accounts," *Harvard Journal of Asiatic Studies* 45, no. 2 (1985): 499–541.

34 Matsuda, *Edo itan bungaku nooto,* p. 304.

35 Morohashi Tetsuji, *Daikanwa jiten,* vol. 7 (Taishūkan shoten, 1989), p. 1133.

36 Ban Kōkei and Mikuma Katen, *Kinsei kijinden: Zoku kinsei kijinden,* ed. Munemasa Isoo (Tōyō bunko, vol. 202, Heibonsha, 1972), pp. 9–12.

37 Katharine Burnett, "A Discourse of Originality in Late Ming Chinese Painting Criticism," *Art History* 23, no. 4 (November 2000): 534.

38 Ujiie Mikito, *Edo kijinden: Hatamoto kawajike no hitobito* (Heibonsha, 2001), p. 241. Anotsu was the name for present-day Tsū in Mie prefecture.

39 Nakano Mitsutoshi, *Kinsei shinkijinden* (Iwanami shoten, 2004), p. 2.

40 Ishikawa Jun, "Kijin," in *Ishikawa Jun zenshū,* vol. 11 (Chikuma Shobō, 1969), pp. 486–489.

41 Koto Yūho, *Shōwa chōjin kijin katarogu* (Raibu shuppan, 1990), p. i.

42 Ibid., pp. iii, vi.

43 Morohashi, *Daikanwa jiten,* vol. 7 (Taishūkan shoten, 1989), p. 676.

44 Munemasa Isoo, *Kokugo kokubun* 31, no. 8 (1962): 54–55.

45 Nakano Mitsutoshi, *Kinsei shin kijinden* (Iwanami shoten, 2004), p. 2.

46 Beerens, *Friends, Acquaintances, Pupils, and Patrons,* pp. 25–28.

47 Lawrence E. Marceau, *Takebe Ayatari: A Bunjin Bohemian in Early Modern Japan* (Ann Arbor: Center for Japanese Studies, University of Michigan, 2004), p. 4.

48 Marceau has referred to this as a "*bunjin* rubric" (ibid., p. 285).

49 Riding on the wind is an allusion to Daoist immortals.

50 W. Puck Brecher, "To Romp in Heaven: A Translation of the *Hōsa kyōshaden,*" *Early Modern Japan: An Interdisciplinary Journal* 13 (Spring 2005): 20–21.

51 The phrase "culture of play" is taken from H. D. Harootunian, "Late Tokugawa Thought and Culture," in *The Cambridge History of Japan,* vol. 5, ed. Marius Jansen (Cambridge: Cambridge University Press, 1989).

52 Quoted in Wu, "The Toleration of Eccentrics," p. 26.

53 Paul Moss, *Eccentrics in Netsuke* (London: Sydney L. Moss, 1982), p. 105.

54 Koto, *Shōwa chōjin kijin katarogu,* p. v.

55 Tsuji, *Kisō no keifu: Matabei—Kuniyoshi* (Bijutsu shuppansha, 1970), p. 77.

56 Takahashi, *Kyoto geien nettowaaku,* p. 49; Oda Susumu, *Nihon no kyōkishi* (Shisakusha, 1990), p. 272.

57 Historiographical debates surrounding the failed *kijin* will be discussed at length in Chapter 7.

58 Maruyama Masao, *Studies in the Intellectual History of Tokugawa Japan* (Princeton, NJ: Princeton University Press, 1974), p. 226.

59 Yajima Arata, Yamashita Yūji, and Tsuji Nobuo, *Nihon bijutsu no hakkenshatachi* (Tokyo daigaku shuppankai, 2003).

60 Motoyama Tekishū, *Zoku zoku meijin kijin* (Genbunsha, 1920). See also Soda Kōichi, *Edo Kijin Kisai Jiten* (Tōkyōdō, 1992) for more on Hōitsu as a *kijin.*

61 Takashina Shūji and Haga Tōru, *Geijutsu no seishinshi* (Dankōsha, 1976), pp. 102–103.

62 Patricia Graham, *Tea of the Sages: The Art of Sencha* (Honolulu: University of Hawai'i Press, 1998), p. 202.

63 Rosenfield and Cranston, *Extraordinary Persons,* p. 36. See also John M. Rosenfield, "Hokusai and Concepts of Eccentricity," in *Hokusai Paintings: Selected Paintings,* ed. Gian Carlo Calza with the assistance of John T. Carpenter (Venice: International Hokusai Research Centre, University of Venice, 1994).

64 Tsuji Nobuo, Saeki Shōichi, Nakano Mitsutoshi, and Satō Yasuhiro, among others, have interpreted *kijin* as modernizers.

65 Tsuji, *Kisō no keifu,* p. 139.

66 Kurozumi Makoto, "The Nature of Early Tokugawa Confucianism," *Journal of Japanese Studies* 20, no. 2 (Summer 1994): 341.

67 Yokota Yōichi, *Ukiyoe avangyarudo to gendai* (Tokyo Station Gallery, 2003).

68 Kawamoto Koji. "The Use and Disuse of Tradition in Bashō's Haiku and Imagist Poetry," *Poetics Today* 20, no. 4 (Winter 1999): 710.

69 Ibid., p. 710.

70 Bürger, *Theory of the Avant-Garde,* pp. 22, 59.

71 Tsuji, *Kisō no keifu,* p. 138.

72   Haruo Shirane, *Traces of Dreams: Landscape, Cultural Memory, and the Poetry of Bashō* (Stanford, CA: Stanford University Press, 1998), p. 289.

73   The art historian John Rosenfield has compiled a three-volume commentary on the art works in the Powers Collection that contains representative works from nearly all the important eccentrics of the Tokugawa period. The third volume is dedicated to biographies of these individuals, and interested readers are referred to this source (Rosenfield 1999) for further biographical information on these *kijin*.

74   See, for instance, Nakano Mitsutoshi, *Kinsei shin-kijinden* (Iwanami shoten, 2004), and Penelope Mason, *Japanese Literati Painters: The Third Generation* (New York: The Brooklyn Museum, 1977).

CHAPTER 2: Contexts of Strangeness in Seventeenth-Century Japan

1   Bernard Leach, *Kenzan and His Tradition: The Lives and Times of Kōetsu, Sōtatsu, Kōrin and Kenzan* (New York: Transatlantic Arts, 1967), p. 46.

2   Nakamura Seishiro, *Edokko-gaku: Shitteru tsumori* (Yamato shuppan, 1994), p. 204.

3   Hong Zicheng, *Vegetable Roots Discourse: Wisdom from China on Life and Living,* trans. Robert Aitken and Daniel W. Y. Kwok (Emeryville, CA: Shoemaker & Hoard, 2006), p. 84.

4   Yagi Sōsaburō, *Ijin to shūyō* (Sūzan-bō, 1912), p. 10.

5   Hara Tokusai, Ban Kōkei, and Yajima Gogaku, *Sentetsu zōden; Kinsei kijinden; Hyakka kikōden* (Yūhōdō shoten, 1927), pp. 680–682.

6   For a discussion of *monotsuki,* see Susan Burns, "Bodies Possessed and Hearts Disordered: Sexuality and Madness in Edo Japan," *Imaging/Reading Eros* (Proceedings of the NEH-funded Conference "Sexuality and Edo Culture, 1750–1850"), ed. Sumie Jones (Bloomington: East Asian Studies Center, University of Indiana, 1996), pp. 72–75.

7   Noriko T. Reider, "The Appeal of '*Kaidan,*' Tales of the Strange," *Asian Folklore Studies* 59, no. 2 (2000): 268, 275.

8   Yoshida Teigo, "The Stranger as God: The Place of the Outsider in Japanese Folk Religion," *Ethnology* 20, no. 2 (April 1981): 95. Pre-Edo folk beliefs ascribe dangerous supernatural abilities to Chinese immigrants. From the Edo period, Europeans replaced Chinese as objects of suspicion.

9   Over five thousand statues have been identified and confirmed as Enkū's.

10   Soda Kōichi, *Edo kijin kisei jiten* (Tōkyōdō, 1992), p. 50.

11   Yajima Arata, Yamashita Yuji, and Tsuji Nobuo, *Nihon bijutsu no hakkensha-tachi* (Tokyo daigaku shuppankai, 2003), p. 73.

12   Such techniques, distinctive to seventeenth-century Japanese aesthetics, have been viewed by modern critics as antecedents to modern abstract art (Soda, *Edo kijin kisei jiten,* pp. 46, 50).

13　Ban Kōkei and Mikuma Katen, *Kinsei kijinden; Zoku kinsei kijinden,* ed. Munemasa Isoo (Heibonsha, 1972), p. 101.

14　Soda, *Edo kijin kisei jiten,* pp. 51–52.

15　W. Puck Brecher, "To Romp in Heaven: A Translation of the *Hôsa Kyôshaden*," *Early Modern Japan: An Interdisciplinary Journal* 13 (Spring 2005): 11–27.

16　Yoshida, "The Stranger as God," p. 94.

17　See Marian Ury, "Recluses and Eccentric Monks: Tales from the Hosshinshu by Kamo no Chomei," *Monumenta Nipponica* 27, no. 2 (Summer 1992): 149–173.

18　Michele Marra, *The Aesthetics of Discontent: Politics and Reclusion in Medieval Japanese Literature* (Honolulu: University of Hawai'i Press, 1991), pp. 9, 62.

19　Michele Marra, "Semi-recluses (*Tonseisha*) and Impermanence (*Mujō*): Kamo no Chōmei and Urabe Kenkō," *Japanese Journal of Religious Studies* 11, no. 4 (December 1984): 338, 343.

20　Kendall H. Brown, *The Politics of Reclusion: Painting and Power in Momoyama Japan* (Honolulu: University of Hawai'i Press, 1997), p. 22. For a comprehensive study of reclusion in China, see Alan J. Berkowitz, *Patterns of Disengagement: The Practice and Portrayal of Reclusion in Early Medieval China* (Stanford, CA: Stanford University Press, 2000).

21　Brown, *The Politics of Reclusion,* p. 29.

22　Nelson Wu, "The Toleration of Eccentrics," *Art News* 57, no. 3 (May 1956): 29.

23　Nakano Mitsutoshi, *Kinsei shin kijinden* (Iwanami shoten, 2004), p. 165. Keiyū authored the prefaces for *Hōsa kyōshaden* (Biographies of Nagoya madmen, 1778) and *Baisaō gego* (Verses of Baisaō, 1763).

24　Subsequent painting genres interpreted Xie He's values differently, but his views were given renewed importance by Ming and then Edo period literati painters. Once Neo-Confucianism had become articulated and embraced, treatise writers adopted its vocabulary. Without meaningfully altering Su's vision, Wang Kai, author of the *Mustard Seed Garden Manual,* for instance, wrote not of inner nature but in terms of apprehending the *ri* (Principle) of the object. Thomas Froncek, *The Horizon Book of the Arts of China* (New York: American Heritage Publishing, 1969), p. 28.

25　Ibid., p. 156.

26　Nakata Yūjirō, *Bunjin garonshū* (Chūō kōronsha, 1982), p. 285.

27　Froncek, *The Horizon Book of the Arts of China,* p. 200.

28　Judith Zeitlin, *Historian of the Strange: Pu Songling and the Chinese Classical Tale* (Stanford, CA: Stanford University Press, 1993), p. 13.

29　Wu, "The Toleration of Eccentrics," p. 53.

30　James Cahill, *Fantastics and Eccentrics in Chinese Painting* (New York: The Asia Society, 1967), p. 87.

31 Jin Nong (1687–1764), Huang Shen (1687–1768), Gao Xiang (1688–1753), Li Fangying (1696—1755), Li Shan (1686?–1756), Luo Pin (1733–1799), Wang Shishen (1686–1759), Hua Yan (1682–1756), and Zheng Xie (1693–1765) are among this group of (more than eight) eighteenth-century literati active in the area surrounding Yanzhou. They are known as antiestablishment figures whose highly creative and individualistic works exemplified literati expressionism.

32 Cahill, *Fantastics and Eccentrics,* p. 96.

33 Zeitlin, *Historian of the Strange,* pp. 10, 199.

34 Ibid., p. 198.

35 Cao Xueqin, *The Story of the Stone,* vol. 3, trans. David Hawkes (Bloomington: Indiana University Press, 1980), pp. 235–236.

36 Wm. Theodore de Bary, "Individualism and Humanitarianism in Late Ming Thought," in *Self and Society in Ming Thought,* ed. Wm. Theodore de Bary and the Conference on Ming Thought (New York: Columbia University Press, 1970), pp. 153, 156.

37 Dorothy Ko, *Teachers of the Inner Chambers: Women and Culture in Seventeenth-Century China* (Stanford, CA: Stanford University Press, 1994), pp. 79–80.

38 Okada Takehiko, "The Zhu Xi and Wang Yang-ming Schools at the End of the Ming and Tokugawa Periods," trans. Robert J. J. Wargo, *Philosophy East and West* 23, nos. 1–2 (January–April 1973): 144.

39 De Bary, "Individualism and Humanitarianism," p. 205. The final phrase is from *The Analects* 17:13.

40 Ibid., p. 219. I am grateful to Peter Nosco for sharing his insights on this point.

41 Okada, "The Zhu Xi and Wang Yang-ming Schools," p. 141.

42 Hua-yuan Li Mowry, *Chinese Love Stories from "Ch'ing-shih"* (Hamden, CT: Archon Books, 1983), p. 3.

43 Hainai is an epithet for China, so in taking this name Feng posits himself as China's eccentric.

44 Nie Fusheng, *Feng Menglong yanjiu* (Studies on Feng Menglong) (Shanghai: Xuelin chubanshe, 2002), p. 35.

45 Pi-Ching Hsu, "Celebrating the Emotional Self: Feng Meng-Lung and Late Ming Ethics and Aesthetics" (Ph.D. diss., University of Minnesota, 1994), p. 15.

46 Mowry, *Chinese Love Stories,* p. 75.

47 Ibid., p. 75.

48 Much has been written about the cult of *qing.* See, for example, Paolo Santangelo, "Reconsidering the 'Cult of *qing*' in Late Imperial China: A 'Romantic Movement' or a Conveyer of Social Values?" *Ming Qing Yanjiu* 2006: 133–163.

49 Cited from Haruo Shirane, *Early Modern Japanese Literature: An Anthology 1600–1900* (New York: Columbia University Press, 2002), p. 368.

50 Peter Nosco, *Remembering Paradise: Nativism and Nostalgia in Eighteenth-Century Japan* (Cambridge, MA: Harvard University Press, 1990), p. 170.

51 Peter Flueckiger contests this interpretation, arguing that Confucian intellectuals (Ogyū Sorai, Hattori Nankaku, and Dazai Shundai) and Nativist thinkers (Kamo no Mabuchi and Mootori Norinaga) all continued to see human emotion, and by extension poetry, as having social and political implications. As such, they continued to understand emotion as requiring regulation and to understand poetry as valuable in its ability to make people's emotions accessible to rulers who, by understanding them better, could become better rulers. Confucians and Nativists, Flueckiger argues, shared common ground on these points (Peter Flueckiger, *Imagining Harmony: Poetry, Empathy, and Community in Mid-Tokugawa Confucianism and Nativism* (Stanford, CA: Stanford University Press, 2011), pp. 30–32.

52 Tōten was the penname of Miyazaki Torazō.

53 Miyazaki Tōten, *Kyōjindan* (Kokkō shobō, 1902), p. 3.

54 Ibid., pp. 5–6.

55 W. Puck Brecher, "Eccentricity as Ideology: Biographies of Meiji *Kijin*," *Japanese Language and Literature* 44, no. 2 (October 2010): 221–222.

56 Brown, *The Politics of Reclusion*, p. 55.

57 Dokkōsai was the son of Confucian scholar Hayashi Razan.

58 Hosokawa Junjirō, *In'itsu zenden* (Hosokawa Junjirō, 1885).

59 Takayama was stripped of his domain in 1587 under Hideyoshi's persecution of Christianity and accepted as a retainer of Maeda Toshiie the following year. The Christian expulsion of 1614 anticipated what would later develop into Japan's "closed country" (*sakoku*) policy.

60 In addition to Furuta Oribe (35,000 *koku*), the *Rikyū shichitetsu* include "Maeda Toshinaga (1562–1614; 1.2 million *koku*); Date Masamune (1567–1636; 620,000 *koku*); Shimazu Yoshihiro (1535–1619; 600,000 *koku*); Ikeda Terumasa (1564–1613; 520,000 *koku*); Fukushima Masanori (1561–1624; 500,000 *koku*); and Hosokawa Tadaoki (1563–1646; 400,000 *koku*)" (Furukawa, "The Tea Master Oribe," p. 102). Other sources include different individuals among the *Rikyū shichitetsu*.

61 For more on Kōetsu and this land grant, see W. Puck Brecher, "Kōetsumura: Of Rhythms and Reminiscence in Hon'ami Kōetsu's Commune," *Japan Review* 22 (2010): 27–53.

62 Hayashiya Tatsusaburō, *Kōetsu* (Dai-ichi hōki, 1964), p. 102.

63 For a comprehensive study of reclusion in medieval Japan, see Brown, *The Politics of Reclusion*, 1997.

64 Patricia Graham, *Tea of the Sages: The Art of Sencha* (Honolulu: University of Hawai'i Press, 1998), pp. 56, 97.

65 Joan Stanley-Baker, *The Transmission of Chinese Idealist Painting to Japan: Notes on the Early Phase (1661–1799)* (Ann Arbor: Center for Japanese Studies, University of Michigan, 1992), p. 70.

66 Ibid., p. 67.

67 Jōzan's and Chōshōshi's entries in this text will be discussed in Chapter 5.

68 For Satake Shozan's (1748–1785) version of this argument, see Kanō Hiroyuki, *Jyūhasseiki no nihon bijutsu: kattō suru biishiki* (Kyoto: Kyoto National Museum, 1990), p. 12.

69 I do not suggest that Sorai introduced this idea. I tend to follow the scholarship of Herman Ooms and Kurozumi Makoto, who have argued that Ancient Learning thinkers such as Itō Jinsai and Ogyū Sorai articulated what people had already begun to experience and thus know intuitively. As Lawrence Marceau puts it: "Jinsai and Sorai were merely articulating already widely held popular beliefs on the relationship between literature and Confucian ethics. Thus the importance of their theoretical writings lies not so much in their novelty, or even their direct influence on later writers, but rather in the fact that they make explicit that which is already implicit in social culture" (Marceau, *Takebe Ayatari*, pp. 7, 15–20).

70 See Chapter 4 for a genealogy of *kyō*.

71 Yagi Akiyoshi, " '*Kyōken' no keifu: Chūgoku kodai shisō ni okeru 'kyō' no shosō*," *Keio gijuku daigaku gengo bunka kenkyūjō kiyō* 37 (March 2006): 123.

72 Arthur Waley, trans., *The Analects of Confucius* (New York: Vintage, 1989), p. 212.

73 Oda Susumu, *Nihon no kyōkishi* (Shisakusha, 1990), p. 36.

74 Takahashi Hiromi, *Kyōto geien no nettowaaku* (Perikansha, 1988), p. 12.

75 Oda, *Nihon no kyōkishi*, p. 145.

76 Differentiation and human character will be further discussed in Chapter 4.

77 Sen Gyōbai, *Tessai no yōmeigaku: Washi no e wo miru nara, mazu san wo yondekure* (Bensei Shuppan, 2004), pp. 35–37.

78 Yagi, " '*Kyōken' no keifu*," p. 125. Wang Yangming gained credence in seventeenth-century Japan through the endorsement of Neo-Confucian scholars like Nakae Tōju (1608–1648) and his student Kumazawa Banzan (1619–1691). See Chapter 4 for a full discussion of Wang Yangming.

79 Burton Watson, trans., *Chuang Tzu: Basic Writings* (New York: Columbia University Press, 1964, 1996), p. 61.

80 Ibid., p. 63. Jieyu also appears in *Zhuangzi* 1:4 and 7:2, and in all cases his uselessness represents dissent against statecraft and moral cultivation.

81 Peipei Qiu, *Bashō and the Dao: The Zhuangzi and the Transformation of Haikai* (Honolulu: University of Hawai'i Press, 2005), p. 37.

82 Karaki Junzō, *Muyōsha no keifu* (Chikua Shobō, 1960), pp. 65–66.

83 Ibid., pp. 63–64. Sōgi was a leading *renga* master of his day.

212   Notes to Pages 48–58

84 Translation from Donald Keene, *Anthology of Japanese Literature* (New York: Grove Press, 1955), pp. 376. The original can be found in *Kōhon Bashō zenshū*, vol. 6 (Kadokawa shoten, 1962), pp. 470–471.

85 Qiu, *Bashō and the Dao*, p. 67.

86 Haruo Shirane, *Traces of Dreams: Landscape, Cultural Memory, and the Poetry of Bashō* (Stanford, CA: Stanford University Press, 1998), p. 73; Karaki, *Muyōsha no keifu*, p. 69.

87 Translation is from Qiu, *Bashō and the Dao*, p. 74.

88 Ibid., p. 74.

89 Peipei Qiu, "Celebrating *Kyō*: The Eccentricity of Bashō and Nanpo," *Early Modern Japan* 16 (2008): 84.

90 Here I use Qiu's translations of these terms. Sato translates *fūkyō* as "poetic dementia." Hiroaki Sato, *Japanese Women Poets: An Anthology* (Armonk, NY, and London: M. E. Sharpe, 2008), p. 144.

91 Peipei Qiu, "Bashō's *Fūryū* and the Aesthetic of *Shōyōyū*: Poetics of Eccentricity and Unconventionality," *Japan Studies Review* 5 (2001): 4.

92 For a full discussion, see Qiu, *Bashō and the Dao*, pp. 98–99.

93 Takahashi Hiromi, *Kyoto geien nettowaaku* (Perikansha, 1988), p. 183.

94 For a complete discussion of *tentori haikai* and commercialization of the *haikai* practice, see Cheryl A. Crowley, *Haikai Poet Yosa Buson and the Bashō Revival* (Leiden: Brill, 2007).

95 Ihara Saikaku, *Life of an Amorous Woman and Other Writings*, trans. Ivan Morris (Norfolk, CT: New Directions, 1963), pp. 20–22, 49–50.

96 Stephen Addiss, ed., *Japanese Quest for a New Vision: The Impact of Visiting Chinese Painters, 1600–1900* (Lawrence: Spencer Museum of Art, University of Kansas, 1986), p. 13.

97 Stanley-Baker, *The Transmission of Chinese Idealist Painting*, p. 47.

98 Brown, *The Politics of Reclusion*, pp. 175–176.

99 Oda, *Nihon no kyōkishi*, pp. 212–213.

100 Hyōta is a contraction of Hyōgushi Tahei (Tahei the screen maker).

101 Ban Kōkei, *Kinsei kijinden*, pp. 193–195.

102 Patti Kameya, "Paupers, Poets, and Paragons: Eccentricity as Virtue in *Kinsei kijinden* (*Eccentrics of our times, 1790*)" (Ph.D. diss., University of Chicago, 2006), pp. 145–146.

103 Imahashi Riko, *Edo ega to bungaku: Byōsha to kotoba no edo bungakushi* (Tokyo University Press, 1999), pp. 52–54.

CHAPTER 3: Strange Tastes

Kanō Hiroyuki, *Jyūhasseiki no nihon bijutsu: Kattō suru biishiki* (Kyoto: Kyoto National Museum, 1990), p. 11.

1 Kenneth Yasuda, *The Japanese Haiku: Its Essential Nature and History* (Tokyo: Tuttle, 2002), p. 244.

2 惟然 (Izen) is also read Inen.

3 Motoyama Tekishū, *Meijin kijin* (Shigensha, 1926), p. 30.

4 Ban Kōkei and Mikuma Katen, *Kinsei kijinden; Zoku kinsei kijinden,* ed. Munemasa Isoo (Heibonsha, 1972), pp. 190–192.

5 Bashō's two verses are: *mazu tanomu / shii no ki mo ari / natsu kodachi* (For now, I will turn to the large oak tree—a grove in summer), trans. Haruo Shirane, in "Matsuo Bashō and The Poetics of Scent" *HJAS* 52, no. 1 (June 1992): 106; and *ikameshiki / oto ya arare no / hinokigasa* (How harsh it sounds! the spattering of the hail on my travelling hat), trans. Makoto Ueda, in *Matsuo Bashō* (Tokyo: Kodansha International, 1982), p. 55.

6 Nakano Mitsutoshi, *Edo Kyōshaden* (Chūō kōron shinsha, 2007), p. 56.

7 Hyakuan's treatises are *Baikarin sōmandan* and *Kayōshū.*

8 Gazoku no kai, ed., with Nakano Mitsutoshi, *Gazoku bunsō: Nakano Mitsutoshi sensei koki kinen shiryōshū* (Kyūko shoin, 2005), pp. 56–57.

9 Harumachi was a poet and ukiyoe artist whose illustrated comic tales written in hiragana and bound with yellow paper came to be called *kibyōshi* (yellow covers). For a translation and discussion of *Kachō kakurenbo* (Hide and seek among flowers and birds), see W. Puck Brecher, "In Appreciation of Buffoonery, Egotism, and the Shōmon School: Koikawa Harumachi's *Kachō kakurenbō,*" *Early Modern Japan: An Interdisciplinary Journal* 18 (2010): pp. 88–102.

10 Translated in Donald Keene, *Travelers of a Hundred Ages* (New York: Columbia University Press, 1999), p. 347.

11 *Haikai daijiten* (Encyclopedic dictionary of *haikai*) also gives Hokka's dates as 1700–1746, but Nakano Mitsutoshi claims that the year of his death cannot be confirmed.

12 Gazoku no kai, *Gazoku bunsō,* pp. 168–169.

13 Comparisons to Cheng Hao (1032–1085), a Neo-Confucian scholar noted for his moral virtue and piety, and Guan Yu (d. 219), a general famous for his long beard, would be considered absurd and therefore humorous.

14 Gazoku no kai, *Gazoku bunsō,* pp. 168–169. Scenting one's clothing with incense, the hairstyle (*kawara*), and the tooth blackening are all women's attributes. For a man, these practices would be considered intentional markers of strangeness.

15 Nakano Mitsutoshi, *Kinsei shin kijinden* (Iwanami shoten, 2004), p. 23.

16 Shūshiki studied under Kikaku, and one of her *haikai* is included in *Kachō kakurenbō.* Sonome studied with Bashō and Kikaku.

17 Gazoku no kai, *Gazoku bunsō,* pp. 168–169.

18 These individuals constitute a representative sample, not a comprehensive list, and I have selected them based on their lasting legacy as eccentrics as judged by commentary from their contemporaries and successors. Collectively they represent both the culmination of *nanga* and the maturation of the *ki* aesthetic.

19 See, for example, Nakano, *Kinsei shin-kijinden;* Penelope Mason, *Japanese Literati Painters: The Third Generation* (New York: The Brooklyn Museum, 1977).

20 Nakata Yūjirō, *Bunjin garonshū* (Chūō kōron-sha, 1982), p. 287.

21 Lawrence E. Marceau, *Takebe Ayatari: A* Bunjin *Bohemian in Early Modern Japan* (Ann Arbor: Center for Japanese Studies, University of Michigan, 2004), pp. 15–20. Amateurism was an ironic calling for Japanese literati, for even the most celebrated painted professionally throughout their careers. Accepting commissions and students much as professional schools did, they embraced amateurism as a designation symbolic of certain attitudes: for example, philosophical opposition to commercialism and stylistic opposition to the technical stringency espoused by the professional schools.

22 Joan Stanley-Baker, *The Transmission of Chinese Idealist Painting to Japan: Notes on the Early Phase (1661–1799)* (Ann Arbor: Center for Japanese Studies, University of Michigan, 1992), p. 47.

23 Ibid., p. 148.

24 Ibid., p. 112. See Sakazaki Shizuka, ed., *Nihon garon taikan,* vol. 1 (Arusu, 1927–1929), pp. 147–148.

25 For a full discussion of reclusion in China, see Alan J. Berkowitz, *Patterns of Disengagement: The Practice and Portrayal of Reclusion in Early Medieval China* (Stanford, CA: Stanford University Press, 2000).

26 Chen Yang and Mitaka Atsuo, "*Nihon injakō,*" *Bungaku* 2, no. 1 (January–February 2001): 61.

27 Nakamura Yukihiko, "*Edo bunjin no seikatsu,*" in *Edo jidai zushi,* vol. 5, ed. Akai Tatsurō (Chikuma shobō, 1976), p. 175.

28 Chen and Mitaka, "*Nihon injakō,*" p. 62.

29 Quoted in Kanō Hiroyuki, *Jyūhasseiki no nihon bijutsu: Kattō suru biishiki* (Kyoto: Kyoto National Museum, 1990), pp. 4–5.

30 For a discussion of this tradition in Chinese painting, see Katharine Burnett, "A Discourse of Originality in Late Ming Chinese Painting Criticism," *Art History* 23, no. 4 (November 2000): 522–558.

31 Nakano Mitsutoshi, "The Role of Traditional Aesthetics," in *Eighteenth Century Japan: Culture and Society,* ed. Andrew C. Gerstle (Richmond, Surrey, UK: Curzon, 2000), p. 130.

32 Kanō, *Jyūhasseiki no nihon bijutsu,* p. 5.

33 Yoshiho Yonezawa and Chu Yoshizawa, *Japanese Painting in the Literati Style,* trans. Betty Iverson Monroe (New York: Weatherhill, 1974), p. 22.

34 Yanagisawa Kien and Mori Senzō, *Unpyō zasshi* (Iwanami shoten, 1936), p. 76.

35 Ban Kōkei, *Kinsei kijinden,* pp. 151–153.

36 Patricia J. Graham, *Tea of the Sages: The Art of Sencha* (Honolulu: University of Hawai'i Press, 1998), pp. 70–71.

37 Takahashi Hiromi, *Kyoto geien nettowaaku* (Perikansha, 1988), p. 21.

38 Quoted in Graham, *Tea of the Sages,* p. 73.

39 Takahashi, *Kyoto geien nettowaaku,* p. 30.

40 Ibid., p. 37.

41 Melinda Takeuchi, "Visions of a Wanderer: The True View Paintings of Ike no Taiga (1723–1776)" (Ph.D. diss., University of Michigan, 1979), p. 41.

42 I refer the interested reader to *Kinsei kijinden* and Melinda Takeuchi's work.

43 Takeuchi, "Visions of a Wanderer," p. 39.

44 Ibid., pp. 46, 48; Akai Tatsuro, *Kinsei no gaka: Sono shiyū to sakuhin* (Kakugawa Shoten, 1976), p. 66.

45 Ueda Akinari, *Taidai shōshin roku,* trans. William E. Clarke and Wendy E. Cobcroft (Sydney: Premodern Japanese Studies, 2009), p. 63.

46 Stanley-Baker, *The Transmission of Chinese Idealist Painting to Japan,* p. 112.

47 Nakata, *Bunjin garonshū,* pp. 315–316.

48 Stanley-Baker, *The Transmission of Chinese Idealist Painting to Japan,* p. 86.

49 Takeuchi, "Visions of a Wanderer," p. 23.

50 Melinda Takeuchi, *Taiga's True Views: The Language of Landscape Painting in Eighteenth-Century Japan* (Stanford, CA: Stanford University Press, 1992), pp. xiii–xiv.

51 Ibid., p. 123.

52 Takeuchi, "Visions of a Wanderer," p. 42.

53 Takeuchi Gengen'ichi, *Haika kijindan*; *Zoku haika kijindan* (Iwanami Shoten, 1987), p. 259.

54 Hugh Wylie, "Nanga Painting Treatises of Nineteenth Century Japan" (Ph.D. diss., University of Kansas, 1991), pp. 58–59.

55 Ibid., p. 142.

56 Cheryl A. Crowley, *Haikai Poet Yosa Buson and the Bashō Revival* (Leiden: Brill, 2007), p. 42.

57 John M. Rosenfield in collaboration with Fumiko E. Cranston, *Extraordinary Persons: Works by Eccentric, Nonconformist Japanese Artists of the Early Modern Era (1580–1868) in the Collection of Kimiko and John Powers,* vol. 2, ed. Naomi Noble Richard (Cambridge, MA: Harvard University Art Museums, 1999), p. 74.

58 For a full discussion of Buson, see Crowley, *Haikai Poet Yosa Buson and the Bashō Revival.*

59 Murakami Mamoru, *Ban Kōkei-sen autosaidaa 119-nin: Kinsei kijinden* (Kyōikusha, 1981), p. 300.

60 Earl Jackson, "The Heresy of Meaning: Japanese Symbolist Poetry," *Harvard Journal of Asiatic Studies* 52, no. 2 (December 1991): 595.

61 Ban Kōkei, *Kinsei kijinden,* p. 234. *KKD* includes Hakuin under the entry for Hakuyūshi, a healer who lives over two hundred years.

62 For this interpretation, see Yajima Arata, Yamashita Yuji, and Tsuji Nobuo, *Nihon bijutsu no hakkensha-tachi* (Tokyo daigaku shuppankai, 2003), p. 194.

63 John C. Maraldo, "Rousseau, Hakuseki, and Hakuin: Paradigms of Self in Three Autobiographers," in *Self as Person in Asian Theory and Practice,* ed. Roger Ames et al. (Albany: SUNY Press, 1994), p. 67.

64 Ibid., p. 67.

65 Ibid., p. 70.

66 Hakuin's self-portraits will be discussed in Chapter 7.

67 Yoshimura Teiji, *Rekishi no naka no kyojintachi* (Sakuhinsha, 1982), p. 238.

68 Yajima et al., *Nihon bijutsu no hakkensha-tachi,* p. 84.

69 J. Hillier, *The Uninhibited Brush: Japanese Art in the Shijō Style* (London: Hugh M. Moss Ltd., 1974), p. 85.

70 Kimura Shigekazu, ed., *Nihon egaron taisei,* vol. 10 (Perikansha, 1998), p. 294.

71 Tsuji Nobuo, *Kisō no keifu* (Perikansha, 1988), pp. 93, 95.

72 Rosenfield and Cranston, *Extraordinary Persons,* vol. 3, p. 89; Money Hickman, "Shōhaku the Eccentric and His Paintings in Indianapolis Museum of Art," *Orientations* 32 (March 2001): 94.

73 Hickman, "Shōhaku the Eccentric," p. 99.

74 Tsuji, *Kisō no keifu,* pp. 90–91.

75 Tsuji Nobuo, *Playfulness in Japanese Art,* trans. Joseph Seubert (Lawrence: Spencer Museum of Art, University of Kansas, 1986), p. 69.

76 Tsuji, *Kisō no keifu,* p. 93.

77 Tsuji Nobuo, "Shōhaku as a Heathen," *Soga Shōhaku Exhibition* (Mie: Mie Prefectural Art Museum, 1987), unpaginated.

78 Satō Yasuhiro, interview by author, Tokyo, April 6, 2004. Cited with permission.

79 Nesaki Mitsuo, "What Underlies Shōhaku's Art—Time and Place," in *Soga Shōhaku Exhibition* (Mie: Mie Prefectural Art Museum, 1987), unpaginated.

80 Money L. Hickman, "Takada Keiho and Soga Shohaku," in *Exhibition Soga Shohaku* (Mie: Mie Prefectural Art Museum, 1998), unpaginated.

81 Satō Yasuhiro, *Jakuchū, Shōhaku: Meihō Nihon no bijutsu,* 27 (Shogakkan, 1991): 105, 140.

82 Nesaki, "What Underlies Shōhaku's Art," unpaginated.

83 Kanō Hiroyuki, "*Soga Shōhaku no koto: Itanteki seishin ni tsuite,*" in *Suibokuga no kyoshō,* vol. 8 (Kodansha, 1995), pp. 90, 97.

84 Tsuji, *Kisō no keifu,* p. 97.

85 Ibid., p. 101.

86 Satō, *Jakuchū, Shōhaku,* p. 3.

87 Tsuji, *Kisō no keifu,* p.100.

88 Quoted in Money Hickman, "Shōhaku the Eccentric," p. 94.

89 Sugimoto Shutarō, "*Uragami Gyokudō: kijin, kisō, kiroku,*" in *Suibokuga no kyoshō,* vol. 13 (Kodansha, 1995), p. 93; Kanō, p. 97.

90 Ibid., p. 94.

91 Tsuji Nobuo, "Life and Works of Itō Jakuchū," in *Itō Jakuchū,* trans. Yasushi Egami (Bijutsu Shuppan-sha, 1974), title page.

92 Satō Yasuhiro, interview by author, Tokyo, April 6, 2004. Cited with permission.

93 *Shirarezaru Nihon ega: Shiatoru hakutakuan korekushon* (Ōtsu-shi: Otsu City Museum of History and the University of Washington Press, 2001), p. 188.

94 Kimura, *Nihon egaron taisei,* vol. 10, p. 279.

95 Elizabeth Lillehoj, ed., *Acquisition: Art and Ownership in Edo-Period Japan* (Warren, CT: Floating World Editions, 2007), p. 13.

96 Some art historians do see evidence of mental instability in Jakuchū. J. Hillier writes that the disparity between Jakuchū's meticulously studied compositions of roosters, fish, and birds and his more personal and satirical works "is hardly one that can be explained on stylistic grounds at all, but only in terms of a split personality, an artistic schizophrenia" (J. Hillier, *The Uninhibited Brush,* p. 83). For similar interpretations, see Yajima Arata, Yamashita Yuji, and Tsuji Nobuo, *Nihon bijutsu no hakkenshatachi* (Tokyo daigaku shuppankai, 2003), p. 199.

97 Suzuki Susumu, *Kinsei itan no geijutsu* (Mariya Shoten, 1973), p. 146.

98 Rosenfield, *Extraordinary Persons,* vol. 3, p. 64.

99 Hillier, *The Uninhibited Brush,* p. 58. Rosetsu maintained a professional relationship with Ōkyo after leaving his tutelage, even collaborating with him on projects (Rosenfield, p. 65).

100 Hillier, *The Uninhibited Brush,* pp. 69–78.

101 Ibid., p. 70.

102 Suzuki, *Kinsei itan no geijutsu,* p. 173; Rosenfield, *Extraordinary Persons,* vol. 1, p. 328.

103 Active in the early nineteenth century, Kinkoku is chronologically anomalous to this section. Though in some ways a transitional figure, his detached aestheticism and intense individualism recall eccentric characteristics distinctive to second-generation *bunjin* from the late eighteenth century.

104 Rosenfield, *Extraordinary Persons,* vol. 3, p. 113; Patricia Fister, "Yokoi Kinkoku: The Life and Painting of a Mountain Ascetic" (Ph.D. diss., University of Kansas, 1983), abstract.

105 Fujimori Seikichi, *Shirazaru kisai tensai* (Shunjūsha, 1965), p. 226.

106 The eighth month would correspond to the seventh month of pregnancy as counted in the West.

107 Yokoi Kinkoku, Fujimori Seikichi, *Kinkoku shōnin gyōjōki* (Heibonsha, 1965), pp. 3–4.

108 Fister, *Yokoi Kinkoku,* p. 239.

109 Ibid., 49–50.

110 *Shirazaru Nihon ega: Shiatoru hakutakuan korekushon* (Ōtsu-shi: Otsu City Museum of History and the University of Washington Press, 2001), p. 155.

111 Fujimori, *Shirazaru kisai tensai,* p. 238.

112 Furukawa quoted in ibid., p. 243.

113 Fister, *Yokoi Kinkoku,* p. 248.

114 Ibid., p. 245.

115 Ibid., p . 65.

116 Ibid., pp. 63–64.

117 For a discussion of aesthetic practice within off-duty spaces, see W. Puck Brecher, "Down and Out in Negishi: Reclusion and Struggle in an Edo Suburb," *Journal of Japanese Studies* 35, no. 1 (Winter 2009): 1–35.

118 For more on this, see Eiko Ikegami, *Bonds of Civility: Aesthetic Networks and the Political Origins of Japanese Culture* (Cambridge: Cambridge University Press, 2005), pp. 153–158, 187–191.

119 Takeuchi's son Seisei produced the sequel *Zoku-haika kijindan* in 1833.

120 See Sato Hiroyuki, *Japanese Women Poets: An Anthology* (Armonk, NY, and London: M. E. Sharpe, 2008), for more on these poets and translations of their *haikai.*

121 Hino Tatsuo, "*Bunjin no kōyū,*" *Bungaku* 4, no. 42 (1974): 59.

122 Stanley-Baker, *The Transmission of Chinese Idealist Painting to Japan,* p. 112.

123 Tajihi Ikuo and Nakano Mitsutoshi, eds., *Shinnihon koten bungaku taikei* (Iwanami Shoten, 2000), p. 411.

124 All three women appear in *Kinsei kijinden,* along with selections of Kaji's poetry. See also Motoyama Tekishū, *Meijin kijin* (Shigensha, 1926), pp. 8–10.

125 Ernest F. Fenollosa, *Epochs of Chinese and Japanese Art: An Outline History of East Asian Design,* vol. 2 (New York: Dover Publications, 1913, 1963), p. 164; and Graham, *Tea of the Sages,* p. 202.

CHAPTER 4: Strange Thoughts

1 Takahashi Hiromi, *Kyoto geien nettowaaku* (Perikansha, 1988), pp. 18–19. For a full treatment of this sociopolitical decline, see Timon Screech, *The Shogun's Painted Culture: Fear and Creativity in the Japanese States 1760–1829* (London: Reaktion, 2000). For a discussion of *Kinsei kijinden* within the context of social upheaval, see Patti Kameya, "Paupers, Poets, and Paragons: Eccentricity as Virtue in *Kinsei kijinden* (*Eccentrics of our times, 1790*)" (Ph.D. diss., University of Chicago, 2006).

2 Screech, *The Shogun's Painted Culture,* p. 93.

3 Ibid., pp. 93, 95, 97.

4 Here I use the term "orthodoxy" in reference to official interpretations of Zhu Xi Neo-Confucianism as established by Hayashi Razan (1583–1657) and reiterated by thinkers like Yamazaki Ansai (1618–1682). I follow the view advanced by Herman Ooms and Kurozumi Makoto that Zhu Xi-ism was far from dominant in mainstream Tokugawa society.

5 Maruyama Masao, *Wabunshū: Maruyama Masao techō no kai hen* (Misuzu Shobō, 2008), pp. 66–73.

6 Takahashi, *Kyoto geien nettowaaku*, p. 20.

7 Maruyama, *Wabunshū*, pp. 50–51.

8 Wm. Theodore de Bary, "Some Common Tendencies in Neo-Confucianism," in *Confucianism in Action*, ed. David S. Nivison and Arthur Wright (Stanford, CA: Stanford University Press, 1959).

9 Tetsuo Najita, "Intellectual Change in Early Eighteenth Century Tokugawa Confucianism," *Journal of Asian Studies* 34, no. 4 (August 1975): 931.

10 Ibid., p. 943.

11 Kurozumi Makoto, "Tokugawa Confucianism and Its Meiji Japan Reconstruction," in *Rethinking Confucianism: Past and Present in China, Japan, Korea, and Vietnam,* ed. Benjamin Elman, John B. Duncan, and Herman Ooms (Los Angeles, CA: UCLA Asian Pacific Monograph Series, 2002), p. 370.

12 Ibid., p. 383.

13 Ibid., p. 379.

14 Herman Ooms, "Human Nature: Singular (China) and Plural (Japan)?" in *Rethinking Confucianism: Past and Present in China, Japan, Korea, and Vietnam,* ed. Benjamin Elman, John B. Duncan, and Herman Ooms (Los Angeles, CA: UCLA Asian Pacific Monograph Series, 2002), pp. 98–99.

15 Charlotte Furth, "Androgynous Males and Deficient Females," *Late Imperial China* 9, no. 2 (December 1988): 8.

16 Ibid., p. 8.

17 There are numerous possible translations of *kyōsha* (*kyōja*) or *kyōjin*. As explained below, translators of Confucius, Mencius, and Zhu Xi have opted for wild, ambitious, impetuous, or ardent. The meaning of 狂 is unspecific or context-specific, but in the context of the Confucian classics it generally connotes unrestrained or egocentric behavior that suggests social criticism; by extension, the *kyōjin* is a self-absorbed or idiosyncratic individual. In early modern Japanese usage, the *kyōjin* is a reckless, lawless, aloof individual who occupies a self-made world in defiance of the social mores. The reader is reminded that this term does not connote the modern implication of insanity or mental illness.

18 Haruo Shirane, ed., *Early Modern Japanese Literature: An Anthology, 1600–1900* (New York: Columbia University Press, 2002), pp. 532–533.

19   Edward Slingerland, trans., *Confucius' Analects: With Selections from Traditional Commentaries* (Indianapolis: Hackett Publishing, 2003), p. 149.

20   Adapted from James Legge, trans., *The Works of Mencius: Translated, and with Critical and Exegetical Notes, Prolegomena, and Copious Indexes* (New York: Dover Publications, 1970), pp. 498–501.

21   Zhu Xi, *Zhuzi youlei* (The words of Zhu Xi), vol. 2, bk. 29 (Beijing: Kuchi Chubanshe, 1992), p. 741.

22   Ibid., p. 1109.

23   E. Bruce Brooks and A. Taeko Brooks, trans., *The Original Analects: Sayings of Confucius and His Successors* (New York: Columbia University Press, 1998), p. 128.

24   Nakano Mitsutoshi, *"Kyōbun ishiki no haikai,"* *Bungaku gogaku* 54 (December 1969): 47.

25   Okada Takehiko, "The Zhu Xi and Wang Yang-ming Schools at the End of the Ming and Tokugawa Periods," trans. Robert J. J. Wargo, *Philosophy East and West* 23, nos. 1–2 (January–April 1973): 141.

26   *Hōsa kyōshaden* is discussed in Chapter 5.

27   Nakano Mitsutoshi, *"Hōsa kyōshaden,"* in *Shinnihon koten bungaku taikei,* ed. Tajihi Ikuo and Nakano Mitsutoshi (Iwanami Shoten, 2000), p. 44.

28   Ibid., p. 48.

29   Shimada Shūjirō, "Concerning the I-p'in Style of Painting," trans. James Cahill, *Oriental Art* 7, no. 2 (Summer 1961): 66–74; 8, no. 3 (Autumn 1962): 130–137; 10, no. 1 (Spring 1964): 19–26.

30   Haruo Shirane, *Traces of Dreams: Landscape, Cultural Memory, and the Poetry of Bashō* (Stanford, CA: Stanford University Press, 1998), p. 289.

31   Takahashi, *Kyoto geien nettowaaku,* pp. 39, 59, 73, 215.

32   Samuel Hideo Yamashita, "Nature and Artifice in the Writings of Ogyū Sorai," in *Confucianism and Tokugawa Culture,* ed. Peter Nosco (Honolulu: University of Hawaiʻi Press, 1984), p. 146.

33   Melinda Takeuchi, *Taiga's True Views: The Language of Landscape Painting in Eighteenth-Century Japan* (Stanford, CA: Stanford University Press, 1992), p. 122.

34   Peter Nosco, *Remembering Paradise: Nativism and Nostalgia in Eighteenth-Century Japan* (Cambridge, MA: Harvard University Press, 1990), p. 142.

35   Ibid., p. 143.

36   Yoshida Tarō, *"Shōheikō ni okeru rekishi kyōiku no kenkyū,"* *Yokohama kokuritsi daigaku kyōiku kiyō,* 4 (December 1964): 41–57. The Shōheikō was a private academy for sons of the *bakufu* elite operated by Hayashi Razan and his heirs between 1630 and 1797, and then by the *bakufu* between 1797 and 1870.

37   Tetsuo Najita, *Japan: The Intellectual Foundations of Modern Japanese Politics* (Chicago: University of Chicago Press, 1974), p. 53.

38   Ibid., pp. 52, 59.

39   Eiko Ikegami, *Bonds of Civility: Aesthetic Networks and the Political Origins of Japanese Culture* (Cambridge: Cambridge University Press, 2005), p. 369.

40   Tetsuo Najita, *Visions of Virtue in Tokugawa Japan: The Kaitokudō Merchant Academy of Osaka* (Chicago: University Chicago Press, 1987), p. 116. For more on Tominaga's attack on Shinto, Confucianism, and Buddhism, see "Okina no fumi" (Jottings of an old man), Tetsuo Najita, trans., in *Readings in Tokugawa Thought: Selected Papers,* vol. 9 (Chicago: The Center for East Asian Studies, University of Chicago, 1993), pp. 69–80.

41   Tetsuo Najita, *Visions of Virtue,* p. 120.

42   Ibid., p. 145.

43   Tetsuo Najita, "History and Nature in Eighteenth-century Tokugawa Japan," in *The Cambridge History of Japan,* vol. 4, ed. John W. Hall (Cambridge and New York: Cambridge University Press, 1991), p. 645.

44   Ibid., p. 646. I use "aesthetes" and "scholars" for convenience, not to isolate literati from the growing class of private scholars and physicians. The *bunjin* arts were standard fare in samurai education, and proficiency was expected. Hayashi Razan, for example, had a hand in determining the subject matter painted by Kanō School artists in service to the *bakufu;* Confucian scholar Arai Hakuseki (1656–1725) published *Gakō Binran* (Handbook on painters), which gave bibliographical details of noted painters beginning with Prince Shōtoku; in "*E no koto*" (On painting; discussed in Chapter 6), Motoori Norinaga bemoaned his apparent lack of talent in painting and poetry, though he did dabble in both.

45   Shōeki withdrew to self-exile; Daini, who advocated rebellion, was executed for treason.

46   We recall that Tominaga Nakamoto was expelled from the Kaitokudō in Osaka in 1730, but that reactions to heterodoxy by the academy and the social mainstream softened considerably following a period of adaptation.

47   Nakano Mitsutoshi, *Edo kyōshaden* (Chūō Kōron-shinsha, 2007), pp. 264–266.

48   Ibid., p. 278. At age forty, Somon discovered the *Zhou yi* (The Changes of the Zhou), the section of the Book of Changes that explains divination using the 64 hexagrams, and became proficient at fortune-telling.

49   Ogawa Kan'ichi, "Somon koji no buhō genryūron," *Ryūkoku shidan* 68–69 (December 1974): 84.

50   As discussed in Chapter 5, Kanga was a collaborator on *Kinsei kijinden* (*KKD*) and received entries in *Ochiguri monogatari* and *Zokukinsei kijinden.* Rikunyo was also involved in the production of *KKD.*

51   For a translation, see Michael Pye, trans., *Emerging from Meditation* (Honolulu: University of Hawai'i Press, 1990).

52   Ogawa, "Somon koji no buhō genryūron," p. 88.

53   Nakano, *Edo kyōshaden,* p. 267.

54   Ogawa, "Somon koji no buhō genryūron," pp. 89–90.

55   Ibid., p. 85; Nakano, *Edo kyōshaden,* p. 289.

56   Nakano, *Edo kyōshaden,* p. 278.

57   Ibid., pp. 276–277.

58   Ibid., p. 286.

59   Ibid., p. 295. Wu Wang was the first emperor of the Zhou dynasty and Li Si was minister under the first Emperor of China.

60   Ibid., pp. 295–296.

61   Gazoku no kai, ed., with Nakano Mitsutoshi, *Gazoku bunsō: Nakano Mitsutoshi sensei koki kinen shiryōshū* (Kyūko shoin, 2005), p. 48. For a translation of *Fūryū Shidōken-den,* see Haruo Shirane, ed., *Early Modern Japanese Literature: An Anthology, 1600–1900* (New York: Columbia University Press, 2002), pp. 486–512. Shidōken's polemics likely generated as much disgust as merriment, an antipathy of impressive longevity. In his treatise *Ijin to kijin no betsu* (The distinction between heroes and eccentrics, 1912), Yagi Sōsaburō concludes that Shidōken was a fake. For Yagi, the fact that Shidōken delivered his sermons while brandishing a phallus-shaped stick and used crude language to produce laughter made the entire performance an exercise in narcissistic self-promotion. Yagi Sōsaburō, *Ijin to shūyō* (Sūzan-bō, 1912), p. 12.

62   Gazoku no kai, *Gazoku bunsō,* p. 665.

63   Ibid., p. 49.

64   Myōraku Daishi (Master Myōraku, C. Miao-le, 711–783) was the ninth patriarch of the Tendai sect in China.

65   Ibid., pp. 53–54.

66   Ibid., p. 53.

67   Dorothy Ko, *Teachers of the Inner Chambers: Women and Culture in Seventeenth-Century China* (Stanford, CA: Stanford University Press, 1994), p. 83.

68   Maruyama Masao, *Studies in the Intellectual History of Tokugawa Japan* (Princeton, NJ: Princeton University Press, 1974), p. 226.

69   Nakano Mitsutoshi, *"Kyōbun ishiki no haikai,"* p. 48.

CHAPTER 5: *Eccentrics of Recent Times* and Social Value

1   Marvin Marcus, *Paragons of the Ordinary: The Biographical Literature of Mori Ōgai* (Honolulu: University of Hawai'i Press, 1993), p. 16.

2   *Kinsei kijinden* was illustrated by Mikuma Katen (1730–1794) and published in Kyoto by Hayashi Bunkindō.

3   Though the term had nominally been used earlier by Ueda Akinari (1776) and Tangai Jikujō (1777), it had not been defined or explained.

4 *KKD* had tremendous historical impact, whereas *HKD* and *Ochiguri monogatari,* not published until much later, did not. *KKD* was written with the clear intention of publication, and its authors deliberately defined the term *kijin* to be both compelling and philosophically acceptable to contemporary readers.

5 For an annotated translation of this text, see W. Puck Brecher, "To Romp in Heaven: A Translation of the *Hōsa Kyōshaden*," *Early Modern Japan: An Interdisciplinary Journal* 13 (Spring 2005): 11–27.

6 Rikurin's manuscript was never published but survives in the Tokyo National Museum; the Historiographical Institute at Tokyo University and the National Diet Library hold the only two publicly accessible extant copies of a 1941 reprint by Nagoya Onkokai Sōsho. These failed attempts at circulation explain why the text was ostensibly unknown until its 2000 publication in *Shinnihon koten bungaku taikei.*

7 Wan Shi, a child prodigy who admired Laozi's *Dao-de Jing,* refused to take the civil service exam and did not pursue any official appointment, instead concentrating on writing poems and books.

8 "Tuo Tuo Song Shi" (Song history), in *Sibu beiyao, Shibu* (The collection of history), book 457, Biography 216, part 1 (Reclusion) (Taipei: Taiwan Zhonghua shuju, 1971), pp. 14042–14043.

9 Li Xueqin and Lu Wenyu, eds., *Siku dacidian,* vol. 1 (Changchun: Jilin Daxue chubanshe, 1996), p. 1522.

10 Chen Jiru, *Kuangfu zhiyan* (Taipei: Iwen, 1965). I am indebted to Chia-Lan Chang for bringing these sources to my attention.

11 Edward Slingerland, trans., *Confucius' Analects: With Selections from Traditional Commentaries* (Indianapolis: Hackett Publishing, 2003), p. 88.

12 Takahashi Hiromi, *Kyoto geien nettowaaku* (Perikansha, 1988), p. 48.

13 Tajihi Ikuo and Nakano Mitsutoshi, eds., *Shinnihon koten bungaku taikei* (Iwanami Shoten, 2000), p. 427.

14 For an alternate theory concerning the participation of Iwagaki Ryūkei (1741–1806) and multiple members of his Kyoto-based poetry circle, see Tajihi and Nakano, *Shinnihon koten bungaku taikei,* pp. 428–431.

15 Over the course of the following century *Heian Jinbutsushi* was published nine times: 1768, 1775, 1783, 1813, 1822, 1830, 1838, 1852, and 1867.

16 Gen Tadamoto (also called Nagata Kanga, 1738–1792) and Tan Bunchū (1732–1790) are the remaining two figures. Tadamoto was a Chinese Learning (*kangaku*) scholar and noted calligrapher, and Bunchū was a poet listed in the *Heian jinbutsushi* as a scholar (*gakusha*). Their friendship with Rikunyo could leave little doubt of their inclusion in *ZKKD.*

17 Ban Kōkei and Mikuma Katen, *Kinsei kijinden; Zoku kinsei kijinden,* Munemasa Isoo, ed. (Heibonsha, 1972), p. 153. I am indebted to Melinda Takeuchi for sharing her own translation of this passage.

18 Jikujō's eulogy reads as follows: "Taiga knows about all sorts of things. He doesn't pander to others. On the outside he appears restless but on the inside he is fastidious. He is humble but not obsequious, and has no need for undue etiquette. He doesn't always do what he ought, and although he may know an answer may not reveal it. Personifying all kinds of righteousness, he is by no means without morals. He shows up in unexpected places and gives alms without ever seeking to receive any, for he cares not whether he makes or loses money. For all these reasons he should be regarded a *kijin* 畸人.
    "He was a brilliant child and highly skilled in all his studies. He was especially good at painting, preferring landscapes (*sansuiga*), and enjoyed climbing famous mountains and venturing into the dark depths of tall peaks. There was nowhere he would not venture. He climbed Mount Fuji several times, always by different routes, and painted numerous distinctive pictures of that mountain. His paintings are unequaled in history. He became ill and died at Kazuhara Hall on the thirteenth day of the fourth month in 1775. . . . As he had no children, Taiga's line was terminated. All knew Taiga's painting but few knew his heart. Those who did, extend it to others. Young people will surely follow in his path." Anzai Unen, *Kinsei meika shogadan,* reproduced in Sugihara Izan, *Nihon meika shogadan* (Matsuyama-dō, 1925).
19 Fujiwara Ietaka, *Ochiguri monogatari,* reprinted in Tajihi Ikuo and Nakano Mitsutoshi, eds, *Shin nihon koten bungaku taikei,* 97 (Iwanami shoten, 2000), pp. 75–76.
20 Mount Feilai Feng is one of the ten famous views of Lake Xi Hu.
21 Fujiwara, *Ochiguri monogatari,* p. 76.
22 Throughout his life Taiga maintained a close relationship with Manpukuji, which commissioned him to paint a total of twenty-nine of its sliding door panels.
23 Patti Kameya, "Paupers, Poets, and Paragons: Eccentricity as Virtue in *Kinsei kijinden* (*Eccentrics of our times, 1790*)" (Ph.D. diss., University of Chicago, 2006), pp. 43, 46.
24 Fujiwara, *Ochiguri monogatari,* p. 108.
25 Ban Kōkei, *Kinsei kijinden,* p. 79.
26 Fujiwara, *Ochiguri monogatari,* p. 103.
27 Ban Kōkei, *Kinsei kijinden,* p. 453.
28 Kendall H. Brown, *The Politics of Reclusion: Painting and Power in Momoyama Japan* (Honolulu: University of Hawai'i Press, 1997), p. 164.
29 This is an error. It was not Gomizunoo (1596–1680) who visited the site of Jōzan's hut, but his heir Emperor Reigen (1654–1732). The *ZKKD* entry corrects this error.
30 Fujiwara, *Ochiguri monogatari,* pp. 103–104.
31 Ban Kōkei, *Kinsei kijinden,* p. 264.

32 Fujiwara, *Ochiguri monogatari,* p. 135. *Jinling huai gu* is an early fifth-century text. As related in Chapter 32 of *Zhuangzi,* the jewel, or pearl, was especially treasured for being unobtainable, or for the fact that obtaining it placed one in mortal danger.

33 Ibid., pp. 131–132.

34 Ban Kōkei, *Kinsei kijinden,* p. 149.

35 I am grateful to the Taiga museum in Kyoto for this insight. Kenkadō's picture is published in Sasaki Yoneyuki, ed., *Ike no Taiga kafu* (Chronology of Ike no Taiga) (Kyoto: Ike no Taiga bijutsukan).

36 Kameya, "Paupers, Poets, and Paragons," p. 45.

37 For a list of supporting documents revealing collaborations among members of this community, see Munemasa Isoo, *Kokugo kokubun* 31, no. 7 (1962): 24–33.

38 Murakami reports that these posters read *Kijin kaimasu* (Will pay for *kijin*).

39 Kōkei's preface and Mikuma Katen's afterword are dated 1788. Kōkei's statement is preceded by a *kanbun* foreword by his friend the Tendai monk and *kanshi* poet Rikunyo Jishū (1734–1801), who explains *kijin* in generalized terms that typify the social outsider. *Kijin,* Rikunyo writes, may live according to personal proclivities in impoverished, temporary dwellings; they may not stay in one place; and they may embrace vulgarity and dispense with any sense of propriety. The hearts of *kijin* are neither predictable nor restrained, but neither are they crooked or perverse; they may possess great artistic talent but do not create art for commercial purposes; they care nothing for appearances and live detached from others without pretensions; and they care nothing for regulations placed upon them. Rikunyo's *kanbun* preface is dated 1790.

40 Ban Kōkei, *Kinsei kijinden,* p. 9.

41 In most cases, the term *kijin* was a laudatory attribution that precluded its usage in self-reference. In fact, self-referential use of the term was often enough evidence for later *kijinden* writers to indict such individuals as self-aggrandizing fakes and disqualify them as "true" *kijin.*

42 Melinda Takeuchi, "Visions of a Wanderer: The True View Paintings of Ike Taiga (1723–1776)" (Ph.D. diss., University of Michigan, 1979), p. 43.

43 Murakami Mamoru, *Ban Kōkei-sen autosaidaa 119-nin: Kinsei kijinden* (Kyōikusha, 1981), pp. 76–77.

44 Ban Kōkei, *Kinsei kijinden,* p. 19.

45 Ibid., p. 25. The philanthropic Zen monk Tōsui (1606–1683) is a colorful figure who helps to recover some of the entertainment value missing in the preceding entries. Tōsui lived his final years running a vinegar stand and doing charity work for beggars.

46 Ibid., pp. 29–30.

47 Patti Kameya, "Yūjo in *Kinsei kijinden,*" *Rikkyō daigaku daigakuin nihon bungaku ronsō* 2 (September 2002): 192.

48 Ishikawa Jun, *Ishikawa Jun zenshū,* vol. 11 (Chikuma Shobō, 1969), pp. 482–483, 487.

49 *Kijin jippen* was a treatise on Roman Catholic ethics rather than eccentricity and was therefore subject to the Tokugawa ban on Christian books, but it is known that Ogyū Sorai, who had been criticizing the prohibition, acquired a copy in 1726.

50 Li Zhizhao, *Jiren shipian* (Ten chapters on eccentrics), *Shenjiao zazhi* (Journal of saint religion), 23, no. 5.

51 Munemasa Isoo, *Kokugo kokubun* 31, no. 8 (1962): 53.

52 Ibid., p. 51.

53 Ishikawa, *Ishikawa Jun zenshū,* pp. 488–89. Ishikawa's view is supported by the fact that entries in *KKD* do not reflect any overtly doctrinal intentions on the part of the authors. *HKD, OM,* and *KKD,* in fact, all contain a number of wholly secular characters whose attraction is purely behavioral. *HKD's* Hechimono, *OM's* Mochizuki Chōkō, and *KKD's* Hyōta, for instance, are depicted as nature-lovers who wander the hills sipping saké and flouting propriety, and for whom religious affiliation is immaterial or secondary to individual will.

54 Patti Kameya, "When Eccentricity is Virtue: Virtuous Deeds in *Kinsei Kijinden* (Eccentrics of Recent Times (1790)," *Early Modern Japan: An Interdisciplinary Journal* 17 (2009): 11.

55 Imahashi Riko, *Edo ega to bungaku: byōsha to kotoba no edo bungakushi* (Tokyo University Press, 1999), p. 49. Indeed, biographies of recluses were common in China and even included in its official dynastic histories. Several such works had been produced in Tokugawa Japan, as well, such as Gensei's *Fusō in'itsuden* (Biographies of Japanese recluses, 1664) and Sairoken Kyōsen's *Kindai yasa inja* (Modern stylish recluses, 1686).

CHAPTER 6: Strangeness in the Early Nineteenth Century

1 For more on this culture of public spectacle, see Andrew L. Markus, "The Carnival of Edo: *Misemono* Spectacles from Contemporary Accounts," *Harvard Journal of Asiatic Studies* 45, no. 2 (1985): 499–541. For a discussion of the critical discourse surrounding this phenomenon, see Nakano Mitsutoshi, "The Role of Traditional Aesthetics," in *Eighteenth Century Japan: Culture and Society,* ed. C. Andrew Gerstle (Richmond, Surrey, UK: Curzon, 1989 [2000]).

2 Patti Kameya, "Paupers, Poets, and Paragons: Eccentricity as Virtue in *Kinsei kijinden* (*Eccentrics of our times, 1790*)" (Ph.D. diss., University of Chicago, 2006), p. 35.

3   Miyatake Gaikotsu, *Hikkashi* (Chōkōya shoten, 1911), pp. 106–107.

4   Hara Tokusai, Ban Kōkei, and Yajima Gogaku, *Sentetsu zōden; Kinsei kijinden; Hyakka kikōden* (Yūhōdō shoten, 1927), pp. 710–713. See Chapter 2 for Yajima's passage on Striped Kanjūrō.

5   Sansantei Arindō is also known as Jōno Saigiku.

6   Kameya, "Paupers, Poets, and Paragons," p. 197.

7   For a description of the process by which an aesthetics of eccentricity is converted to a set of behaviors, see W. Puck Brecher, "In Appreciation of Buffoonery, Egotism, and the Shōmon School: Koikawa Harumachi's *Kachō kakurenbō*," *Early Modern Japan: An Interdisciplinary Journal* 18 (2010): 88–102.

8   Haruo Shirane, ed., *Early Modern Japanese Literature: An Anthology, 1600–1900* (New York: Columbia University Press, 2002), p. 565.

9   Nakano, "The Role of Traditional Aesthetics," p. 126.

10 Pierre Bourdieu, *Outline of a Theory of Practice,* trans. Richard Nice (Cambridge: Cambridge University Press, 1977), p. 197.

11 Katharine P. Burnett, "A Discourse of Originality in Late Ming Chinese Painting Criticism," *Art History* 23, no. 4 (November 2000): 523.

12 Nakano Kōji, *Seihin no shisō* (Sōshisha, 1992), p. 81.

13 As Timon Screech notes, artists were cognizant that eccentricity could yield commercial rewards: "Jakuchū ran away and hid until they thought he was dead; Shōhaku rode backwards on his horse; Taiga forgot the money due on his pictures. . . . [I]ndependent artists needed [such] legends to cultivate their clients." Timon Screech, *The Shogun's Painted Culture: Fear and Creativity in the Japanese States 1760–1829* (London: Reaktion Books, 2000), p. 184.

14 Ibid., p. 185.

15 Sugita Kozō, *Edo bunjin omoshiro shiwa* (Mainichi shinbun-sha, 1993), p. 185.

16 Nakano Kōji, *Seihin no shisō,* p. 81.

17 Kobayashi Issa, *Ora ga haru, waga haru shū* (Iwanami Shoten, 1927), p. 120.

18 Ueda Akinari, *Taidai shōshin roku,* trans. William E. Clarke and Wendy E. Cobcroft (Sydney: Premodern Japanese Studies, 2009), pp. 92–93.

19 Ibid., pp. 65–66.

20 Sakazaki Shizuka, ed., *Nihon garon taikan,* vol. 2 (Tokyo: Arusu, 1929), p. 1292; Ueda Akinari, *Taidai shōshin roku,* pp. 65–66, 69.

21 Elizabeth Lillehoj, ed., *Acquisition: Art and Ownership in Edo-Period Japan* (Warren, CT: Floating World Editions, 2007), p. 12.

22 Yokota Yōichi, *Ukiyoe avangyarudo to gendai* (Tokyo: Tokyo Station Gallery, 2003), p. 7.

23 Franchini, Rosenfield, and Vandi all discuss Hokusai as a *kijin.*

24 John M. Rosenfield, "Hokusai and Concepts of Eccentricity," in *Hokusai Paintings: Selected Paintings,* ed. Gian Carlo Calza with the assistance of John

T. Carpenter (Venice: International Hokusai Research Centre, University of Venice, 1994), pp. 21–22.

25 Yoshimura Teiji, *Rekishi no naka no kyojintachi* (Sakuhinsha, 1982), p. 184.

26 Chiara Benedicta Franchini, *"Katsushika Hokusai: Un eccentrico della pittura"* (Katsushika Hokusai: Painting's eccentric), Nipponico.com (accessed May 9, 2004). http://www.nipponico.com/tesi/franchini_chiara_benedicta/.

27 Rosenfield, "Hokusai and Concepts of Eccentricity," p. 21.

28 Chiara Benedicta Franchini, *"Katsushika Hokusai: Un eccentrico della pittura."*

29 Cinzia Vandi, *"Vivere come un 'fiore di loto nel fango': La vicenda personale ed artistic di Katsushika Hokusai"* (Living like "a lotus in the mud": The personal and artistic affairs of Katsushika Hokusai), http://xoomer.virgilio.it/iporpor/pensieri/nozioni/Articoli/hokusai.htm (accessed Dec. 6, 2010).

30 Rosenfield, "Hokusai and Concepts of Eccentricity," p. 17.

31 Christine Guth, *Art of Edo Japan: The Artist and the City, 1651–1868* (New York: Harry M. Abrams, 1996), p. 118.

32 The fact that the Tokugawa claimed ancestry from the Genji clan indeed suggests this as political satire.

33 Miyatake, *Hikkashi,* p. 146.

34 Rosenfield, "Hokusai and Concepts of Eccentricity," p. 20.

35 Isao Toshihiko, *Kuniyoshi no ehon* (Iwasaki bijutsusha, 1989), p. 184.

36 *Nihon rekishi daijiten,* vol. 5 (Kawade Shobō shinsha, 1961), p. 48; *Nihon rekishi daijiten,* vol. 12 (Kawade Shobō shinsha, 1961), p. 133.

37 Arakawa Hiroshi, *"Kansei no sankijin to yūreki no jidai," Jinbun ronshū* 55, no. 2 (January 2005): 31–34.

38 As controversial figures, this trio remained largely unheralded until their accomplishments were highlighted in 1842 when, on the fiftieth anniversary of his death, Hayashi received an official pardon. In the Meiji period, historians held up Hayashi, Takayama, and Gamō as heroes of a dark, feudal era who had fought to revere the emperor (*sonnō*), strengthen the country (*kyōhei*), and open to Western knowledge (*kaika*).

39 Hayashiya Tatsusaburō, *Bakumatsu bunka no kenkyuu* (Iwanami Shoten, 1974), p. 38.

40 Ibid., p. 144.

41 Naramoto Tatsuya, *Rekishi no kōotsu* (Kyoto: Shibunkaku shuppan, 1982), p. 153.

42 Details of Chikuden's petitions will be discussed in Chapter 7.

43 Tetsuo Najita, "History and Nature in Eighteenth-century Tokugawa Japan," in *The Cambridge History of Japan,* vol. 4, ed. John W. Hall (Cambridge: Cambridge University Press, 1991), p. 645.

44 This author's name is also read Sakazaki Tan. Before the glut of *nanga* treatises in the nineteenth century, nearly all Edo period pedagogical writings were by

Kanō and Tosa School professional painters; Nakata Yūjirō, *Bunijinga suihen,* vol. 15 [Gyokudō] (Chūō kōron, 1978), p. 126. These were openly composed in imitation of Chinese treatises and amounted to little more than accounts of Chinese painting and painters. Produced mainly in schools and studios for pedagogical purposes, their existence was generally unknown. *Garon* were thus domesticated as the sole intellectual property of master and pupil; Sakazaki Shizuka, *Nihonga no seishin* (Tokyo: Perikan-sha. 1995), p. 156.

45 Sakazaki, *Nihonga no seishin,* 1995, p. 1.

46 Patricia J. Graham, *Tea of the Sages: The Art of* Sencha (Honolulu: University of Hawaiʻi Press, 1998), p. 152.

47 Paul Allan Berry, "Tanomura Chikuden: Man amidst the Mountains" (Ph.D. diss., University of Michigan, 1985), p. 384.

48 Hugh Wylie, "Nanga Painting Treatises of Nineteenth-century Japan" (Ph.D. diss., University of Kansas, 1991), p. 417.

49 Nakata, *Bunijinga suihen,* p. 127. Shunkin, Gyokudō's son, had distanced himself from his father's pronounced individualism to compose *garon* and create more authentically Chinese works. Hankō (1802–1846), the son of reclusive, individualistic *nanga* artist Okada Beisanjin (1744–1820), followed Shunkin's example and began copying Chinese paintings despite his father's opposition.

50 This credo was taken from Dong Qichang's (1555–1636) *Huachan shi supi.*

51 Taketani Chōjirō, *Bunjin garon: Uragami Shunkin 'Rongashi' hyōshaku* (Meiji Shoin, 1988), pp. 9–12.

52 Sakazaki, *Nihon garon taikan,* p. 171.

53 Sakazaki, *Nihonga no seishin,* pp. 148–149.

54 Wylie, "Nanga Painting Treatises," p. 415.

55 Quoted in ibid., p. 79.

56 Quoted in ibid., pp. 54–55 (cited here with Wylie's brackets). This last axiom is from *The Analects,* 14:25.

57 Motoori Norinaga, "E no koto," in Sakazaki, *Nihon garon taikan,* pp. 189–195.

58 Rosemary Mercer, *Deep Words: Miura Baien's System of Natural Philosophy,* translation and philosophical commentary by Rosemary Mercer (Leiden: E. J. Brill, 1991), p. 195. *Jōri* is the non-dualistic notion of the indistinguishability between opposites. Baien's point here is that making distinctions between things leads to a logic of binary opposition that obscures the essential unity of the physical world.

59 Sources disagree on Yūhi's birth year. While most report it as 1693, other credible sources cite it as 1712.

60 Sakazaki, *Nihonga no seishin,* p. 62.

61 Sugimoto Shutarō, *"Uragami Gyokudō: Kijin, kisō, kiroku,"* in *Suibokuga no kyoshō,* vol. 13 (Kodansha, 1995), pp. 16–17.

62 Wylie, "Nanga Painting Treatises," pp. 80–81. Modern historians find it difficult to determine what in his works to attribute to alcohol and what to his unique style.

63 Umehara Takeshi, *Bi to rinri no mujun: Umehara Takeshi chosakushū 19* (Shūeisha, 1983), p. 330.

64 Kubo Michio, *Uragami Gyokudō-den* (Shinchōsha, 1996), pp. 212–215.

65 Satō Yasuhiro, *Uragami Gyokudō* (Shinchōsha, 1997), p. 77.

66 Sugimoto, "*Uragami Gyokudō,*" pp. 18–19.

67 Satō, *Uragami Gyokudō,* p. 73.

68 Ibid., p. 74. Articulated by Xie He (5th c.), the Six Laws were widely embraced as the standard aesthetic criteria for painting.

69 We recall a similar statement in a poem by Yokoi Kinkoku in which he ruminates on his isolation and devotion to artistic independence.

70 Ikezawa Ichirō, *Edo bunjinron: Ōta Nanpo wo chūshin ni* (Kyūko shoin, 2000), pp. 48–50.

71 Timothy Bradstock and Judith N. Rabinovitch, *An Anthology of Kanshi (Chinese Verse) by Japanese Poets of the Edo Period* (Lewiston, NY: Edwin Mellen Press, 1997), p. 194.

72 John M. Rosenfield in collaboration with Fumiko E. Cranston, *Extraordinary Persons: Works by Eccentric, Nonconformist Japanese Artists of the Early Modern Era (1580–1868) in the Collection of Kimiko and John Powers,* vol. 3, ed. Naomi Noble Richard (Cambridge, MA: Harvard University Art Museums, 1999), p. 107.

73 Kubo, *Uragami Gyokudō-den,* p. 215.

74 Satō, *Uragami Gyokudō,* pp. 74–75.

75 Sugimoto, "*Uragami Gyokudō,*" p. 19.

76 Stephen Addiss, *Tall Mountains and Flowing Waters: The Arts of Uragami Gyokudō* (Honolulu: University of Hawai'i Press, 1987), p. 10; Rosenfield, *Extraordinary Persons,* vol. 3, p. 107.

77 Rosenfield, *Extraordinary Persons,* vol. 2, p. 172.

78 Takagi Ichinosuke and Hisamatsu Sen'ichi, *Kinsei waka-shū* (Iwanami shoten, 1966), p. 37.

79 Kanekiyo Masanori, *Kagawa Kageki* (Yoshikawa Hirobunkan, 1973), p. 72.

80 Donald Keene, *World within Walls: Japanese Literature of the Pre-Modern Era, 1600–1867* (New York: Grove Press, 1976), p. 488.

81 Ibid., p. 489.

82 Roger K. Thomas, *The Way of Shikishima: Waka Theory and Practice in Early Modern Japan* (Lanham, MD: University Press of America, 2008), p. 121.

83 Translation is from Thomas, *The Way of Shikishima,* p. 121.

84 Ibid., p. 113.

85 Kanekiyo, *Kagawa Kageki,* p. 28.

86 Ibid., pp. 28–29.

87 In 1812 Kageki composed *Hyakushū iken* (A divergent view of the Hyakunin isshū) as a response to Keichū's *Hyakunin isshū kaikanshō* and Kamo no Mabuchi's *Hyakunin isshū shogaku*. His use of the word *iken* (divergent view), Kanekiyo holds, is a reassertion of independence.

88 Kanekiyo, *Kagawa Kageki*, pp. 80, 90.

89 Keene, *World within Walls*, p. 489.

90 Anna Beerens, *Friends, Acquaintances, Pupils, and Patrons: Japanese Intellectual Life in the Late Eighteenth Century: A Prosopographical Approach* (Leiden: Leiden University Press, 2006), p. 78.

91 Kanekiyo, *Kagawa Kageki*, p. 78.

92 Munemasa Isoo, *Kinsei no gabungaku to bunjin: Nihon kinsei bun'en no kenkyū, zokuhen* (Dōbōsha, 1995), p. 134.

93 Ibid., pp. 137–138.

94 In addition to mountain goblin, tengu carried multiple meanings, including eccentricity. Tengu Kōhei (d. 1817), for example, a middle-ranking samurai who claimed descent from Confucius, was so named for his fondness for eccentric acts.

95 Roger K. Thomas, "'High' versus 'Low': The *Fude no saga* Controversy and Bakumatsu Poetics," *Monumenta Nipponica* 49, no. 4 (Winter 1994): 461.

96 Kanekiyo, *Kagawa Kageki*, pp. 34–38.

97 Ibid., p. 29.

98 Sugihara Izan, *Nihon meika shogadan* (Matsuyamadō, 1925), p. 46.

99 Nakata Yūjirō, "*Watanabe Kazan no garon*," *Bunijinga suihen*, vol. 19 (Chūō kōron, 1975), p. 131.

100 Bonnie Abiko, "Watanabe Kazan: The Man and His Times" (Ph.D. diss., Princeton University, 1982), pp. 246–250.

101 Donald Keene, *Frog in the Well: Portraits of Japan by Watanabe Kazan, 1793–1841* (New York: Columbia University Press, 2006), p. 232; Doris Croissant, "In Quest of the Real: Portrayal and Photography in Japanese Painting Theory," in *Challenging Past and Present: The Metamorphosis of Nineteenth-century Japanese Art*, ed. Ellen P. Conant (Honolulu: University of Hawai'i Press, 2006), p. 156.

102 Nakata, "*Watanabe Kazan no garon*," p. 131.

103 Keene, *Frog in the Well*, pp. 15, 84, and 265.

Chapter 7: Reevaluating Strangeness

1 Here I borrow H. D. Harootunian's phrase from his "Late Tokugawa Thought and Culture," in *The Cambridge History of Japan*, vol. 5, ed. Marius Jansen (Cambridge: Cambridge University Press, 1989).

2 Ernest F. Fenollosa, *Epochs of Chinese and Japanese Art: An Outline History of East Asian Design*, vol. 2 (New York: Dover Publications, 1963 [orig. 1913]), p. 165.

3   Nakano Mitsutoshi, "The Role of Traditional Aesthetics," in *Eighteenth Century Japan: Culture and Society*, ed. C. Andrew Gerstle (Richmond; Surrey, UK: Curzon, 2000 [1989]), p. 128.

4   Ibid., p. 126.

5   Takeuchi Gengenichi, *Haika kijindan: Zoku haika kijindan* (Iwanami Shoten, 1987), p. 11.

6   Nakano, "The Role of Traditional Aesthetics," p. 129.

7   For comprehensive discussions of social hierarchies and the status system generally, see Herman Ooms, *Tokugawa Village Practice: Class, Status, Power, Law* (Berkeley: University of California Press, 1996); and David L. Howell, *Geographies of Identity in Nineteenth-Century Japan* (Berkeley: University of California Press, 2005).

8   Harootunian, "Late Tokugawa Thought and Culture," pp. 172–173.

9   Saeki Shōichi, "Images of Eccentrics: East and West," in *Biography East and West: Selected Conference Papers*, ed. Carol Ramelb (Honolulu: East–West Center and University of Hawai'i, 1989), p. 10.

10 Nakanishi Susumu, *Kyō no seishinshi* (Kōdansha, 1978), p. 218.

11 See John M. Rosenfield in collaboration with Fumiko E. Cranston, *Extraordinary Persons: Works by Eccentric, Nonconformist Japanese Artists of the Early Modern Era (1580–1868) in the Collection of Kimiko and John Powers*, 3 vols., ed. Naomi Noble Richard (Cambridge, MA: Harvard University Art Museums, 1999); and John M. Rosenfield, "Hokusai and Concepts of Eccentricity," *Hokusai Paintings: Selected Paintings*, ed. Gian Carlo Calza with the assistance of John T. Carpenter (Venice: International Hokusai Research Centre, University of Venice, 1994).

12 Rosenfield, *Extraordinary Persons*, vol. 1, p. 35.

13 Ibid., p. 36.

14 Saeki, "Images of Eccentrics," p. 11.

15 Yoshimura Teiji, *Rekishi no naka no kyojintachi* (Sakuhinsha, 1982), p. 49.

16 Ishikawa Jun, *Ishikawa Jun zenshū*, vol. 11 (Chikuma Shobō, 1969), pp. 486–489.

17 Sugiura Minpei, "*Nihon no inja, chūgoku no inja*," *Kokubungaku: Kaishaku to kyōzai no kenkyū* 19, no. 14 (December 1974): 73–75.

18 Sakurai Yoshirō, *Inja no fubō: inton seikatsu to sono seishiin* (Hanawa Shobō, 1967), pp. 14–15.

19 Ibid., p. 261.

20 Matsuda Osamu, *Edo itan bungaku nooto* (Seidōsha, 1993), p. 345.

21 Masakatsu Gunji, *Kabuki* (Kodansha, 1985), p. 13.

22 The conventionalization of kabuki performance did not preclude artistic interests among actors themselves, many of whom formed close associations with poetry salons and *bunjin* networks, and became accomplished literati in

their own right. For a discussion, see C. Andrew Gerstle, *Kabuki Heroes on the Osaka Stage 1780–1830* (Honolulu: University of Hawai'i Press, 2005), pp. 16–26.

23 Matsuda, *Kabuki*, pp. 348–355; Yoshimura, *Rekishi no naka no kyojintachi*, p. 51.

24 Quoted in Nelson Wu, "The Toleration of Eccentrics," *Art News* 57, no. 3 (May 1956): 27.

25 Motoyama Tekishū, *Meijin kijin*, vol. 1 (Shigensha, 1926), p. 1.

26 Carl Jung, *Modern Man in Search of a Soul* (New York: Harcourt Brace & Co., 1933), p. 237.

27 For a review and analysis of the discourse on relationships between artistic creativity and public life, see Sander Gilman, "The Mad Man as Artist: Medicine, History, and Degenerate Art," *Journal of Contemporary History* 20, no. 4 (October 1985): 575–597; Patricia Waugh, "Creative Writers and Psychopathology: The Cultural Consolations of 'The Wound and the Bow' Thesis," in *Madness and Creativity in Literature and Culture,* ed. Corinne Saunders and Jane Macnaughton (Hampshire, UK: Palgrave, 2005), pp. 177–193; and, in the same volume, Al Alvarez, "The Myth of the Artist," pp. 194–201.

28 Ishida Takao, *Sengo bundan kijin retsudan* (Fujiwara Shoten, 2002), pp. 213–215.

29 Takayama Hikokurō Kinenkan, *"Kansei no sankijin no keifu,"* (Ōta: Takayama Hikokurō Kinenkan, 1999).

30 Sawada Fujiko, *"Zokubutsu to kijin,"* *Hongō* 55 (January 2005): 4.

31 Miyatake Gaikotsu, *Hikkashi* (Chōkōya shoten, 1911), p. 198.

32 Mao Zedong, cited in Thomas Froncek, *The Horizon Book of the Arts of China* (New York: American Heritage Publishing, 1969), p. 197.

33 Sigmund Freud, *Civilization and Its Discontents* (New York: W. W. Norton & Co., 1961), pp. 49–51, 73.

34 Pierre Bourdieu, *The Rules of Art: Genesis and Structure of the Literary Field,* trans. Susan Emanuel (Stanford, CA: Stanford University Press, 1995), p. 256.

35 Ibid., p. 253.

36 Jay Rubin, *Injurious to Public Morals: Writers and the Meiji State* (Seattle: University of Washington Press, 1984), p. 120.

37 Quoted in Peter Bürger, *Theory of the Avant-Garde,* trans. Michael Shaw (Minneapolis: University of Minnesota Press, 1984), p. 25.

38 Anne Walthall, *The Weak Body of a Useless Woman: Matsuo Taseko and the Meiji Restoration* (Chicago: University of Chicago Press, 1998), pp. 12, 13. This phenomenon is also examined in Eiko Ikegami, *Bonds of Civility: Aesthetic Networks and the Political Origins of Japanese Culture* (Cambridge: Cambridge University Press, 2005).

39 Yoshizawa Chū, *Nihon nanga ronkō* (Kodansha, 1977), pp. 439–470.

40 Richard Edwards, "The Orthodoxy of the Unorthodox," in *Artists and Traditions: Uses of the Past in Chinese Culture*, ed. Christian F. Murck (Princeton, NJ: Princeton University Press, 1976), p. 186.

41 Ian Gregson, *Contemporary Poetry and Postmodernism: Dialogue and Estrangement* (New York: St. Martin's Press, 1996), pp. 130–131.

42 Ibid., p. 2.

43 Benjamin Sher contends that the term "defamiliarization" misinterprets Shklovsky's intention. Estrangement, he argues, does not transfer the known into the unknown, but calls into question the knowability of all things and in the process familiarizes us to "real knowledge" that expands and complicates our perceptual process. Viktor Shklovsky, *Theory of Prose*, trans. Benjamin Sher (Elmwood Park, IL: Dalkey Archive Press, 1990), p. xix.

44 Shklovsky, *Theory of Prose*, pp. 2–3, 148–149. I do not suggest that this is a uniquely Japanese phenomenon. The literary goal of jolting a reader out of conventional thinking, in fact, seems a nearly universal phenomenon: Bertolt Brecht's examination of alienation serves this purpose; Tolstoy creates an estranging perception by telling a story, "Kholstomer," from the point of view of a horse—a technique later adopted by Natsume Soseki in *I Am a Cat*; Roseline Crowley finds in the poetry of Mallarmé (1842–1898) a use of juxtaposition and defamiliarization that creates new linguistic and aesthetic effects by breaking from traditional uses of the language (Roseline Crowley, "Toward the Poetics of Juxtaposition: L'Après-Midi d'un Faune," *Yale French Studies*, no. 54 [1977]: p. 44); and avant-garde movements of all eras and genres intentionally disgust, bore, and alienate their audiences for the same reason.

45 Shklovsky, *Theory of Prose*, p. 12. Literary deceleration involves parallelisms and repetitions of words and stanzas to slow the pace of the narrative. It serves to minimize action and maximize form in order to create a literature of maximal perceptual richness. Nō plays commonly use deceleration (repetition) and time compression to minimize the pace and the extent of the dramatic action.

46 J. Thomas Rimer, *On the Art of the Nō Drama: The Major Treatises of Zeami* (Princeton, NJ: Princeton University Press, 1984), p. 120.

47 Earl Miner, *Comparative Poetics: An Intercultural Essay on Theories of Literature* (Princeton, NJ: Princeton University Press, 1990), p. 45.

48 Ibid.

49 Robert, Brower, "Fujiwara Teika's *Maigetsushō*," *Monumenta Nipponica* 40, no. 4 (1985): 415.

50 Nakata Yūjirō, "*Watanabe Kazan no garon*," *Bunijinga suihen*, vol. 19 (Chūō kōron, 1975), p. 131.

51 Bürger, *Theory of the Avant-Garde*, pp. xxxvi–xxxvii.

52 Rudolf Arnheim, *Entropy and Art: An Essay on Disorder and Order* (Berkeley and Los Angeles: University of California Press, 1971), p. 25.

53 Wai-kam Ho, "Tung Ch'i-Ch'ang's New Orthodoxy and the Southern School Theory," in *Artists and Traditions: Uses of the Past in Chinese Culture,* ed. Christian F. Murck (Princeton, NJ: Princeton University Press, 1976), p. 118.

54 Ban Kōkei and Mikuma Katen, *Kinsei kijinden: Zoku kinsei kijinden,* ed. Munemasa Isoo (Tōyō bunko 202, Heibonsha, 1972), p. 10.

55 For more on "betweenness," see Dennis McCort, *Going Beyond the Pairs: The Coincidence of Opposites in German Romanticism, Zen, and Deconstruction* (Albany: SUNY Press, 2001), p. 84.

56 Cleopatra Papapavlou, "The Haiga Figure as a Vehicle of Buson's Ideal: With Emphasis on the Illustrated Sections of '*Oku no hosomichi*' and '*Nozarashi kiko*'" (Ph.D. diss., University of California, Berkeley, 1981), p. 171.

57 Lawrence E. Marceau, *Takebe Ayatari: A* Bunjin *Bohemian in Early Modern Japan* (Ann Arbor: Center for Japanese Studies, University of Michigan, 2004), p. 284.

58 Victor Koschmann, ed., *Authority and the Individual in Japan: Citizen Protest in Historical Perspective* (Tokyo: University of Tokyo Press, 1978), p. 25.

59 See, for example, Kitazawa Noriaki, *Kishida Ryūsei to taishō avangyarudo* (Iwanami shoton, 1993); and Satō Yasuhiro, "*Nihonega to jigazō,*" in Miura Atsushi, ed., *Jigazō no bijutsushi* (Tokyo daigaku shuppankai, 2003), p. 132.

60 Kuwahara Sumio, *Nihon no jigazō* (Nanbokusha, 1966), p. 3.

61 Ibid., p. 16.

62 Ibid., pp. 11–12; Grisha F. Dotzenko, *Enku: Master Carver* (Tokyo, New York, San Francisco: Kodansha International, 1976), p. 42.

63 Yoshizawa Chū, "*Okada Beisanjin no fude ni naru santen no jigazō ni tsuite,*" *Kokka* 1097 (1986): 9.

64 Ibid., pp. 10–11.

65 Satō, "*Nihonega to jigazō,*" pp. 155–156.

66 Stephen Addiss, *Haiga: Takebe Sōchō and the Haiku-painting Tradition* (Honolulu: Marsh Art Gallery, University of Richmond in association with University of Hawai'i Press, 1995), p. 98.

67 Satō, "*Nihonega to jigazō,*" pp. 158–161.

68 For a discussion of Yokoi Kinkoku's self-portraits, see Patricia Fister, "Yokoi Kinkoku: The Life and Painting of a Mountain Ascetic" (Ph.D. diss., University of Kansas, 1983).

69 Kuwahara, *Nihon no jigazō,* p. 5.

70 Ibid., p. 1.

71 This is not to side with Japanist writer Kamei Katsuichirō and the many postwar Japanese writers who argue that early modern painting represented a Japanization rather than a modernization of native identities.

72 For more comparisons with Heian court diaries, see Saeki Shōichi, *Denki no naka no erosu* (Chikuma shoten, 1990), pp. 230–233.

73 Donald Keene, *World within Walls: Japanese Literature of the Pre-Modern Era, 1600–1867* (New York: Grove Press, 1976), p. 498.

74 Takagi Ichinosuke and Hisamatsu Sen'ichi, *Kinsei waka-shū* (Iwanami shoten, 1966), p. 38.

75 Katsuya Hirano, "Social Networks and Production of Public Discourse in Edo Popular Culture," in *Acquisition: Art and Ownership in Edo-Period Japan*, ed. Elizabeth Lillehoj (Warren, CT: Floating World Editions, 2007), pp. 124–125.

76 Kanō Hiroyuki, *"Jūhasseiki to iu jidai," Jūhasseiki no nihon bijutsu* (Kyoto: Kyoto Kokuritsu Hakubutsukan, 1990), p. 4.

77 See Chapter 3 for Nankai's original statement.

78 Saeki, "Images of Eccentrics: East and West," p. 6.

79 As already noted, alcohol consumption was generally limited to social occasions. Cannabis had long been used to treat a range of ailments but was rarely used as a recreational drug. Matsuura Seizan's (1760–1841) *Kasshi Yawa* (Tales from the night of the rat, 1827) and Murata Harumi's (1746–1811) *Nishigorinoya zuihitsu* (Essays by Nishigorinoya, 1806) give accounts of the only known incident of cannabis being used in a recreational capacity. In the year 1800, a lower monk at the Saikōji temple in Yanaka discovered cannabis plants in the temple's garden. He mentioned it to the others, saying: "Their young leaves are delicious and we love eating them in the provinces. Don't you eat them here in Edo?" After an evening of raucous merrymaking that drew crowds of curious onlookers, one monk reported that "inebriation from saké is nothing compared to the buzz one gets from cannabis"; Oda Susumu, *Nihon no kyōkishi* (Shisakusha, 1990), p. 238. *Kokon yōran* (Handbook of the ancient and modern; date unknown) by Yashiro Hirokata (1758–1841), in addition, notes cannabis' medicinal applications and that "eating it makes one unable to stop laughing uproariously" (Oda, *Nihon no kyōkishi*, p. 237). Regardless of the monk's claim that cannabis was a common food for provincial folk, little documented evidence suggests its recreational use in the Edo period, or even that its psychotropic effects were known. Indeed, despite its ubiquity in Japanese material culture (in rope, clothing, medicine, etc.), its effects appear to have been largely unknown. Given its ready availability, one expects that cannabis would have been widespread had demand for a psychotropic drug existed.

GLOSSARY

bakufu 幕府, shogunate

biwahōshi 琵琶法師, blind lute-playing priests who often recited vocal literature

bunjin (C. *wenren*) 文人, amateur, independent artist

bunjinga 文人画, see *nanga*

butsudan 仏壇, family altar

chanoyu 茶の湯, tea ceremony

darumauta 達磨歌, unconventional ("mad") verses; Zen poems (associated with Fujiwara Teika, among others)

dengaku 田楽, "field music"; folk performance considered a precursor to Nō theater; *see* **sarugaku**

fūga 風雅, "windblown elegance"; literary, often poetic, elegance and refinement

fūkyō 風狂, "windblown madness"; aesthetic eccentricity

fūryū 風流, aesthetic, often literary, elegance, sophistication, and taste

ga (also *miyabi*) 雅, elevated; refined (*see* **zoku**)

garon 画論, treatise on painting

gekokujō 下克上, the low overcoming the high

gesaku 戯作, comic fiction

gyōja 行者, Buddhist ascetic; magico-religious adept

haikai 俳諧, 17-syllable poetry

hijiri 聖, itinerant monk

hōben 方便, expedient means of attaining Buddhist salvation

hongaku 本覚, original enlightenment (in Buddhism)

honzen no sei 本然の性, original nature (in Neo-Confucianism)

i 異, different; strange; heterodox (*see* **sei**)

iki 粋, sophisticated; stylish; refined (in Edo region; *see* **sui**)

in'itsu 隠逸, reclusion; rejection of the world

inja 隠者, hermit; recluse

insei 隠棲 (also *inton* 隠遁), seclusion; retirement

intonsha 隠遁者, hermit; recluse

ippin 逸品, excellence or untrammeled style (in painting)

itsujin 逸人, hermit; recluse

jinsei 人性, human nature

jōi 攘夷, expulsion of foreigners; isolationism

kabukimono 歌舞伎者, street toughs who emulated styles of kabuki actors

kaidan 怪談, tales of the strange

kaika 開化, enlightenment; opening

kakekotoba 掛詞, pivot word or pun (in poetry)

kami 神, Shinto deity

kanbun 漢文, writing in literary Chinese

kanshi 漢詩, Chinese poetry

ki (C. *qi*) 気, material force (in Neo-Confucianism); spirit consonance

ki 畸; 奇, eccentric; strange

kibyōshi 黄表紙, "yellow covers"; satirical illustrated books popular in the late 18th century

kichigai 気違い, lunacy

kijin 畸人; 奇人, eccentric person

kijinden 畸人伝; 奇人伝, biographies of eccentric people

kōan 公案, paradox; nonsensical riddle used as a pedagogical device (in Zen Buddhism)

kodō 古道, the ancient (Japanese) Way

koku 石, unit of volume (roughly 180 liters) for rice; currency used for samurai salaries

kokugaku 国学, National Learning; Nativism

koto 琴, zither, usually with thirteen strings

kyō 狂, "madness," referring to eccentric behaviors or styles

kyōgen 狂言, comic drama

kyōjin 狂人, eccentric ("mad") person

kyōka 狂歌, comic ("mad") *waka*

kyōken 狂狷, eccentric and nonconforming

kyōsha 狂者; *see* **kyōjin**

kyōsha no bun (also *kyōbun*) 狂者文, comic ("mad") prose

kyōsō 狂僧, "mad" monk

makoto 誠, sincerity

mingei 民芸, folk art

monogurui 物狂い, derangement; madness

monotsuki 物憑, spirit or animal possession

muga 無我, no-self (in Zen Buddhism)

muyō 無用, useless; uselessness

muyōsha 無用者, useless person

nanga 南画 (also *bunjinga* [C. *wenrenhua*] 文人画), genre of painting
    popularized in Japan by literati emulating Southern School Chinese paintings

nenbutsu 念仏, Pure Land Buddhist prayer invoking Amida Buddha: "*Namu
    Amida Butsu*" (Praise Amida)

nihonjinron 日本人論, discourse on Japaneseness

nyūjō 入定, process of self-mummification performed by certain Buddhist priests

omomuki 趣, elegant taste; charm

Ōyōmeigaku 王陽明学; see **Yōmeigaku**

qing (J. *jō*) 情, emotion

rakugo 落語, comic storytelling

rangaku 蘭学, Dutch studies

renga 連歌 (or *haikai no renga* 俳諧の連歌), comic-linked verse *ri* (C. *li*) 理, Principle (in Neo-Confucianism)

rinpa 琳派, school of painting and decorative arts established in 17th-century Kyoto

rōjū 老中, elder statesman

ryōchi 良知, moral intuition; intuitive knowledge (in Wang Yangming thought)

sakoku 鎖国, "closed country" policy enacted in the 1630s

sarugaku 猿楽, folk theater, dance, and/or entertainment popular in the medieval period (*see dengaku*)

sei 正, correct; orthodox (*see i*)

sencha 煎茶, infused green tea

seppuku 切腹, ritual suicide

shirabe 調, "tuning"

shishi 志士, "men of high purpose"; activists instrumental in carrying out the Meiji Restoration

shogakai 書画会, calligraphy and painting party

shōyōyū 逍遥遊, carefree wandering

shugendō 修験道, Buddhist sect that practices mountain asceticism

shugenja 修験者, mountain ascetic

sonnō 尊王, revere the emperor; royalism

sonnō jōi 尊王攘夷, "Revere the Emperor, Expel the Barbarian"

Soraigaku 徂徠学, the Ogyū Sorai School (of Neo-Confucianism)

sui 粋, sophisticated; stylish; refined (in Kamigata region; *see iki*)

ten 天, Heaven

tenja 点者, professional *haikai* and *renga* poetry grader

tentori haikai 点取り俳諧, point-procuring *haikai*

terakoya 寺子屋, private temple school

tokkō 徳行, virtue

tsū 通, connoisseurship of the arts and social graces

ukiyoe 浮世絵, pictures of the floating world (*ukiyo*)

ushin renga 有心連歌, serious-linked verse (as opposed to *haikai no renga*, comic-linked verse)

wabun 和文, writing in Japanese

waka 和歌, 31-syllable poetry

wenren 文人; *see* **bunjin**

wu-wei (J. *mui*) 無為, effortless action (in Daoism)

yamabushi 山伏, mountain ascetic; *see also* **shugenja**

yojō 余情, emotional overtones (in poetry)

yōkyō 佯狂, feigned madness

Yōmeigaku 陽明学 (or *Ōyōmeigaku* 王陽明学), the Wang Yangming School (of Neo-Confucianism)

yūgen 幽玄, "mysterious depths" (in poetry and Nō); suggestive yet profound

yūjo 遊女, prostitute

za 座, artists' guild; poetry circle or salon

zoku 俗, coarse; vulgar (*see* **ga**)

BIBLIOGRAPHY

The place of publication for Japanese sources is Tokyo unless otherwise indicated.

Abiko, Bonnie. "Watanabe Kazan: The Man and His Times." Ph.D. diss., Princeton University, 1982.

Addiss, Stephen. *Haiga: Takebe Sōchō and the Haiku-painting Tradition.* Honolulu: Marsh Art Gallery, University of Richmond in association with University of Hawai'i Press, 1995.

———, ed. *Japanese Quest for a New Vision: The Impact of Visiting Chinese Painters, 1600–1900.* Lawrence: Spencer Museum of Art, University of Kansas, 1986.

———. *Tall Mountains and Flowing Waters: The Arts of Uragami Gyokudō.* Honolulu: University of Hawai'i Press, 1987.

Akai Tatsuro. *Kinsei no gaka: Sono shiyū to sakuhin.* Kakugawa Shoten, 1976.

Arakawa Hiroshi. "Kansei no sankijin to yūreki no jidai." *Jinbun ronshū* 55, no. 2 (January 2005): 1–41.

Arnheim, Rudolf. *Entropy and Art: An Essay on Disorder and Order.* Berkeley and Los Angeles: University of California Press, 1971.

Aston, W. G. *Nihongi: Chronicles of Japan from the Earliest Times to A.D. 697.* Vol. 2. Rutland, VT, and Tokyo: Charles E. Tuttle, 1998.

Ban Kōkei and Mikuma Katen. *Kinsei kijinden; Zoku kinsei kijinden.* Ed. Munemasa Isoo. Tōyō bunko 202. Heibonsha, 1972.

Beerens, Anna. *Friends, Acquaintances, Pupils, and Patrons: Japanese Intellectual Life in the Late Eighteenth Century: A Prosopographical Approach.* Leiden: Leiden University Press, 2006.

Berkowitz, Alan J. *Patterns of Disengagement: The Practice and Portrayal of Reclusion in Early Medieval China.* Stanford, CA: Stanford University Press, 2000.

Berry, Paul Allan. "Tanomura Chikuden: Man amidst the Mountains." Ph.D. diss., University of Michigan, 1985.

Bourdieu, Pierre. *Outline of a Theory of Practice.* Trans. Richard Nice. Cambridge: Cambridge University Press, 1977.

———. *The Rules of Art: Genesis and Structure of the Literary Field.* Trans. Susan Emanuel. Stanford, CA: Stanford University Press, 1995.

Bradstock, Timothy, and Judith N. Rabinovitch. *An Anthology of Kanshi (Chinese Verse) by Japanese Poets of the Edo Period.* Lewiston, NY: Edwin Mellen Press, 1997.

Brecher, W. Puck. "Down and Out in Negishi: Reclusion and Struggle in an Edo Suburb." *Journal of Japanese Studies* 35, no. 1 (Winter 2009): 1–35.

————. "Eccentricity as Ideology: Biographies of Meiji *Kijin.*" *Japanese Language and Literature* 44, no. 2 (October 2010): 213–237.

————. "In Appreciation of Buffoonery, Egotism, and the Shōmon School: Koikawa Harumachi's *Kachō kakurenbō.*" *Early Modern Japan: An Interdisciplinary Journal* 18 (2010): 88–102.

————. "Kōetsumura: Of Rhythms and Reminiscence in Hon'ami Kōetsu's Commune." *Japan Review* 22 (2010): 27–53.

————. "To Romp in Heaven: A Translation of the *Hōsa Kyōshaden.*" *Early Modern Japan: An Interdisciplinary Journal* 13 (Spring 2005): 11–27.

Brooks, E. Bruce, and A. Taeko Brooks, trans. *The Original Analects: Sayings of Confucius and His Successors.* New York: Columbia University Press, 1998.

Brower, Robert. "Fujiwara Teika's *Maigetsushō.*" *Monumenta Nipponica* 40, no. 4 (1985): 399–425.

Brown, Kendall H. *The Politics of Reclusion: Painting and Power in Momoyama Japan.* Honolulu: University of Hawai'i Press, 1997.

Bürger, Peter. *Theory of the Avant-Garde.* Trans. Michael Shaw. Minneapolis: University of Minnesota Press, 1984.

Burnett, Katharine. "A Discourse of Originality in Late Ming Chinese Painting Criticism." *Art History* 23, no. 4 (November 2000): 522–558.

Burns, Susan. "Bodies Possessed and Hearts Disordered: Sexuality and Madness in Edo Japan." *Imaging/Reading Eros* (Proceedings of the NEH-funded Conference "Sexuality and Edo Culture, 1750–1850"). Ed. Sumie Jones. Bloomington: East Asian Studies Center, University of Indiana, 1996.

Cahill, James. *Fantastics and Eccentrics in Chinese Painting.* New York: The Asia Society, 1967.

Cao Xueqin. *The Story of the Stone.* Vol. 3. Trans. David Hawkes. Bloomington: Indiana University Press, 1980.

Chen Jiru. *Kuangfu zhiyan.* Taipei: Iwen, 1965.

Chen, Yang, and Mitaka Atsuo. "*Nihon injakō.*" *Bungaku* 2, no. 1 (Jan.–Feb. 2001).

Croissant, Doris. "In Quest of the Real: Portrayal and Photography in Japanese Painting Theory." In *Challenging Past and Present: The Metamorphosis of Nineteenth-century Japanese Art,* ed. Ellen P. Conant. Honolulu: University of Hawai'i Press, 2006.

Crowley, Cheryl A. *Haikai Poet Yosa Buson and the Bashō Revival.* Leiden: Brill, 2007.

Crowley, Roseline. "Toward the Poetics of Juxtaposition: L'Après-midi d'un Faune." *Yale French Studies,* no. 54 (1977): 32–44.

De Bary, Wm. Theodore. "Individualism and Humanitarianism in Late Ming Thought." In *Self and Society in Ming Thought,* ed. Wm. Theodore de Bary and the Conference on Ming Thought. New York: Columbia University Press, 1970.

———. "Some Common Tendencies in Neo-Confucianism." In *Confucianism in Action,* ed. David S. Nivison and Arthur Wright. Stanford, CA: Stanford University Press, 1959.

De Certeau, Michel. *The Practice of Everyday Life.* Trans. Steven Rendall. Berkeley and Los Angeles: University of California Press, 1984.

Dotzenko, Grisha F. *Enku: Master Carver.* Tokyo, New York, San Francisco: Kodansha International, 1976.

Edwards, Richard. "The Orthodoxy of the Unorthodox." In *Artists and Traditions: Uses of the Past in Chinese Culture,* ed. Christian F. Murck, pp. 185–199. Princeton, NJ: Princeton University Press, 1976.

Fenollosa, Ernest F. *Epochs of Chinese and Japanese Art: An Outline History of East Asian Design.* Vol. 2. 1913. Reprint. New York: Dover Publications, 1963.

Fister, Patricia. "Yokoi Kinkoku: The Life and Painting of a Mountain Ascetic." Ph.D. diss., University of Kansas, 1983.

Flueckiger, Peter. *Imagining Harmony: Poetry, Empathy, and Community in Mid-Tokugawa Confucianism and Nativism.* Stanford, CA: Stanford University Press, 2011.

Foucault, Michel. *Madness and Civilization: A History of Insanity in the Age of Reason.* New York: Pantheon Books, 1965.

Franchini, Chiara Benedicta. "Katsushika Hokusai: Un eccentrico della pittura" (Katsushika Hokusai: A painting eccentric). Nipponico.com. May 9, 2004. http://www.nipponico.com/tesi/franchini_chiara_benedicta.

Freud, Sigmund. *Civilization and Its Discontents.* New York: W. W. Norton & Co., 1961.

Froncek, Thomas. *The Horizon Book of the Arts of China.* New York: American Heritage Publishing, 1969.

Fujimori Seikichi. *Shirazaru kisai tensai.* Shunjūsha, 1965.

Fujiwara Ietaka. *Ochiguri monogatari.* Reprinted in Tajihi Ikuo and Nakano Mitsutoshi, eds. *Shin nihon koten bungaku taikei,* 97. Iwanami Shoten, 2000.

Furth, Charlotte. "Androgynous Males and Deficient Females." *Late Imperial China* 9, no. 2 (December 1988): 1–31.

Furukawa, Hideaki. "The Tea Master Oribe." In *Turning Point: Oribe and the Arts of Sixteenth-Century Japan,* ed. Miyeko Murase. New York: Metropolitan Museum of Art, 2003.

Gazoku no kai, ed., with Nakano Mitsutoshi. *Gazoku bunsō: Nakano Mitsutoshi sensei koki kinen shiryōshū.* Kyūko Shoin, 2005.

Gerstle, Andrew C., ed. *Eighteenth Century Japan: Culture and Society.* Richmond, Surrey, UK: Curzon, 2000.

Gerstle, C. Andrew, with Timothy Clark and Akiko Yano. *Kabuki Heroes on the Osaka Stage 1780–1830.* Honolulu: University of Hawai'i Press, 2005.

Graham, Patricia J. *Tea of the Sages: The Art of* Sencha. Honolulu: University of Hawai'i Press, 1998.

Gregson, Ian. *Contemporary Poetry and Postmodernism: Dialogue and Estrangement.* New York: St. Martin's Press, 1996.

Gunji, Masakatsu. *Kabuki.* Tokyo: Kodansha, 1985.

Guth, Christine. *Art of Edo Japan: The Artist and the City, 1651–1868.* New York: Harry M. Abrams, 1996.

Hara Tokusai, Ban Kōkei, and Yajima Gogaku. *Sentetsu zōden; Kinsei kijinden; Hyakka kikōden.* Yūhōdō Shoten, 1927.

Harootunian, H. D. "Late Tokugawa Thought and Culture." In *The Cambridge History of Japan,* ed. Marius Jansen, vol. 5, pp. 168–258. Cambridge: Cambridge University Press, 1989. Hayashiya Tatsusababurō. *Bakumatsu bunka no kenkyū.* Iwanami Shoten, 1974.

———. *Kōetsu.* Dai-ichi hōki, 1964.

Hess, Thomas, ed. *The Grand Eccentrics: Five Centuries of Artists Outside the Main Currents of Art History.* New York: The Macmillan Company, 1966.

Hickman, Money. "Shōhaku the Eccentric and His Paintings in the Indianapolis Museum of Art." *Orientations* 32 (March 2001): 93–102.

Hickman, Money L. "Takada Keiho and Soga Shohaku." *Exhibition Soga Shohaku.* Mie: Mie Prefectural Art Museum, 1998.

Hillier, J. *The Uninhibited Brush: Japanese Art in the Shijō Style.* London: Hugh M. Moss Ltd., 1974.

Hino Tatsuo. "Bunjin no kōyū" *Bungaku* 4, no. 42 (1974): 52–65.

Hiraga Gennai. "*Hōhiron.*" Trans. William F. Sibley. *Readings in Tokugawa Thought: Selected Papers.* Vol. 9. Chicago: The Center for East Asian Studies, University of Chicago, 1993.

Ho, Wai-kam. "Tung Ch'i-Ch'ang's New Orthodoxy and the Southern School Theory." In *Artists and Traditions: Uses of the Past in Chinese Culture,* ed. Christian F. Murck. Princeton, NJ: Princeton University Press, 1976.

Hong Zicheng. *Vegetable Roots Discourse: Wisdom from China on Life and Living.* Trans. Robert Aitken and Daniel W. Y. Kwok. Emeryville, CA: Shoemaker & Hoard, 2006.

Hosokawa Junjirō. *In'itsu zenden.* Hosokawa Junjirō, 1885.

Hotta Rikurin. "Hōsa kyōsha-den." In *Shinnihon koten bungaku taikei,* 97, ed. Tajihi Ikuo and Nakano Mitsutoshi. Iwanami Shoten, 2000.

Howell, David L. *Geographies of Identity in Nineteenth-Century Japan.* Berkeley: University of California Press, 2005.

Hsu, Pi-Ching. "Celebrating the Emotional Self: Feng Meng-Lung and Late Ming Ethics and Aesthetics." Ph.D. diss., University of Minnesota, 1994.

Idemitsu Bijutsukan. *Tanomura Chikuden.* Idemitsu Bijutsukan, 1997.

Ihara Saikaku. *Life of an Amorous Woman and Other Writings.* Trans. Ivan Morris. Norfolk, CT: New Directions, 1963.

Ikegami, Eiko. *Bonds of Civility: Aesthetic Networks and the Political Origins of Japanese Culture.* Cambridge: Cambridge University Press, 2005.

Ikezawa Ichirō. *Edo bunjinron: Ōta Nanpo wo chūshin ni.* Kyūko Shoin, 2000.

Imahashi Riko. *Edo ega to bungaku: Byōsha to kotoba no edo bungakushi.* Tokyo University Press, 1999.

Isao Toshihiko. *Kuniyoshi no ehon.* Iwasaki Bijutsusha, 1989.

Ishida Takao. *Sengo bundan kijin retsudan.* Fujiwara Shoten, 2002.

Ishikawa Jun. *Shokoku kijinden.* Chikuma Shoten, 1966.

Izutsu Toshihiko and Izutsu Toyo. *The Theory of Beauty in the Classical Aesthetics of Japan.* The Hague: Martinus Nijhoff Publishers, 1981.

Jackson, Earl. "The Heresy of Meaning: Japanese Symbolist Poetry." *Harvard Journal of Asiatic Studies* 52, no. 2 (December 1991): 561–598.

Jansen, Marius. *Japan and Its World: Two Centuries of Change.* Princeton, NJ: Princeton University Press, 1995.

Jung, Carl. *Modern Man in Search of a Soul.* New York: Harcourt Brace & Co., 1933.

Kameya, Patti. "Paupers, Poets, and Paragons: Eccentricity as Virtue in *Kinsei kijinden* (*Eccentrics of our times, 1790*)." Ph.D. diss., University of Chicago, 2006.

———. "When Eccentricity Is Virtue: Virtuous Deeds in *Kinsei kijinden.*" *Early Modern Japan: An Interdisciplinary Journal* 17 (2009): 7–21.

———. "Yūjo in Kinsei kijinden." *Rikkyō daigaku daigakuin nihon bungaku ronsō* 2 (September 2002): 180–192.

Kanekiyo Masanori. *Kagawa Kageki.* Yoshikawa Hirobunkan, 1973.

Kanō Hiroyuki. "Soga Shōhaku no koto: Itanteki seishin nit suite." *Suibokuga no kyoshō.* Vol. 8. Kodansha, 1995.

———. *Jyūhasseiki no nihon bijutsu: Kattō suru biishiki.* Kyoto: Kyoto National Museum, 1990.

Karaki Junzō. *Muyōsha no keifu.* Chikua Shobō, 1960.

Kawamoto Koji. "The Use and Disuse of Tradition in Bashō's Haiku and Imagist Poetry." *Poetics Today* 20, no. 4 (Winter 1999): 709–721.

Keene, Donald. *Frog in the Well: Portraits of Japan by Watanabe Kazan, 1793–1841.* New York: Columbia University Press, 2006.

———. *The Japanese Discovery of Europe: Honda Toshiaki and Other Discoverers, 1720–1798.* New York: Grove Press, 1954.

———. *Travelers of a Hundred Ages.* New York: Columbia University Press, 1999.

———. *World within Walls: Japanese Literature of the Pre-Modern Era, 1600–1867.* New York: Grove Press, 1976.

Kimura Shigekazu, ed. *Nihon egaron taisei.* Vol. 10. Perikansha, 1998.

Kitazawa Noriaki. *Kishida Ryūsei to taishō avangyarudo.* Iwanami Shoten, 1993.

Ko, Dorothy. *Teachers of the Inner Chambers: Women and Culture in Seventeenth-Century China.* Stanford, CA: Stanford University Press, 1994.

Kobayashi Issa. *Ora ga haru, waga haru shū.* Iwanami Shoten, 1927.

Koschmann, Victor, ed. *Authority and the Individual in Japan: Citizen Protest in Historical Perspective.* Tokyo: University of Tokyo Press, 1978.

Koto Yūho. *Shōwa chōjin kijin katarogu.* Raibu Shuppan, 1990.

Kubo Michio. *Uragami Gyokudōden.* Shinchōsha, 1996.

Kurozumi Makoto. "Tokugawa Confucianism and Its Meiji Japan Reconstruction." In *Rethinking Confucianism: Past and Present in China, Japan, Korea, and Vietnam,* ed. Benjamin Elman, John B. Duncan, and Herman Ooms. Los Angeles: UCLA Asian Pacific Monograph Series, 2002.

Kuwahara Sumio. *Nihon no jigazō.* Nanbokusha, 1966.

Leach, Bernard. *Kenzan and His Tradition: The Lives and Times of Kōetsu, Sotatsu, Kōrin and Kenzan.* New York: Transatlantic Arts, 1967.

Legge, James. *The Works of Mencius: Translated, and with Critical and Exegetical Notes, Prolegomena, and Copious Indexes.* New York: Dover Publications, 1970.

Li Mowry, Hua-yuan. *Chinese Love Stories from "Ch'ing-shih."* Hamden, CT: Archon Books, 1983.

Li Xueqin and Lu Wenyu, eds. *Siku dacidian* (The great dictionary of the four collections). 2 vols. Changchun: Jilin Daxue Chubanshe, 1996.

Lillehoj, Elizabeth, ed. *Acquisition: Art and Ownership in Edo-Period Japan.* Warren, CT: Floating World Editions, 2007.

Mair, Victor H. *Wandering on the Way: Early Taoist Tales and Parables of Chuang Tzu.* Honolulu: University of Hawai'i Press, 1994.

Maraldo, John C. "Rousseau, Hakuseki, and Hakuin: Paradigms of Self in Three Autobiographers." In *Self as Person in Asian Theory and Practice,* ed. Roger Ames et al., pp. 57–79. New York: SUNY Press, 1994.

Marceau, Lawrence E. *Takebe Ayatari: A* Bunjin *Bohemian in Early Modern Japan.* Ann Arbor: Center for Japanese Studies, University of Michigan, 2004.

Marcus, Marvin. *Paragons of the Ordinary: The Biographical Literature of Mori Ōgai.* Honolulu: University of Hawai'i Press, 1993.

Markus, Andrew L. "The Carnival of Edo: *Misemono* Spectacles from Contemporary Accounts." *Harvard Journal of Asiatic Studies* 45, no. 2 (1985): 499–541.

Marra, Michele. *The Aesthetics of Discontent: Politics and Reclusion in Medieval Japanese Literature.* Honolulu: University of Hawai'i Press, 1991.

———. "Semi-recluses (*Tonseisha*) and Impermanence (*Mujō*): Kamo no Chōmei and Urabe Kenkō," *Japanese Journal of Religious Studies* 11, no. 4 (December 1984): 313–350.

Maruyama Masao. *Wabunshū: Maruyama Masao techō no kai hen.* Misuzu Shobō, 2008.

———. *Studies in the Intellectual History of Tokugawa Japan.* Trans. Mikiso Hane. Princeton, NJ: Princeton University Press, 1974.

Mason, Penelope E. *Japanese Literati Painters: The Third Generation.* New York: The Brooklyn Museum, 1977.

Matsuda Osamu. *Edo itan bungaku nooto.* Seidōsha, 1993.

McCort, Dennis. *Going Beyond the Pairs: The Coincidence of Opposites in German Romanticism, Zen, and Deconstruction.* Albany: SUNY Press, 2001.

McKelway, Matthew P., et al. *Traditions Unbound: Groundbreaking Painters of Eighteenth Century Kyoto.* San Francisco: Asian Art Museum, 2005.

Mercer, Rosemary. *Deep Words: Miura Baien's System of Natural Philosophy.* Translation and philosophical commentary by Rosemary Mercer. Leiden: E. J. Brill, 1991.

Miner, Earl. *Comparative Poetics: An Intercultural Essay on Theories of Literature.* Princeton, NJ: Princeton University Press, 1990.

Miyatake Gaikotsu. *Hikkashi.* Chōkōya Shoten, 1911.

Miyazaki Tōten. *Kyōjindan.* Kokkō Shobō, 1902.

Morohashi Tetsuji. *Daikanwa jiten.* Vol. 7. Taishūkan Shoten, 1989.

Moss, Paul. *Eccentrics in Netsuke.* London: Sydney L. Moss, 1982.

Motoori Norinaga. "E no koto." *Nihon garon taikan.* Vols. 1 and 2, ed. Sakazaki Shizuka. Arusu, 1927–1929.

Motoyama Tekishū. *Meijin kijin.* Vol. 1. Shigensha, 1926.

———. *Zoku zoku meijin kijin.* Genbunsha, 1920.

Munemasa Isoo. "Kinsei kijinden no seiritsu." *Kokugo kokubun* 31, no. 7 (1962): 16–36.

———. "Kinsei kijinden no seiritsu." *Kokugo kokubun* 31, no. 8 (1962): 50–60.

———. *Kinsei no gabungaku to bunjin: Nihon kinsei bun'en no kenkyū, zokuhen.* Dōbōsha, 1995.

Murakami Mamoru. *Ban Kōkei-sen autosaidaa 119-nin: Kinsei kijinden.* Kyōikusha, 1981.

Najita, Tetsuo. "History and Nature in Eighteenth-century Tokugawa Japan." In *The Cambridge History of Japan,* vol. 4, ed. John W. Hall. Cambridge: Cambridge University Press, 1991.

———. "Intellectual Change in Early Eighteenth Century Tokugawa Confucianism." *Journal of Asian Studies* 34, no. 2 (August 1975): 931–944.

———. *Visions of Virtue in Tokugawa Japan: The Kaitokudō Merchant Academy of Osaka.* Chicago: University of Chicago Press, 1987.

Nakamura Seishiro. *Edokko-gaku: Shitteru tsumori.* Yamato Shuppan, 1994.

Nakamura Yukihiko. "Edo bunjin no seikatsu." In *Edo jidai zushi,* vol. 5, ed. Akai Tatsurō. Chikuma Shobō, 1976.

Nakanishi Susumu. *Kyō no seishinshi.* Kōdansha, 1978.

Nakano Kōji. *Seihin no shisō.* Sōshisha, 1992.

Nakano Mitsutoshi. *Edo kyōshaden.* Chūō Kōron-shinsha, 2007.

———. *Kinsei shin-kijinden.* Iwanami Shoten, 2004.

————. "Kyōbun ishiki no haikai." *Bungaku gogaku* 54 (December 1969): 41–50.

————. "The Role of Traditional Aesthetics." In *Eighteenth Century Japan: Culture and Society,* ed. Andrew C. Gerstle. Richmond, Surrey, UK: Curzon, 2000 [1989].

Nakata Yūjirō. *"Watanabe Kazan no garon." Bunijinga suihen.* Vol. 19. Chūō Kōronsha, 1975.

————. *Bunijinga suihen.* Vol. 15. Chūō Kōronsha, 1978.

————. *Bunjin garonshū.* Chūō Kōronsha, 1982.

Naramoto Tatsuya. *Rekishi no kōotsu.* Kyōto: Shibunkaku Shuppan, 1982.

Nesaki Mitsuo. "What Underlies Shōhaku's Art—Time and Place." *Soga Shōhaku Exhibition.* Mie: Mie Prefectural Art Museum, 1987.

Nie Fusheng. *Feng Menglong yanjiu* (Studies on Feng Menglong). Shanghai: Xuelin Chubanshe, 2002.

Nihon rekishi daijiten. Kawade Shobō Shinsha, 1961.

Nihongi: Chronicles of Japan from the Earliest Times to A.D. 697. Trans. W. G. Aston. Rutland, VT, and Tokyo: Charles E. Tuttle, 1998.

Nosco, Peter. *Remembering Paradise: Nativism and Nostalgia in Eighteenth-Century Japan.* Cambridge, MA: Harvard University Press, 1990.

Oda Susumu. *Nihon no kyōkishi.* Shisakusha, 1990.

Ogawa Kan'ichi. *"Somon koji no buhō genryūron." Ryūkoku shidan* 68–69 (December 1974): 82–94.

Okada Takehiko. "The Zhu Xi and Wang Yang-ming Schools at the End of the Ming and Tokugawa Periods." Trans. Robert J. J. Wargo. *Philosophy East and West* 23, nos. 1–2 (January–April 1973): 139–162.

Ooms, Herman. "Human Nature: Singular (China) and Plural (Japan)?" In *Rethinking Confucianism: Past and Present in China, Japan, Korea, and Vietnam,* ed. Benjamin Elman, John B. Duncan, and Herman Ooms. Los Angeles: UCLA Asian Pacific Monograph Series, 2002.

————. *Tokugawa Village Practice: Class, Status, Power, Law.* Berkeley and Los Angeles: University of California Press, 1996.

Papapavlou, Cleopatra. "The Haiga Figure as a Vehicle of Buson's Ideal: With Emphasis on the Illustrated Sections of 'Oku no hosomichi' and 'Nozarashi kiko.'" Ph.D. diss., University of California, Berkeley, 1981.

Pickover, Clifford A. *Strange Brains and Genius: The Secret Lives of Eccentric Scientists and Madmen.* New York: Plenum Press, 1998.

Qiu, Peipei. *Bashō and the Dao: The Zhuangzi and the Transformation of Haikai* (Honolulu: University of Hawai'i Press, 2005).

————. "Celebrating *Kyō:* The Eccentricity of Bashō and Nanpo." *Early Modern Japan* 16 (2008): 84–91.

————. "Bashō's *Fūryū* and the Aesthetic of *Shōyōyū:* Poetics of Eccentricity and Unconventionality." *Japan Studies Review* 5 (2001): 1–36.

Reider, Noriko T. "The Appeal of 'Kaidan,' Tales of the Strange." *Asian Folklore Studies* 59, no. 2 (2000): 265–283.

Rimer, J. Thomas. *On the Art of the Nō Drama: The Major Treatises of Zeami.* Princeton, NJ: Princeton University Press, 1984.

Rosenfield, John M. "Hokusai and Concepts of Eccentricity." In *Hokusai Paintings: Selected Paintings,* ed. Gian Carlo Calza with the assistance of John T. Carpenter. Venice: International Hokusai Research Centre, University of Venice, 1994.

Rosenfield, John M., in collaboration with Fumiko E. Cranston. *Extraordinary Persons: Works by Eccentric, Nonconformist Japanese Artists of the Early Modern Era (1580–1868) in the Collection of Kimiko and John Powers,* ed. Naomi Noble Richard. 3 vols. Cambridge, MA: Harvard University Art Museums, 1999.

Rubin, Jay. *Injurious to Public Morals: Writers and the Meiji State.* Seattle: University of Washington Press, 1984.

Saeki Shōichi. *Denki no naka no erosu.* Chikuma Shoten, 1990.

Saeki, Shōichi. "Images of Eccentrics: East and West." In *Biography East and West: Selected Conference Papers,* ed. Carol Ramelb. Honolulu: East–West Center and University of Hawai'i, 1989.

Sakazaki Shizuka, ed. *Nihon garon taikan.* Vols. 1 and 2. Arusu, 1927–1929.

———. *Nihonga no seishin.* Perikansha. 1995.

Sakurai Yoshirō. *Inja no fubō: Inton seikatsu to sono seishiin.* Hanawa Shobō, 1967.

Santangelo, Paolo. "Reconsidering the 'Cult of *qing*' in Late Imperial China: A 'Romantic Movement' or a Conveyer of Social Values?" *Ming Qing Yanjiu* (2006): 133–163.

Sasaki Yoneyuki, ed. *Ike no Taiga kafu* (Chronology of Ike no Taiga). Kyoto: Ikeno Taiga bijutsukan.

Sato, Hiroaki. *Japanese Women Poets: An Anthology.* Armonk, NY, and London: M. E. Sharpe, 2008.

Satō Yasuhiro. "*Edo bijutsu no kijintachi.*" *Bijutsushi ronsō* 24 (2008): 17–45.

———. *Jakuchū, Shōhaku: Meihō Nihon no bijutsu,* 27. Shogakkan, 1991.

———. "*Nihonega to jigazō.*" In *Jigazō no bijutsushi,* ed. Miura Atsushi. Tokyo Daigaku Shuppankai, 2003.

———. "*Shōhaku no iru bijutsushi.*" *Chiba-shi bijutsukan nyūsu* 5 (March 1998): 3–5.

———. *Uragami Gyokudō.* Shinchōsha, 1997.

Saunders, Corinne, and Jane Macnaughton, eds. *Madness and Creativity in Literature and Culture.* Hampshire, UK: Palgrave, 2005.

Sawada Fujiko. "*Zokubutsu to kijin.*" *Hongō* 55 (January 2005): 2–4.

Screech, Timon. *The Shogun's Painted Culture: Fear and Creativity in the Japanese States 1760–1829.* London: Reaktion Books, 2000.

Sen Gyōbai. *Tessai no yōmeigaku: Washi no e wo miru nara, mazu san wo yondekure.* Bensei Shuppan, 2004.

Shimada Shūjirō. "Concerning the I-p' in Style of Painting." Trans. James Cahill. *Oriental Art* 7, no. 2 (Summer 1961): 66–74; 8, no. 3 (Autumn 1962): 130–137; 10, no. 1 (Spring 1964): 19–26.

Shioda Junichi. *Japanese Outsider Art: Inhabitants of Another World.* Tokyo: Setagaya Art Museum, 1993.

Shirane, Haruo, ed. *Early Modern Japanese Literature: An Anthology, 1600–1900.* New York: Columbia University Press, 2002.

————. "Matsuo Bashō and the Poetics of Scent." *Harvard Journal of Asiatic Studies* 52, no.1 (June 1992): 77–110.

————. *Traces of Dreams: Landscape, Cultural Memory, and the Poetry of Bashō.* Stanford, CA: Stanford University Press, 1998.

Shirarezaru nihon ega: Shiatoru hakutakuan korekushon. Ōtsu: Ōtsu City Museum of History and the University of Washington Press, 2001.

Shklovsky, Viktor. *Theory of Prose.* Trans. Benjamin Sher. Elmwood Park, IL: Dalkey Archive Press, 1990.

Slingerland, Edward, trans. *Confucius' Analects: With Selections from Traditional Commentaries.* Indianapolis: Hackett Publishing, 2003.

Soda Kōichi. *Edo Kijin, Kisai Jiten.* Tōkyōdō, 1992.

————. *Nihon Kijin, Kijin Jiten.* Tōkyōdō, 1991.

Stanley-Baker, Joan. *The Transmission of Chinese Idealist Painting to Japan: Notes on the Early Phase (1661–1799).* Ann Arbor: Center for Japanese Studies, University of Michigan, 1992.

Sugihara Izan. *Nihon meika shogadan.* Matsuyamadō, 1925.

Sugimoto Shutarō. "*Uragami Gyokudō: Kijin, kisō, kiroku.*" *Suibokuga no kyoshō.* Vol. 13. Kodansha, 1995.

Sugita Kozō. *Edo bunjin omoshiro shiwa.* Mainichi Shinbunsha, 1993.

Sugiura Minpei. "*Nihon no inja, chūgoku no inja.*" *Kokubungaku: Kaishaku to kyōzai no kenkyū.* 19, no.14 (December 1974): 72–75.

Suzuki Susumu. *Kinsei itan no geijutsu.* Mariya Shoten, 1973.

Tajihi Ikuo and Nakano Mitsutoshi, eds. *Shinnihon koten bungaku taikei.* Iwanami Shoten, 2000.

Takagi Ichinosuke and Hisamatsu Sen'ichi. *Kinsei waka-shū.* Iwanami Shoten, 1966.

Takahashi Hiromi. *Kyōto geien no nettowaaku.* Perikansha 1988.

Takano Kiyoshi. *Kawarimono no Nihonshi.* Kosaidō Shuppan, 1980.

Takashina Shūji and Haga Tōru. *Geijutsu no seishinshi.* Dankōsha, 1976.

Takayama Hikokurō Kinenkan. *Kansei no sankijin no keifu.* Ōta: Takayama Hikokurō Kinenkan, 1999.

Taketani Chōjirō. *Bunjin garon: Uragami Shunkin 'Rongashi' hyōshaku.* Meiji Shoin, 1988.

Takeuchi Gengen'ichi. *Haika kijindan; Zoku haika kijindan.* Iwanami Shoten, 1987.

Takeuchi, Melinda. *Taiga's True Views: The Language of Landscape Painting in Eighteenth-Century Japan.* Stanford, CA: Stanford University Press, 1992.

———. "Visions of a Wanderer: The True View Paintings of Ike Taiga (1723–1776)." Ph.D. diss., University of Michigan, 1979.

Thomas, Roger K. "'High' versus 'Low': The *Fude no saga* Controversy and Bakumatsu Poetics." *Monumenta Nipponica* 49, no. 4 (Winter 1994): 455–469.

———. *The Way of Shikishima: Waka Theory and Practice in Early Modern Japan.* Lanham, MD: University Press of America, 2008.

Tanemura Suehiro. *Tōkaidō shoyū gojyūsan tsuji.* Asahi Shinbunsha, 2001.

Tominaga Nakamoto. "*Okina no fumi.*" In *Readings in Tokugawa Thought: Selected Papers,* vol. 9, trans. Tetsuo Najita. Chicago: The Center for East Asian Studies, University of Chicago, 1993.

Tsuji Nobuo. *Kisō no keifu.* Perikansha, 1988.

———. "Life and Works of Itō Jakuchū." In *Itō Jakuchū,* trans. Yasushi Egami. Bijutsu Shuppan-sha, 1974.

———. *Playfulness in Japanese Art.* Trans. Joseph Seubert. Lawrence: Spencer Museum of Art, University of Kansas, 1986.

———. "Shōhaku as a Heathen." *Soga Shōhaku Exhibition.* Mie: Mie Prefectural Art Museum, 1987.

"Tuo Song Shi" (Song History). In *Sibu beiyao, Shibu* (The Collection of History). Book 457, Biography 216, part 1 (Reclusion). Taipei: Taiwan Zhonghua Shuju, 1971.

Ueda Akinari. *Taidai shōshin roku.* Trans. William E. Clarke and Wendy E. Cobcroft. Sydney: Premodern Japanese Studies, 2009.

Ueda Makoto. *Literary and Art Theories in Japan.* Cleveland, OH: The Press of Case Western Reserve University, 1967.

Ueda, Makoto. *Matsuo Bashō.* Tokyo: Kodansha International, 1982.

Ujiie Mikito. *Edo kijinden: Hatamoto kawajike no hitobito.* Heibonsha, 2001.

Umehara Takeshi. *Bi to rinri no mujun: Umehara Takeshi chosakushū 19.* Shūeisha, 1983.

Ury, Marian. "Recluses and Eccentric Monks: Tales from the Hosshinshu by Kamo no Chomei." *Monumenta Nipponica* 27, no. 2 (Summer 1992): 149–173.

Vandi, Cinzia. "*Vivere come un 'fiore di loto nel fango': La vicenda personale ed artistic di Katsushika Hokusai*" (Living like "a lotus in the mud": The personal and artistic affairs of Katsushika Hokusai). http://xoomer.virgilio.it/iporpor/pensieri/nozioni/oli/Artic hokusai.htm (accessed November 6, 2010).

Waddell, Norman. *The Old Tea Seller: Baisaō: Life and Zen Poetry in Eighteenth Century Kyoto.* Berkeley, CA: Counterpoint, 2008.

Waley, Arthur, trans. *The Analects of Confucius.* New York: Vintage, 1989.

Walthall, Anne. *The Weak Body of a Useless Woman: Matsuo Taseko and the Meiji Restoration.* Chicago: University of Chicago Press, 1998.

Washburn, Dennis. "Ghostwriters and Literary Haunts: Subordinating Ethics to Art in Ugetsu Monogatari." *Monumenta Nipponica* 48, no.1 (Spring 1990): 39–74.

Watson, Burton. *Chinese Lyricism: Shih Poetry from the Second to the Twelfth Century.* New York: Columbia University Press, 1971.

Watson, Burton, trans. *Chuang Tzu: Basic Writings.* New York: Columbia University Press, 1964, 1996.

Weeks, David, and Jamie James. *Eccentrics: A Study of Sanity and Strangeness.* New York, Tokyo, and London: Kodansha, 1996.

Wu, Nelson. "The Toleration of Eccentrics." *Art News* 57, no. 3 (May 1956): 26–29, 52–54.

Wylie, Hugh. "Nanga Painting Treatises of Nineteenth-century Japan." Ph.D. diss., University of Kansas, 1991.

Yagi Akiyoshi. "'Kyōken' no keifu: Chūgoku kodai shisō ni okeru 'kyō' no shosō." *Keio gijuku daigaku gengo bunka kenkyūjō kiyō* 37 (March 2006): 111–127.

Yagi Sōsaburō. *Ijin to shūyō.* Sūzan-bō, 1912.

Yajima Arata, Yamashita Yuji, and Tsuji Nobuo. *Nihon bijutsu no hakkensha-tachi.* Tokyo Daigaku Shuppankai, 2003.

Yamashita, Samuel Hideo. "Nature and Artifice in the Writings of Ogyū Sorai." In *Confucianism and Tokugawa Culture,* ed. Peter Nosco. Honolulu: University of Hawai'i Press,1984.

Yanagisawa Kien and Mori Senzō. *Unpyō zasshi.* Iwanami Shoten, 1936.

Yasuda Kenneth. *The Japanese Haiku: Its Essential Nature and History.* Tokyo: Tuttle, 2002.

Yokoi, Kinkoku. *Yokoi Kinkoku-ten: Tokubetsuten.* Otsu-shi: Shiga Kenritsu Biwako Bunkakan, 1984.

Yokota Yōichi. *Ukiyoe avangyarudo to gendai.* Tokyo Station Gallery, 2003.

Yonezawa, Yoshiho, and Chu Yoshizawa. *Japanese Painting in the Literati Style.* Trans. Betty Iverson Monroe. New York: Weatherhill, 1974.

Yoshida Tarō. "Shōheikō ni okeru rekishi kyōiku no kenkyū." *Yokohama kokuritsu daigaku kyōiku kiyō* 4 (December 1964): 41–57.

Yoshida, Teigo. "The Stranger as God: The Place of the Outsider in Japanese Folk Religion." *Ethnology* 20, no. 2 (April 1981): 87–99.

Yoshimura Teiji. *Rekishi no naka no kyojintachi.* Sakuhinsha, 1982.

Yoshizawa Chū. *Nihon nanga ronkō.* Kodansha, 1977.

———. "Okada Beisanjin no fude ni naru santen no jigazō ni tsuite." *Kokka* 1097 (1986): 9–11.

Zeitlin, Judith. *Historian of the Strange: Pu Songling and the Chinese Classical Tale.* Stanford, CA: Stanford University Press, 1993.

Zhu Xi. *Zhuzi Youlei* (The Words of Zhu Xi: The Four Books). Shanghai: Kuchi Chupanshe, 1992.

INDEX

Bold page numbers refer to figures.

ABOUT THE AUTHOR

W. Puck Brecher (Ph.D., University of Southern California) is an assistant professor of Japanese at Washington State University. His research interests focus on thought, aesthetics, literature, urban history, and art history in Japan's early modern period, as well as environmental activism in Japan. His recent articles have been published in *Journal of Japanese Studies; Japanese Language and Literature; Japan Review; Early Modern Japan: An Interdisciplinary Journal; Japan Studies Review;* and *The European Legacy.*

Production Notes for Brecher | *The Aesthetics
of Strangeness: Eccentricity and Madness
in Early Modern Japan*

Jacket design by Julie Matsuo-Chun

Text design and composition by Jansom with
display type in Euclid and text type in
Adobe Garamond Pro and MS PMincho

Printing and binding by Sheridan Books, Inc.

Printed on 60 lb. House White, 444 ppi.